PITCHFORKS
and
TORCHES

PITCHFORKS
and
TORCHES

The Worst of the Worst,
from Beck, Bill, and Bush
to Palin and Other
Posturing Republicans

KEITH OLBERMANN

WILEY

John Wiley & Sons, Inc.

Published by John Wiley & Sons, Inc., Hoboken, New Jersey
Published simultaneously in Canada

No part of this publication may be reproduced, stored in a retrieval system, or transmitted in any form or by any means, electronic, mechanical, photocopying, recording, scanning, or otherwise, except as permitted under Section 107 or 108 of the 1976 United States Copyright Act, without either the prior written permission of the Publisher, or authorization through payment of the appropriate per-copy fee to the Copyright Clearance Center, 222 Rosewood Drive, Danvers, MA 01923, (978) 750-8400, fax (978) 646-8600, or on the web at www.copyright.com. Requests to the Publisher for permission should be addressed to the Permissions Department, John Wiley & Sons, Inc., 111 River Street, Hoboken, NJ 07030, (201) 748-6011, fax (201) 748-6008, or online at http://www.wiley.com/go/permissions.

Limit of Liability/Disclaimer of Warranty: While the publisher and the author have used their best efforts in preparing this book, they make no representations or warranties with respect to the accuracy or completeness of the contents of this book and specifically disclaim any implied warranties of merchantability or fitness for a particular purpose. No warranty may be created or extended by sales representatives or written sales materials. The advice and strategies contained herein may not be suitable for your situation. You should consult with a professional where appropriate. Neither the publisher nor the author shall be liable for any loss of profit or any other commercial damages, including but not limited to special, incidental, consequential, or other damages.

For general information about our other products and services, please contact our Customer Care Department within the United States at (800) 762-2974, outside the United States at (317) 572-3993 or fax (317) 572-4002.

Wiley also publishes its books in a variety of electronic formats. Some content that appears in print may not be available in electronic books. For more information about Wiley products, visit our web site at www.wiley.com.

Library of Congress Cataloging-in-Publication Data:

Olbermann, Keith, date.
 Pitchforks and torches : the worst of the worst, from Beck, Bill, and Bush to Palin and other posturing Republicans / Keith Olbermann.
  p. cm.
 ISBN 978-0-470-61447-1 (acid-free paper); ISBN 978-0-470-76960-7 (ebk);
 ISBN 978-0-470-76961-4 (ebk); ISBN 978-0-470-76962-1 (ebk)
  1. United States–Politics and government–2009—Anecdotes.
 2. Republican Party (U.S. : 1854-)–Anecdotes. 3. Conservatism–United States–Anecdotes. 4. Fox News–Anecdotes. I. Title.
 E907.O53 2010
 973.932—dc22

                                                        2010034984

Printed in the United States of America

10 9 8 7 6 5 4 3 2 1

For my father,
who taught me as much when I was 50
as he did when I was 5

Republicans Shoot, Democracy Saves

NOVEMBER 6, 2008

Number three: I could write a book–gate. Rumors murmuring at the White House: having seen the success of his predecessor's tome, Mr. Bush wants to write *his* autobiography. Bill Clinton's publishers are quoted as saying, "Given how the public feels about him right now, I think patience is something I would encourage." Curtis Sittenfeld, who has already written a novel about Laura Bush, says she should write an autobiography and quickly. "Personally," Sittenfeld adds, "I would find a memoir by President Bush resistible."

Number two: International diplomacy–gate. President Medvedev of Russia not even waiting until the ink was dry on the Obama election to warn that if this administration continues Mr. Bush's plan to install a missile defense system in Eastern Europe, he will put short-range missiles pointed at Europe on Russia's border. First, dude, chill; it's been two days. Second—wait a minute, did I misunderstand conservatives and Mr. Bush and all them there guys all these years? Ronald Reagan won the Cold War, remember? Russia can't be a problem forever and ever, remember?

Number one: ICE-gate. Like everything else they threw at him, it didn't stick, and it got very little public attention. Just before the election, a "federal law enforcement official" leaked to reporters the fact that one of Barack Obama's aunts was living illegally in this country, information that most likely came from Mr. Bush's Department of Immigration and Customs Enforcement, ICE.

Guess who has suddenly handed in her two-week notice as assistant secretary of Homeland Security, chief of ICE? Julie Myers, the Bush appointee, who just happens to be the niece of the former chairman of the Joint Chiefs. She was in charge when ICE arrested the family of a Vietnamese immigrant who three days earlier had been quoted in a newspaper article as being critical of this nation's immigration policies. And she was also the clear-headed executive who awarded the most original costume trophy to a guy at the Homeland Halloween party last year who was dressed up like this: dreadlocks, blackface, prison stripes.

There's your last Bush legacy, the head of ICE, Little Miss Nepotism, Little Miss Racial Sensitivity, and very possibly the source of a last-minute leak that was a clear violation of federal statute in your effort to try to fix the outcome of the presidential election. I've said it before and I'll say it again: this nation has survived the evil of the Bush administration these last eight years not principally because truth has prevailed, nor because of anybody's courage, but rather because most of the people in the Bush administration are about as nitwitted and careless as this Myers woman. Democracy saved because its enemies were too stupid to realize that they were stupid!

We, the People; You, the Worst
NOVEMBER 7, 2008

The bronze to radio sports yakker Mike Francesa, who also does a local TV show in New York. You may have heard that an under-informed Fox sideline reporter was taping an interview with a new football coach about whether he still talked to an old mentor. Unfortunately the old mentor is dead. The reporter had to restart the interview. It's dumb, but it happens. It was embarrassing enough that this was seen on the raw Fox feed, seen by all the other networks.

You know what this Francesa does? He takes the mistake from the interview, the interview which was not shown live or on tape on Fox or anywhere else. He plays it on his show. Now Fox is rightly not letting the other TV networks watch its raw feeds anymore, so we don't get to show you extra replays or funny shots from the crowd. Nice job.

Our runner-up: Joe Wurzelbacher. This guy's hypocrisy is already the stuff of legend. No plumber's license, but he's got a publicist. He lied about trying to buy a business, but he is trying to get a recording contract. Add one to the list. Fixed News, of all places, pointing out that a man who tried to equate Obama with Karl Marx because he wanted to spread the wealth was, himself, twice on welfare. He explained that he deserved it because he had paid into the system. Yes, except he didn't completely pay into it. A tax lien against Wurzelbacher in Ohio for nearly $1,200 is still officially unresolved.

But our winner . . .
Michele Bachmann, about to begin her second term as your least stable member of the U.S. House of Representatives. It was just three weeks ago tonight that she went on *Hardball* and suggested that there were members of the House and the Senate, including Senator Obama, who held anti-American views, and the media should investigate. Now Congresswoman Bachmann has told Politico.com that she is "extremely grateful that we have an African American who has won this year." She called Obama's election "a tremendous signal we sent."

Exactly who is this "we," Congresswoman? The people who voted for him? I'm thinking you weren't one of that "we." The people who viewed him as an appropriate and patriotic choice for executive? You called him anti-American, so clearly you weren't one of that "we," either. The collective voice of the United States? Yes, you're in that "we." And, in fact, you deserve some credit for Obama's election. Thanks for reminding the rest of us how quickly things can go horribly wrong when unscrupulous hypocrites get into the mix, and how vigilant we have to be when they start trying to divide us.

Congresswoman Michele Bachmann of Minnesota—by the way, nice face, both of them—today's worst person in the world!

A Question of Love

NOVEMBER 10, 2008

This isn't about yelling, and this isn't about politics, and this isn't really just about Prop 8. I don't have a personal investment in this: I'm not gay. I had to strain to think of one member of even my very extended family who is. I have no personal stories of close friends or colleagues fighting prejudice that still pervades their lives.

And yet to me this vote is horrible. Horrible. Because this isn't about yelling, and this isn't about politics. This is about the human heart, and if that sounds corny, so be it.

If you voted for this proposition or support those who did or the sentiment they expressed, I have some questions because, truly, I do not understand. Why does this matter to you? What is it to you? In a time of impermanence and fly-by-night relationships, these people want the same chance at permanence and happiness that is your option. They don't want to deny you yours. They don't want to take anything away from you. They want what you want: a chance to be a little less alone in the world.

Only now you are saying to them, "No, you can't have it on these terms." Maybe something similar if they behave, if they don't cause too much trouble. You'll even give them all the same legal rights, even as you're taking away the legal right which they already had. A world around them still anchored in love and marriage, and you are saying, "No, you can't marry."

What if somebody passed a law that said *you* couldn't marry?

I keep hearing this term "redefining" marriage. If this country hadn't redefined marriage, black people still couldn't marry white people. Sixteen states had laws on the books which made that illegal in 1967.

1967!

The parents of the president-elect of the United States couldn't have married in nearly one-third of the states in the country their son grew up to lead. But it's worse than that. If this country had not "redefined" marriage, some black people still couldn't marry black people. It is one of the most overlooked and cruelest parts of our sad history of slavery. Marriages were not legally recognized if the people were slaves. Since slaves were property, they could not legally be husband and wife, or mother and child. Their marriage vows were different: not "Until death do you part," but "Until death or distance do you part." Marriages among slaves were not legally recognized. You know, just like marriages today in California are not legally recognized if the people are gay.

And uncountable in our history are the number of men and women forced by society into marrying the opposite sex in sham marriages, or marriages of convenience, or just marriages of not knowing; centuries of men and women who have lived their lives in shame and unhappiness and who have, through a lie to themselves or others, broken countless other lives—of spouses and children—all because we said a man couldn't marry another man, or a woman couldn't marry another woman. The sanctity of marriage.

How many marriages like that have there been, and how on earth do they *increase* the "sanctity" of marriage rather than render the term meaningless?

What is this to you? Nobody is asking you to embrace their expression of love. But don't you, as human beings, have to embrace that love? The world is barren enough. It is stacked against love, and against hope, and against those very few and precious emotions that enable us, all of us, to go forward.

Your marriage only stands a 50-50 chance of lasting, no matter how much you feel and how hard you work. And here are people overjoyed at the prospect of just that chance, and that work, just for the hope of having that feeling. With so much hate in the world, with so much meaningless division, and people pitted against each other for no good reason, this is what your religion tells you to do? With your experience of life and this world and all its sadnesses, this is what your conscience tells you to do? With your knowledge that life, with endless vigor, seems to tilt the playing field on which we all live in favor of unhappiness and hate, this is what your heart tells you to do?

You want to sanctify marriage? You want to honor your God and the universal love you believe he represents? Then spread happiness, this tiny, symbolic, semantical grain of happiness. Share it with all those who seek it. Quote me anything from your religious leader or a book of your choosing that tells you to stand against this. And then tell me how you can believe both that statement and another statement, which reads only "Do unto others as you would have them do unto you."

You are asked now, by your country, and perhaps by your creator, to stand on one side or another. You are asked now to stand, not on a question of politics, not on a question of religion, not on a question of gay or straight. You are asked now to stand on a question of love. All you need to do is stand, and let the tiny ember of love meet its own fate.

You don't have to help it. You don't have to applaud it. You don't have to fight for it. Just don't put it out. Just don't extinguish it. Because while it may at first look like that love is between two people you don't know and you don't understand and maybe you don't even want to know, that love is, in fact, the ember of your love for your fellow person, because this is the only world we have, and the other guy counts, too.

This is the second time I have found myself in ten days concluding by turning to, of all things, the closing plea for mercy by Clarence Darrow in a murder trial. But what he said fits what is really at the heart of this. He said, "I was reading last night of the aspiration of the old Persian poet Omar Khayyam." This is what he told the judge: "It appealed to me as the highest that I can vision. I wish it was in my heart. I wish it was in the hearts of all: So I be written in the Book of Love; I do not care about that Book above. Erase my name, or write it as you will, so I be written in the Book of Love."

He Did Not Have Sex with That Page

NOVEMBER 12, 2008

The bronze to the traffic wardens of Hounslow, England. Veterans Day—Remembrance Day there—is a far more grave affair in that country. In commemoration of the 11th hour of the 11th day, when the First World War ended, the nation still observes two minutes of motionless silence. It was during that two minutes of silence yesterday that motorist Stephanie Jost says she was standing next to her car and watched as one of the metermen placed a $90 parking ticket on her windshield.

Our runner-up: Bill-O the Clown, again reading the conservative talking points, trying to pin the victory of Proposition 8 in California on black voters. "The African American community came out for Obama. While they were in that booth, they said, 'You know what—gay marriage, I don't think so.' So why aren't they protesting in front of the African American church?" Maybe because they're not racists and you are.

Our friend Nate Silver, who relies on statistics rather than on things he heard in the hallway, has dispensed with this version of reality, simplified for the Bill-Os of the world. Nate writes, "The notion that Prop 8 passed because of the Obama turnout surge is silly. Exit polls suggest that first-time voters, the vast majority of whom were driven to turn out by Obama, voted against Prop 8 by a 62 to 38 margin. If California's electorate had been the same as it was in 2004, Prop 8 would have passed by a wider margin." Nate Silver, Bill. FiveThirtyEight.com. Learn something. Well, try.

But our winner . . .
Former congressman Mark Foley. In his first interview since he resigned in September 2006 after the sex scandal involving underage male pages, Foley said he did nothing illegal, never had any sexual contact with the teens, just inappropriate Internet conversation. He says what he did was extraordinarily stupid, but that he wasn't a pedophile. Quoting Foley: "It hits me right in the gut, because it's absolutely false and inaccurate. A pedophile is someone having sex with a prepubescent person. I mean, that is an outrage to be called that."

He also said the 17-year-old kids never said, "Stop," or "I'm not enjoying this," or "This is inappropriate." "It's not what I envisioned," the Florida Republican concluded. "Working this hard all my life to end up in an ash heap because of a momentary lapse of judgment."

A *momentary* lapse of judgment that lasted from no later than late 2005 until well into the summer of 2006.

Former congressman Mark Foley of Florida—besides everything else, he can't tell what time it is or how long something takes or how "pedophile" is defined—today's worst person in the world!

The Oxygen Is Not Getting Through

NOVEMBER 14, 2008

The bronze to Bill-O the Clown. As suggested by his inability to tell a toy panda from a toy bear, the sensory apparatus seems to be breaking down on the model 15-C Bill-O-Matic. "The debate over gay marriage is now a full-fledged national battle. As Talking Points said last night, the election of Barack Obama has emboldened secular progressives who feel it's their time. Gay marriage is just the beginning. Other cultural war issues will also be on display shortly. These include limited gun possession, legalizing narcotics, unrestricted abortion, and the revocation of the Patriot Act." Bill, this debate over gay marriage—Prop 8 in California—this was started by the religious right along with the support of enablers like you. And you all started it quite a long time before Obama was the front-runner, let alone the nominee or the president-elect. If it blows back on you and costs you any of your precious phony-baloney culture war issues, or if it costs the Mormon Church its tax-exempt status, you will have no one to blame but yourself.

Runner-up: Rick Davis, erstwhile campaign manager for John McCain. Our old pal the deep-breathing Rich Lowry interviews him for the *National Review* and quotes Davis as follows on Sarah Palin's disastrous interview with Katie Couric: "She was under the impression the Couric thing was going to be easier than it was. Everyone's guard was down for the Couric interview." Lowry also paraphrases Davis as adding—these are Lowry's words—"the Couric interview, which Davis says Palin thought would be softer because she was being interviewed by a woman." Seriously. So, far from all of you being wrong about that, you are also sexist, condescending, pandering, patronizing, and trying to find your vice presidential candidate a soft interview on a national broadcast TV network.

But our winners . . .
A Mr. Dick Scharff of Coronado, California, who wrote the following letter to the editor, which was published by his cowinner, the *San Diego Union Tribune*: "Veterans, active duty, retired military, alarm, alarm. President-elect Obama is proposing a national security force with allegiance, paid benefits provided by the executive branch to him. Come on, some really bad guys have tried that in the past, and we know where that went. Not while I draw a breath." Mr. Scharff, if you are that paranoid over Obama's seeking to expand the Peace Corps and the USA Freedom Corps, which was created by George W. Bush, then the oxygen is already not getting through. So threatening to hold your breath is not going to affect you or the rest of us. But this incitement in there to some kind of military rebellion, violent overthrow kind of thing of the, you know, lawfully elected government of the United States, that's kind of illegal. The *San Diego Union Tribune* newspaper should not have printed it, and should be correcting the fact that they did.

Dick Scharff of Coronado, California, and the *San Diego Union Tribune*, today's worst persons in the world!

Worst of Bush

Bubble, Bubble, Toil and Trouble
NOVEMBER 24, 2008

Number three: Privatize this–gate. The journal *Health Affairs* published a study today by Mathematical Policy Research on the effects of the administration's 2003 gambit in which about a fourth of all Medicare programs were privatized. Want to make one last guess? What do you suppose happened to care? Improved or not? How about complexity, filling out forms and stuff? More or less? How about costs, up or down? Quality of care dropped slightly. The amount of paperwork increased sharply. And the price jumped 13 percent. Who would ever have thought that giving private business a profit motive to make the process more complicated, less effective, and more expensive could have driven up the cost?

Number two: Once a Bushy–gate, Press Secretary Dana Perino kind of painted herself into a corner over the last week, stating from her podium, "We did not torture." When it was pointed out to her that the administration has acknowledged having water-boarded prisoners and that even John McCain said that's torture, she chose not to retract her statement. "I absolutely feel comfortable with what I said." That means she's lying and she feels comfortable about lying. She added, "I stopped reading blogs about me. I told my mom to stop because it was so vitriolic." She also denied she's actually Kristen Wiig's character from *Saturday Night Live*, the one who claims she can become invisible at will or instantly grow a foot-long beard.

Number one: Well, that went well–gate. The Iraq war was a success. We have that from no less an authority than President George W. Bush, appearing on the *Sunday Project* program on the Japanese TV network Asahi. "I think the decision to remove Saddam Hussein was right. People have been able to take their troops out of Iraq because Iraq is becoming successful. I'm very pleased with what is taking place there now. We are bringing troops home because of the success in Iraq, but Iraq is not yet completely safe." The president added, "So there will be a U.S. presence for a while there at the request of the Iraqi government." And then he concluded, "Most countries there within a very broad coalition have come home, but we want to help this government."

In short, nobody still, not even his friends, has told him the truth.

Someone's Not Ready to Lead

NOVEMBER 24, 2008

The bronze to Mark Halperin from *Time* magazine speaking at a Politico.com journalism conference at the University of Southern California, announcing that media bias in the presidential campaign was at its highest in years—bias in favor of President-elect Obama. "It's the most disgusting failure of people in our business since the Iraq War," he said. "It was extreme bias, extreme pro-Obama coverage."

Seriously. This is the man who insisted that when Senator McCain couldn't or wouldn't say how many houses he owned, it would "wind up being one of the worst moments in the entire campaign for Obama." This is the man who looked at the 2007 presidential questionnaire in which Obama promised to try to negotiate a deal with a Republican opponent to use public financing and, as late as a month ago, he said this had been an ironclad promise by Obama to use public financing. In short, here is a guy who lied to support the Republican nominee claiming bias against the Republican nominee.

Our runner-up: Nice to see Bill-O the clown has stayed in shape during my absence. He has called the media-watchdog site Media Matters "the most dishonest Web site in the country," because, well, it accurately quoted him. "We said the other day that in Minnesota the election commission had certified the election and that what's-his-name—[Norm] Coleman, the senator—had won by 215 votes. So what I said was Coleman's victory was certified by the state because it was. He had 215 more votes, which is absolutely true, absolutely true, okay. Rock solid, in stone. That's what they did."

Except they didn't. The Minnesota State Canvassing Board has not only *not* certified that election, last Tuesday it specifically said that "except for the offices of U.S. senator, state senator District 16, state representatives Districts 12-B and 16-A, the candidates

11

who received the highest number of votes cast for each office voted in more than one county is hereby declared elected." There is, in fact, a Minnesota law, 204-C.40, that specifically demands that if there is a recount, "no certificate of election shall be prepared or delivered until after the recount is completed."

The only thing rock-solid here is Bill-O's head.

But our winner . . .
Good old Senator Joe Lieberman. This is the senator on a public affairs program on WTIC, the Fox station in Hartford, Connecticut, yesterday: "I never felt that Barack Obama was unready."

And from *Meet the Press*, August 3, 2008: "Is he ready to lead or as ready as John McCain? No. There's a very serious point to that ad. And it gets right to it, which is, is, notwithstanding his celebrity status, Barack Obama ready to lead? My answer is no."

So the question is, when the senator said he never felt that Barack Obama was unready, was he telling the truth? And *my* answer is no. Senator Joe Lieberman, they called Senator John Frémont the old pathfinder.

They can call Senator Lieberman the old backpedaler: today's worst person in the world!

Worst Person in the World

Ain't Pat a Shame
DECEMBER 8, 2008

The bronze to the latest incarnation of the Baseball Hall of Fame veterans committees. They finally corrected one of the mistakes of their many predecessors by electing Joe Gordon today. He was the second baseman of the 1930s and 1940s; he was that era's equivalent of Ryne Sandberg. But they once again bypassed for election the likes of Ron Santo and Jim Kaat and Dick Allen and especially Gil Hodges. Hodges was merely the National League's all-time leader in home runs by right-handed batters the day he retired.

Then he managed the so-called miracle Mets to the world championship in 1969, and he died young at just 47. And yet he has now been ignored by Hall of Fame voters for 40 consecutive elections.

The runner-up: Pat Boone. The singer and failed basketball entrepreneur has become quite the paranoid lately, but this is remarkable. Running a column suggesting that the Mumbai massacre will be repeated here, to quote him: "Look around. Watch your evening news. Read your newspaper. Are you unaware of the raging demonstrations in our streets, in front of our churches and synagogues? Even spilling into these places of worship, and many of these riots turning defamatory and violent? Have you not seen the angry, distorted faces of the rioters, seen their derogatory and threatening placards and signs, heard their vows to overturn the democratically expressed views of voters, no matter what it costs, no matter what was expressed at the polls? Twice? I refer to California's Proposition 8. Let me ask you, have you not seen the awful similarity between what happened in Mumbai and what's happening right now in our cities?" Yes, the terrorists randomly murdering people on the streets of Mumbai, and the Prop 8 backlash protesters. Same thing. They're in fact so far apart that it's like comparing Pat Boone the singer to Pat Boone the thinker.

But our winner . . .
"Evil secular progressive," as Bill-O might call such a person in his latest blatherings about the imaginary war on Christmas, the author of *Parade*'s great American holiday quiz, distributed in hundreds of Sunday newspapers yesterday. Not a great American Christmas quiz, but a great American *holiday* quiz; complete with secular progressive questions that have nothing to do with Christmas. Like who started Kwanzaa and what does Hanukkah mean in Hebrew? Just another slide down the slippery slope to the eventual banishment of Christmas by the evil nonsectarians who will not recognize the rightful dominant place of Christmas in a Christian nation. And which evildoer spewed his multiculturalist bile in *Parade*'s great American holiday quiz? That's right, Bill-O

the Christmas Benedict Arnold. The winner even gets a free copy of O'Reilly's new book, *A Bold Fresh Piece of Christmas Treason*. Losers get two copies.

Bill-O the Hypocrite, today's worst person in the world!

Regrets, He Had a One

DECEMBER 9, 2008

Number three: Harriet-gate. The president expressing one of the great regrets of his tenure, the nomination of Harriet Miers to the Supreme Court. You mean how dumb it was? Oh, no. That he had to withdraw it. In his words: "There's no doubt in my mind that my dear friend Harriet Miers would have had the same judicial philosophy twenty years after I went home, and had the intellectual fire power to do the job." He then described the nomination and the withdrawal process: "This really, really good person got chucked out there, and, man, the lions tore her up." Mr. Bush said this in an interview with the ultraconservative *National Review*, the same publication that, of course, called for the withdrawal of the Miers nomination 11 days after Mr. Bush proposed it, dismissing her as one of the "president's cronies."

Number two: Gitmo-gate. So you set up this extralegal cockamamie detention center and you don't even think through the scenario. Khalid Sheikh Mohammed and four other accused 9/11 plotters want to plead guilty so they can get the death penalty and be executed, but nobody knows for sure whether or not detainees who plead guilty can be executed. So the judge has to tell them that, and they withdraw their pleas? So you tear up the Constitution and torture these people so you can find 9/11 plotters guilty, but you screw it up so badly that when they save you the trouble and plead guilty, you might have to say, "No thanks." President Wile E. Coyote, supergenius!

And number one: IED-gate, one of the top ten most disturbing realities of the war in Iraq. The concept, evidently a surprise to all on our side, of the improvised explosive device. The use of roadside bombs by insurgents to kill Americans. Well, it was not a surprise after all. The Pentagon's inspector general has issued a 72-page report revealing that the military was aware of the threat posed by mines and improvised explosive devices and of the availability of mine-resistant vehicles years before the insurgent actions began in Iraq in 2003. Which makes the report's other finding—that Marine Corps leaders simply stopped processing an urgent request from combat commanders in Anbar Province for MRAPs, the IED-resistant vehicles in 2005—even more heinous. So not only did the Bush administration and the Bush Pentagon ignore the prewar intel that the WMD we sought to recover were not in Iraq. But the Bush administration and the Pentagon ignored the likelihood that if we removed Saddam Hussein, an insurgency of some sort would develop in Iraq. And now we learn the Bush administration and the Bush Pentagon ignored the prewar intel that when an insurgency did develop, it would use roadside bombs to kill the troops we needlessly sent there. I don't know what, if any, religion you belong to, but I suspect you will agree that the people who ignored so many warnings that resulted in preventable deaths should have a long time to think about it in hell!

Worst Person in the World

The Comedian Doesn't Get His Own Joke

DECEMBER 16, 2008

The bronze to the CEO of the infamous Blackwater USA, Eric Prince. If you want to read one gigantic huge rationalization, see his op-ed in the *Wall Street Journal*, in which he excuses everything he and his company have ever done in Iraq with one line: "Unlike politicians who visit, the question for me has never been why the U.S. ever got into Iraq. Instead, as the CEO of Blackwater, the urgent question was, how the company I head could perform the duties asked of us by the U.S. State Department."

Wow! an oldie but a goody, the "I was just following orders" defense.

Our runner-up: Karl Rove trying to sell Fixed News viewers on the premise that the Blagojevich scandal is now somehow sticking to the president-elect and that Obama should ignore prosecutor Patrick Fitzgerald's instructions not to release his investigation into staff contacts with Blagojevich's staff until next Monday. "The president-elect," Rove says, "ought to decide what's in his best interest." This puts Mr. Rove in slight disagreement with a Fox analyst who said last Tuesday that the Republicans would not try to link Obama to Blagojevich because "I think we have to be careful about this because, look, I think Fitzgerald went out of his way today to basically say none of this touches President-elect Obama." The Fox analyst who made that cogent observation: Karl Rove—the other Karl Rove.

But our winner . . .
Comedian Rush Limbaugh, clearly on the ropes after Colin Powell's plea to Republicans, "Can we continue to listen to Rush Limbaugh? Is this really the kind of party that we want to be when these kinds of spokespersons seem to appeal to our lesser instincts, rather than to our better instincts?" Comedian's clear and insightful response was "Powell's not a Republican. McCain's not a Republican. These guys aren't even mavericks."

And you are? You, the guy who admitted to carrying water for a candidate you didn't really support in 2006? Who belched out venom on McCain's behalf up until last month? You know what they call people who advocate things and individuals in which they don't believe, apart from frauds, shills, phonies, and snake oil salesmen, shams, posers, impostors, and con artists, prostitutes, whores, hookers, and streetwalkers?

They also call them comedian Rush Limbaugh, today's worst person in world!

Since When Does a Republican Want a Judge to Be Generous?

DECEMBER 18, 2008

Number three: People will love him when he's dead–gate. Vice President Cheney becoming the latest to insist that history will generously judge Mr. Bush, and thus his administration and thus Mr. Cheney, too. His "place in history will likely grow during the next 20 to 30 years." He trotted out the argument about how Gerald Ford was vilified for pardoning Richard Nixon, but now he's not anymore. "By the time of his passing a couple of years ago, opinion had totally turned on that. In fact, most people by then, even many who had been very critical 30 years before, were in agreement that, in fact, it was a good decision. It was the right thing to do from the standpoint of the country."

Apart from the reality that the act of pardoning a crooked president to soothe a ruptured nation bears no resemblance to lying that nation into an unnecessary war and getting 4,000 of our troops killed, apart from the fact that 30 years from now, rather, Bush is much more likely to be considered asleep at the switch on 9/11 than he is now, Cheney's also wrong about the idea that Gerald Ford is viewed favorably 32 years after he left office. The last polling on overall presidential popularity done by Rasmussen for July 4, 2007, still had Ford in a tie for the 12th most unpopular president of all time, even though he was only in office for 30 months.

Number two: Nexus of politics and terror–gate. The president's ever-changing number of how many domestic acts of terrorism he prevented is back up to numerous. Officially, that would be four, based on his speech at the War College. "We prevented numerous terrorist attacks, including an attempt to bomb fuel tanks at JFK Airport, a plot to blow up airliners bound for the East Coast, a scheme to attack a shopping mall in the Chicago area, and a plan to destroy the tallest skryscraper in Los Angeles." It's *skyscraper*, but okay.

17

The skyscraper was the one where Mr. Bush got the name wrong while announcing it to the world, before he told local authorities in Los Angeles that he was going to tell everybody, setting off mild panic there. The airliners one is the reason you can't bring liquid in your carry-on, the British-based scheme for which the plotters had not obtained a ticket, nor passport, and chemists laughed at the idea anyway. The mall was the deal in '06 where the guy got no further than trying to buy a hand grenade from an undercover FBI agent. And the JFK plot, that was the mutant who thought he could cause an airport to blow up by starting a fire at a fuel pipeline 30 miles away.

So thanks for stopping all these. Nice work, Jack Armstrong.

Number one: Insult the dead–gate. This is a White House talking point still, even though your average three-year-old could disprove it using only an Etch-A-Sketch. Spokesman Tony Fratto was on the air with Fixed News parent Jon Scott. Scott gave the setup line about how 9/11 was unforeseeable and thus not even slightly Bush's responsibility and said, "Nobody was thinking that there would be terrorists flying 767s into buildings at that point."

Mr. Fratto replied, "That's true. I mean, no one could have anticipated that kind of attack, or very few people." Yes, well, it ain't true, and out of respect for the people who died that day, you damn well better stop saying it. A President's Daily Brief as far back as December 1998 says bin Laden was preparing to hijack U.S. aircraft in hopes of trading hostages for jailed radicals. The August 6, 2001, brief, of course, told President Bush, if he read it, that there were patterns of suspicious activities in this country, consistent with preparations for hijackings.

The FBI agent John O'Neill repeatedly warned of the prospect of suicide hijackings and basically got drummed out of the Bureau for saying it. In a bitter and cosmic irony, he started a private security job in the World Trade Center just in time to become one of the victims there. The FAA had distributed a CD-ROM early in 2001 to the airlines and the airports warning that terrorists might hijack a plane in order to use it as a weapon. That Mr. Fratto's employers might not have been expected to know the exact hour of these attacks does not give him or anyone else the right to perpetuate the lie that 9/11 was impossible to conceive. Clearly, many inside this nation's government anticipated it. It was Mr. Bush and his gang who chose to ignore them.

What's a Good Résumé Word for "Disgrace"?

JANUARY 9, 2009

The bronze to two unnamed students at Woonsocket High School in Woonsocket, Rhode Island. Here's the mixed message of all mixed messages: two boys, 15 and 16, were desperate not to be late for school, so they stole a car, the keys to which were found in the pocket of one of the guys as he sat in the detention room because he was late for school anyway.

Runner-up: Alberto Gonzales, the disgraced former attorney general, apparently does not realize he is the disgraced former attorney general. He admits he has been looking for work in the private sector since last April with no luck. But at least the current downturn has provided him with a new rationalization. "It is a rough economy right now," he tells a newspaper in Austin, "and it's a tough time for a lot of law firms. Greater opportunities will present themselves once the story's out there."

Part of the problem might be Mr. Gonzales's expectations. "I'm very fortunate that I'm at a point in my life where if I wanted to do something completely different, be baseball commissioner, for example," he says, "seriously, I would love a job in baseball, a plug there, I can do it."

Speaking as a lifelong baseball fan, historian, reporter, and customer, I would rather see the game banished from the face of the earth.

Speaking of which, our winner . . .
Glenn Beck. After he lost his show on CNN, he's got a perfect
fit over there on Fox Noise. In advertisements for the new show,
Beck says, "I'm tired of the politics of left and right, right and
wrong. We argue back and forth. If you haven't voted for the
donkey, you're just a hatemonger. The other side, those donkeys,
trying to turn us into communist Russia, stop."

Seems to be a complex psychological, hypocritical, self-hate
phenomenon going here, because it is Beck who is the one who
constantly claims that Democrats are communists. In August, he
called Obama a "Marxist." A year ago, he called Hillary Clinton
"Comrade Clinton" and said a plan of hers "sounds like the Soviet
Union."

Beck said of John Edwards, "He is a communist." He called
a Harvard professor "Stalin." After John McCain sewed up
the Republican nomination last winter, Beck said, "It's not just
a fear slogan to say Democrats are communist. We are on a collision course with socialism, communism, here in the United
States."

Unfortunately for Mr. Beck and the rest of us, he is not on a
collision course with sanity. Glenn, if it is hypocritical self-hate, at
least you have plenty of company—Beck, today's worst person in
the world!

Special Comment

We Have Tortured People
JANUARY 19, 2009

We have tortured people, you and I. This is the people's democracy. We are the people. These are our elected officials. That they
did not come to us and ask to act thusly in our names is unfortunate, indeed criminal, but it is also almost irrelevant. They work
for us—they work for us and they tortured people, and so we have
tortured people.

You and I know we have tortured Khalid Sheikh Mohammed. We not only know about it. We have now heard it boasted about by one of the men who, as of tomorrow, will no longer work for us, George Walker Bush.

"The techniques were necessary and are necessary to be used on a rare occasion to get information necessary to protect the American people," Mr. Bush said to Fox News on January 11. "One such person who gave us information was Khalid Sheikh Mohammed. I'm in the Oval Office. I'm told that we have captured Khalid Sheikh Mohammed and the professionals believe he has information necessary to secure the country. So I asked what tools are available for us to find information from him. They give me a list of tools. And I said are these tools deemed to be legal. We got legal opinions before the decision was made.

"I think when people study the history of this particular episode, they will find out we gained good information from Khalid Sheikh Mohammed in order to protect our country. We believe that the information we gained helped save lives on American soil."

Never mind Mr. Bush's delusions here, never mind all primary sources who witnessed the interrogation of Khalid Sheikh Mohammed said they got nothing from him until they started buddying up to him, never mind that Mr. Bush's supporters' favorite torture construction, the mythical ticking time bomb scenario not only did not transpire here, but Mr. Bush has not even had the imagination to pretend it did just in order to slightly cover his moral tracks.

The key is that this statement, if it had been under oath, would have been a confession to a war crime. Mr. Bush is proactive. "I asked what tools are available." Mr. Bush is aware of the legal haze in which he steps. "And I said, are these tools deemed to be legal."

Mr. Bush realizes the tools he has chosen have been used. "We gained good information from Khalid Sheikh Mohammed."

Since we know from previous admissions at the Pentagon that Khalid Sheikh Mohammed was waterboarded, we can infer that Mr. Bush knew he would be waterboarded and knew afterward that he *had been* waterboarded.

Mr. Bush is guilty. He is guilty as sin.

Mr. President-elect, you were first asked about all this on the 18th of April last. I am proud to say you were asked about it by a fellow who got onto his high school newspaper while I was the editor, Will Bunch of the *Philadelphia Daily News*.

"I think you are right," you told him. "If crimes have been committed, they should be investigated. You are also right that I would not want my first term consumed by what was perceived on the part of Republicans as a partisan witch hunt, because I think we have too many problems we have to solve. So this is an area where I would want to exercise judgment."

Good. Amen. But in that brief interview was born, or at least elucidated, a loophole, genuine crimes, as opposed to really bad policies. Vice President Biden echoed this on December 21, in a statement to which your transition team has directed all those to whom this is a paramount issue.

He said, "The questions of whether or not a criminal act has been committed or a very, very bad judgment has been engaged in is something the Justice Department decides."

After his comment last week, with straightforwardness that was like water to a lost soul in the Sahara, that waterboarding is torture, your nominee at Justice, Mr. Eric Holder, echoed all this. "We don't want to criminalize policy differences that might exist between the outgoing administration and the administration that is about to take over."

But, Mr. President-elect, you have a confession. Since this statement of a structure of policy prefacing policy itself from Mr. Biden, you have had Mr. Bush's confession. Moreover, since Mr. Biden's statement, you have a legal assessment from within the bowels of the Bush administration itself.

"We tortured Mohammed al-Qahtani," Judge Susan Crawford told the *Washington Post* a week ago. "His treatment met the legal definition of torture." That was why, Judge Crawford added, as the Bush administration official in charge of deciding whether or not to bring detainees at Guantanamo Bay to trial, she decided in Qahtani's case not to.

This, Mr. President-elect, was not the obvious waterboarding of Khalid Sheikh Mohammed. This was a more insidious combination of legally approved procedures that still nearly killed this man Qahtani.

"The techniques were all authorized," Judge Crawford continued, "but the manner in which they applied them was overly aggressive and too persistent. This was not any one particular act. It was just a combination of things that had a medical impact on him, that hurt his health."

In fact, Mr. President-elect, the records at Gitmo showed that Qahtani's heartbeat eventually slowed to 35 beats per minute.

"It was abusive and uncalled for and coercive, clearly coercive. I sympathize with the intelligence gatherers in those days after 9/11 not knowing what was coming next and trying to gain information to keep us safe. But there still has to be a line that we should not cross. Unfortunately, what this has done, I think, has tainted everything going forward."

If you are worried about the Republicans viewing any torture prosecution in the way you postulated to Will Bunch, a partisan witch hunt, you can remind them that the woman who said all that, Susan Crawford, is a lifelong Republican.

So Mr. President-elect, beyond whatever else will come out, as the whistle-blowers begin just after noon tomorrow, you have your predecessor's unofficial confession and you have this singular evaluation by a principal in your predecessor's administration, this kind of line-level confession.

They are guilty of this, Mr. President-elect. They are guilty as sin.

Since he talked to my friend Bunch in April, Mr. Obama's only lengthy comments about this were made to George Stephanopoulos on January 11 of this year. See if a disturbing theme becomes evident. "Obviously, we are going to be looking at past practices. I don't believe that anybody is above the law. On the other hand, I also have a belief that we need to look forward, as opposed to looking backwards."

Later, "My instinct is to focus on how do we make sure that moving forward we are doing the right thing."

Later still, "My orientation is going to be to move forward."

Finally, "What we have to focus on is getting things right in the future, as opposed to looking at what we got wrong in the past."

Sadly, as commendable as the intention here might seem, this country has never moved forward without first cleansing itself of its mistaken past. In point of fact, every effort to merely draw a line in the sand and declare the past dead has served only to keep the past alive and often to strengthen it.

We compromised with slavery in the Declaration of Independence. And four score and nine years later, we had buried 600,000 of our sons and brothers in a Civil War.

After that war's ending, we compromised with the social restructuring and protection of the rights of minorities in the South. And a century later, not only had we not resolved anything, but black leaders were still being assassinated in the cities of the South.

We compromised with Germany in the reconstruction of Europe after the First World War. Nobody even arrested the German kaiser, let alone conducted war crimes trials then. And 19 years later, there was an indescribably more evil Germany and a more heartrending Second World War.

We compromised with the trusts of the early 1900s. Today, we have corporations too big to fail.

We compromised with the Palmer Raids and got McCarthyism. And we compromised with McCarthyism and got Watergate. We compromised with Watergate, and junior members of the Ford administration realized how little was ultimately at risk. They grew up to be Paul Wolfowitz and Donald Rumsfeld and Dick Cheney.

But, Mr. President-elect, you are entirely correct. As you say, what we have to focus on is getting things right in the future, as opposed to looking at what we got wrong in the past. That means prosecuting all those involved in the Bush administration's torture of prisoners and starting at the top.

You are also right that you should not want your first term consumed by what would be perceived on the part of Republicans as a partisan witch hunt. But your only other option might be to let this set and fester indefinitely. Because, Mr. President-elect, someday there will be another Republican president, or even a Democrat just as blind as Mr. Bush to ethics and this country's moral force. He will look back to what you did about Mr. Bush or what you did not do. And he will see precedent. Or as Cheney saw, he will see how not to get caught next time.

Prosecute, Mr. President-elect. Even if you get not one conviction, you will still have accomplished good for generations unborn. Merely by acting, you will deny Mr. Bush what he most wants. Right now, without prosecutions, without this nation standing up and saying this was wrong and we will atone, Mr. Bush's version of what happened goes into the historical record of this nation.

Torture was legal. It worked. It saved the country. The end.

We have tortured people, you and I, Mr. President-elect. This is the people's democracy. We are the people. These were our elected officials. That they did not come to us and act thusly in our names is unfortunate and indeed criminal, but it is almost irrelevant. They worked for us. They tortured people, and so we have tortured people.

Thus, beginning tomorrow, it is up to you not just to discontinue this but to prevent it. At the end of his first year in office, Mr. Lincoln tried to contextualize the Civil War for those who still wanted to compromise with the evils of secession and slavery. "The struggle of today," Lincoln wrote, "is not altogether for today. It is for a vast future also."

Mr. President-elect, you have been handed the beginning of that future. Use it to protect our children and our distant descendants from anything like this ever happening again.

Worst of Bush

A Very Different Thousand Days

JANUARY 21, 2009

Number three: Vacation-gate. It's final now. The *Washington Post* has calculated how much time off the 43rd president took; 149 visits to Camp David for a total of 487 days, 77 visits to Crawford, Texas, for a total of 490 days, 11 visits to Kennebunkport, Maine, for a total of 43 days.

Total, 1,020 days, more than a third of his entire presidency. I know what you're thinking, 34 percent of his days in office Mr. Bush took off. It seemed like so much more.

Number two: Farewell-gate. No wave of last-minute pardons, but the administration may require some forgiveness itself for its closing-out bash at Glen Echo Park in Maryland. Slate.com somehow got inside. It says the invitation e-mail read, "Due to the historic nature of the venue, there are limitations on what can be done in terms of climate control. Do wear layers and coats." In other words, there was no heat.

Karl Rove, Dana Perino, Alberto Gonzales, Condi Rice, and all the gang were present. So was Mr. Bush. He said, "This is objectively the finest group of people ever to serve our country." He added, "We never shruck." Then somebody helped out, "Shirked."

What do they all do now? I mean until the trials? *Slate* reports, quoting here, "One outgoing treasury employee had already landed a job as a manger at Abercrombie and Fitch."

Number one: Torture-gate. A gentleman named Manfred Nowak said on German television last night, "Judicially speaking, the United States has a clear obligation to prosecute members of the administration for war crimes." That the U.S. had signed the UN Convention on torture, which reads, in part, "that all means, particularly penal law, will be used to punish individual government figures who violate that convention."

This Mr. Nowak specifically mentioned Donald Rumsfeld and President Bush. And so what? A German commentator demanding war crimes trials? Manfred Nowak is not a commentator. He is, in fact, an Austrian who works for the United Nations. He is, in fact, its investigator. His special title is Special Rapporteur on torture.

The UN says Mr. Nowak, unlike its human rights monitors, does not have to wait for domestic remedies, for national prosecutions to run out before he can recommend that the UN intervene. In short, it may not matter whether or not the Obama administration chooses to prosecute torture by the Bush administration. The United Nations might be able to start something on its own.

Not Smarter Than a Fifth-Grader

JANUARY 21, 2009

The bronze to Bill-O the Clown; "The far left editor of *Newsday*, John Mancini, apparently has been fired by the paper's new owners. He printed an absurd column saying that the Factor promoted violence because one of my books was found in the home of an accused killer. Mancini deserved to be removed. He ruined a once fine newspaper. Enough is enough with this kind of kooky stuff."

Newsday now reports that after a brief dispute with the new owners, Mr. Mancini has now returned to his job as editor of *Newsday*. It also hints that the dispute was about the paper's coverage of a scandal involving the basketball team also owned by the paper's new owners. As usual with Bill-O's delusions, it had nothing to do with him, even though he is the center of the universe.

Our runner-up: Frontier Airlines, its flight attendant, Amy Fleming, and the authorities who the carrier pushed to prosecute a passenger named Tamera Jo Freeman. On flight, her two kids quarreled about the window shade. They managed to spill mom's drink on her. She swatted each of them on the thigh as punishment. The flight attendant came over and told her to stop spanking her kids. Ms. Freeman was not pleased. She swore. She threw what was left of a can of juice on the floor.

She was then accused of a terrorist act, spent three months in jail, pleaded guilty, now has lost custody of her kids. A passenger nearby said, "It was a nasty loud exchange, but Ms. Freeman capitulated and offered no resistance." Flight attendant is unrepentant:

"Absolutely, she deserved a felony conviction." Did she deserve to lose her children, Ms. Fleming? How are you sleeping at night, by the way?

But our winner . . .

Chris Wallace of Fixed News. The fumbling over the oath of office yesterday, precipitated by Chief Justice John Roberts, led to that do-over tonight. But Mr. Wallace said, "I have to say, I'm not sure that Barack Obama really is president of the United States, because the oath of office is said in the Constitution, and I wasn't at all convinced that even after he tried to amend it, that John Roberts ever got it out straight and that Barack Obama ever said the prescribed words."

Even though by the Constitution the new president becomes the new president at noon on January 20, whether he is swearing the oath at the hour or taking a bath. Honestly, Chris, what are you, 11 years old?

Chris Wallace of Fox Noise, today's worst person in the world!

She Bought the Ruby Slippers during Katrina

JANUARY 23, 2009

Number three: Wicked Witch of the West–gate. We are beginning to understand the context of the uproarious welcome at State yesterday for new Secretary Clinton. The careerists over there really didn't like the old secretary. *Harper's* reported that one of them has said she was looking forward to the Glenda party. That was yesterday's arrival of Secretary Clinton.

Scott Horton writes that he asked the employee, "If Hillary is Glenda, the Good Witch of the South from *The Wizard of Oz*, did that make Condoleezza Rice the Wicked Witch of the West?" The answer he got was "You're on to it."

Another 20-year vet at State said that upon Rice's confirmation as secretary, the tone of internal department publications had changed. They began to praise and glorify Rice. No prior secretary did anything like this.

Number two: VA-gate. Walter Reed, the billion-dollar shortfall, and now the missing 25,000. The Government Accountability Office today releasing an analysis of the Veterans Affairs Administration's long-term budget plan, devised under Mr. Bush's leadership in 2007 and carrying into 2013. It not only underestimates costs by millions. It also completely miscounts the number of its patients who receive care at nursing homes operated by the VA or by state governments. The budget says there are about 6,000 of these vets. In fact, there are about 31,000. They didn't budget for 25,000 veterans. That is one way of keeping costs down.

Number one: Terrorist-gate. The *New York Times*, of all outfits, reporting that a guy we released from Guantanamo Bay a year ago is now the deputy leader of Al Qaeda's group in the nation of Yemen. Said Ali al-Shihri was sent home to Saudi Arabia in 2007. Went through this Saudi rehab program. Supposedly went to work in the family business. But he is now a suspect in the bombing of our embassy in Yemen last September.

The *Times* wrote that this "has underscored the potential complications in carrying out the executive order President Obama signed Thursday that the detention center"—that would be Gitmo—"be shut down within a year." Conservative politicians have gone nuts, saying this shows you can't close Gitmo ever and you certainly can't release anybody from Gitmo. They were right, and they told you so. Bill O'Reilly tonight led his newscast with this as a warning to President Obama.

All this is based on one really big assumption. In fact, it would see a commentary as bass-ackward. The Bush administration detained this man and claimed he had gone to an urban warfare tactics training camp in Kabul, had been injured in an air raid just after we went into Afghanistan in 2001, had met with extremists in Iran and smuggled some of them into Afghanistan, and had tried to carry out a fatwa on a writer.

But before he was freed from Gitmo—please remember, he was not freed as part of the panicky flushing of the innocent of the last months of the administration—the Bushies let him go in 2007. Shihri said he had gone to Afghanistan to do relief work, and his trip to Iran, that was to buy carpets for his family's furniture store in Riyadh. The ultimate question here is not, Doesn't this prove we can never ever close Gitmo? but rather, If he was really trafficking tourists of terrorism and not a guy buying rugs, why did the Bush people let him go? Or why was he never put on trial? Or why did the permanent solution to terrorism the Bushies claimed Gitmo was, fail so utterly here?

And, perhaps worst of all, if Shihri was once just a guy trying to get a deal on some carpets, which is suggested by the fact that Bush's people let him go, did his detention at Gitmo, in fact, turn him into a terrorist? Did we perhaps create in Said Ali al-Shihri his reason for hating us?

Worst Person in the World

RushFAIL, HainesWIN

JANUARY 29, 2009

The bronze to the First Choice Liquor Store in Springfield, Queensland, Australia. A clerk thought an unnamed 40-year-old woman was shoplifting using a fake pregnancy belly. He said if she did not pull up her shirt and prove she really was pregnant, he would call the cops. She complied. She was pregnant, really pregnant, eight months, two weeks. The store has made an undisclosed settlement with the woman. And state legislators are pushing to make it illegal in that part of Australia to strip-search anybody in public.

The silver: Republican congressman Phil Gingrey of Georgia. He told Politico.com that it was counterproductive for conservative radio talkers, like Comedian Rush Limbaugh, to "stand back and throw bricks, rather than offer real leadership." Mr. Gingrey may be the chairman of the conservative Republican Study Committee, but to paraphrase *Catch-22*, everybody works for Rush-bo.

Gingrey now says he received a high volume of phone calls and correspondence. So now he is saying, "I see eye to eye with Rush Limbaugh." He even cowed enough to have phoned in and apologized to Limbaugh personally. He added that Sean Hannity and Newt Gingrich were the voices of the conservative movement's conscience. Parenthetically, that explains everything. The congressman then added baa, baa, baa.

But our winner . . .
The comedian himself. Some people are not afraid of the big bad mediocre announcer. Our CNBC colleague Mark Haines, anything but a raging liberal, today schooled the comedian in flawless fashion over his pretense at being nonpartisan in a newspaper article after he said he hoped President Obama failed.

Haines asked Rush: "A week after the inauguration, you said you hope he fails. Are you now admitting that that was a stupid and mean-spirited thing to say?"

Rush replied: "No, it was an accurate thing to say. It was an honest thing to say. As a conservative, I want liberalism to fail. I want the country to succeed. That is what I meant. That's what I said over and over again. You have to stop reading these left-wing liberal media sites."

To which Haines responded: "I just listen to you, Rush. I don't read anybody. I listen to you. And what I hear is hypocrisy."

A thing of beauty is a joy forever, Mark Haines.

Comedian Rush Limbaugh, today's worst person in the world!

Special Comment

In the Name of God, Go
FEBRUARY 5, 2009

Regarding former vice president Cheney's remarks about the prospects of future terrorist attacks in this country, it may be time for Mr. Cheney to leave this country.

The partisanship, divisiveness, and naivete to which he ascribed every single criticism of his and President Bush's delusional policies of the last eight years have now roared forth in a destructive and uninformed diatribe from Mr. Cheney that can only serve to undermine the nation's new president, undermine the nation's effort to thwart terrorism, and undermine the nation itself.

Mr. Cheney's remarks were posted yesterday at Politico.com. They are a reiteration of all the manias of his vice presidency. Only they now come without the authority of office. They insist—he insists—on the imminence of attack, on the maintenance of Gitmo, on the necessity of waterboarding, on the efficacy of torture.

Time does not wither nor custom stale your infinite variety, Mr. Cheney. You will say it and be wrong, and you will still say it anew. You will say it and undercut a president 17 days on the job, and you will still say it anew. You will say it and help terrorists, and you will still say it anew.

"The United States needs to be not so much loved as it needs to be respected. Sometimes, that requires us to take actions that generate controversy. I'm not at all sure that that's what the Obama administration believes."

The first glimmer, in years, of sanity in any your remarks, sir. That's not at all what the Obama administration appears to believe. It seems to be ready to use all avenues and all emotions, seeking love, respect, fear, diplomacy, shared experience, education, principle, and, yes, even rational thought. This president, unlike yours, seems intent on living in the real world, rather than trying to reshape an imaginary one by force.

"When we get people who are more concerned about reading the rights to an Al Qaeda terrorist than they are with protecting the United States against people who are absolutely committed to do anything they can to kill Americans, then I worry."

More concerned, Mr. Cheney? What delusion of grandeur makes you think you have the right to say anything like that? Because a president, or an ordinary American, demands that we act as Americans and not as bullies; demands that we play by our rules; that we preserve, protect, and defend the Constitution of the United States; you believe we have chosen the one and not the other? We can be Americans, or we can be what you call "safe," but not both?

"If it hadn't been for what we did with respect to the terrorist surveillance program, or enhanced interrogation techniques for high-value detainees, the Patriot Act, and so forth, then we would have been attacked again. Those policies we put in place, in my opinion, were absolutely crucial to getting us through the last seven-plus years without a major-casualty attack on the U.S."

Mr. Cheney, you are lying. As the cloud of fear you deliberately fostered in this good-hearted and courageous nation finally begins to dissipate, the nonsense that you and Mr. Bush presented as "evidence" of this childish claim, this perverse example of wishful-nightmare-thinking, has become apparent, and it should shame you.

The "major-casualty attacks" on the U.S. you think you stopped, involved would-be hijackers who were under constant surveillance by at least two nations and had neither passports nor plane tickets. They involved feeble-minded braggarts, so clueless as to even the most obvious steps of organization that they believed they could enter Fort Dix in New Jersey disguised as pizza delivery men, kill hordes of Americans, and get out alive, even though Fort Dix teems with soldiers who have an almost inexhaustible supply of weapons.

They involved embittered ex-airport-employees so uninformed about where they used to work that they thought dropping a match in a fuel supply line 30 miles away would cause the airport to explode. These are the plots that by your own proud, strutting, crazy admissions, were the ones you "got us through."

You and Mr. Bush, sir, you are the old men who cried wolf. The *Politico* story continues:

"Citing intelligence reports, Cheney said at least 61 of the inmates who were released from Guantanamo during the Bush administration—'that's about 11 or 12 percent'—have 'gone back into the business of being terrorists.'"

Mr. Cheney, you made this statistic up. Perhaps not you personally, but your people made this statistic up! As the new reality-based administration has discovered, there are not enough records of the detainees still at Gitmo to suggest that there is any reliable database of those who have been released. That McCarthy-esque number, sir, is also as fluid as the infamous senator's was.

As Professor Mark Denbeaux of Seton Hall University noted on this network last month:

"The government has given its 43rd attempt to describe the number of people who have left Guantanamo and returned to the battlefield. Forty-one times they have done it orally, as they have this last time. And their numbers have changed from 20 to 12 to 7 to more than 5 to 2 to a couple to a few, 25, 29, 12 to 24. Every time, the number has been different. In fact, every time they give a number, they don't identify a date, a place, a time, a name, or an incident to support their claim."

Mr. Cheney, which orifice are you pulling these numbers from? You know, in the movie *The Manchurian Candidate*, the character based loosely on Joe McCarthy had trouble remembering all the different numbers. His Lady Macbeth–like wife pointed out to him that the reason she kept changing the number of purported communists in the State Department was so that people would no longer be asking, "Are there communists in the State Department?" but would begin only asking, "How many communists are there?"

Eventually she picked one number that her husband could remember, fifty-seven. She found it on the bottle of catsup on the room service tray.

Of course, Mr. Cheney, it is also impossible to prove that any of those released detainees actually were terrorists before we captured them, because you never presented any evidence against them, sir, and they were released. Which makes something else you said seem almost the product of a split personality.

"If you release the hard-core Al Qaeda terrorists that are held at Guantanamo, I think they go back into the business of trying to kill more Americans and mount further mass-casualty attacks. If you turn them loose and they go kill more Americans, who's responsible for that?"

Well, right now? That'd be you and Mr. Bush. You released those supposed repeat terrorists, all 61 of them, or 12. You. If Gitmo worked so well and you really had the devils in a cage, why did you release them, without trial, without any second effort at proving their guilt? You just released them. If you turned them loose and they go kill more Americans, who's responsible for that, Dick?

And six years and more since General Powell and Dr. Rice, and all the rest, played the trump card of terrorizing this nation, the mighty Cream of Mushroom Cloud soup, you played it again: nuclear weapon, biological agent, deaths of perhaps hundreds of thousands.

"I think there's a high probability of such an attempt. Whether or not they can pull it off depends on whether or not we keep in place policies that have allowed us to defeat all further attempts, since 9/11, to launch mass-casualty attacks against the United States."

"The Bush System," as John Yoo so aptly rechristened it the other day: start the wrong war, detain the wrong people, employ the wrong methods, pursue the wrong leads, utilize the wrong emotions. Beat them up first, ask questions later. You know, just like Al Qaeda does, or Iran. Save this nation from the terrorists by doing the terrorists' work for them, Mr. Cheney.

To your credit, sir, you have added a new monster under a new bed to try to continue to foment a national policy of panic. It's the terrorists-on-our-streets ploy.

"Is that really a good idea to take hardened Al Qaeda terrorists who've already killed thousands of Americans and put them in San Quentin or some other prison facility, where they can spread their venom even more widely than it already is?"

As opposed to keeping them in an extralegal facility mixed in with some unknown number of innocents mistaken for terrorists. Who is likelier to be more influenced by terrorist venom, Mr. Cheney? The characters from the TV series *Oz* or a bunch of guys who we're holding in chains without trial and without even some token attempt at rehabilitation?

And by the way, what about Ahmed Ressam, sir? Benni Noris, if you prefer, the Millennium Bomber. Caught at a ferry crossing from Canada to Washington State in December 1999, on his way to blow up Los Angeles International Airport. He had a car, a legit passport, nitroglycerin, and timing devices.

And what did we do to him, Mr. Cheney? Did we send him to Gitmo? Or pre-Gitmo? As "high a value" terrorist as ever we've caught in this country, trained by Abu Zubaydah, days away from his target and ready to go. We tried him in U.S. courts, with U.S. lawyers. Part of the case went to the U.S. Supreme Court. He got 22 years in U.S. prisons.

No torture, no gulag, no stories of him proselytizing fellow prisoners. Oh, but he did cooperate long enough to tell his prosecutors, who didn't beat the hell out of him, about Al Qaeda cells in this country.

That was his info they stuck in the President's Daily Brief of August 6, 2001. That's probably news to you, since obviously you and Mr. Bush didn't read it, stalking Saddam Hussein as you were.

Of course, none of that mattered to Mr. Cheney, just as none of this matters to Mr. Cheney. Because, at heart, Mr. Cheney is not interested foremost in protecting this country. He is interested foremost in protecting Mr. Cheney. And the business of being Dick Cheney, of rationalizing one's own existence after one of the most reprehensible, myopic, unprincipled, and even un-American careers in the history of our government, depends on continuing to convince the gullible among us to live in abject fear and not with vigilance and common sense and principles.

We, sir, will most completely ensure our security not by maintaining the endless, demoralizing, draining, life-denying blind fear and blind hatred which you so thoroughly embody. We will most easily purchase our safety by repudiating the "Bush System." We will reserve the violence for which you are so eager, sir, for any battlefield to which we truly must take, and not for unconscionable wars which people like you goad and scare and lie us into.

You, Mr. Cheney, *you* terrified more Americans than did any terrorist in the last seven years. And now it is time for you to desist, or to be made to desist. With damnable words like these, sir, you help no American. You protect no American. You serve no American. You only aid and abet those who would destroy this nation from within or without.

More than 400 years ago, when a British Parliament attempted to govern after its term had expired, it was dispersed by the actions and the words of Oliver Cromwell:

"You have sat too long for any good you have been doing lately," he told them—exactly as, Mr. Cheney, exactly as a nation now tells you:

"Depart, I say, and let us have done with you. In the name of God, go!"

Standard Operating Procedures

FEBRUARY 6, 2009

Number three: Burrowing-gate. This is the definition of Still Bushed. Senator Dianne Feinstein of California is pushing an investigation of at least three Bush political appointees who may have found loopholes permitting them to keep influential jobs in their government departments despite the change of government. Feinstein's keeping the names quiet, just in case these are innocent bystanders somehow. But the Associated Press says one of them is Tara Jones, special assistant to the Pentagon Office of Detainees.

Now, if that name sounds vaguely familiar, it is because it was her e-mails, obtained by the *New York Times*, that outlined the so-called Pentagon pundits scandal, in which the Bush administration and the Pentagon were pushing a series of ex-generals onto TV networks and feeding them talking points, even those generals who might still have had business relationships with the Pentagon. And Tara Jones is now considered perhaps a civil service employee at the Obama Pentagon.

Number two: Bailout-gate and the story of how the banks we bailed out are treating their customers, their dead customers. This is from Paul Kelleher, who called to advise Bank of America that his mother, B of A credit card holder Theresa Hatt, had just passed away. Mr. Kelleher says that the Bank of America representative he talked to briefly expressed condolences, then asked how Kelleher planned to pay the small balance remaining on his mother's card. "I'm not going to," he told the bank. "She has no estate to speak of, but you should feel free to go through the standard probate procedure. I'm certainly not legally obligated to pay for her."

Kelleher says the rep responded, "You mean you're not going to help her out?" Kelleher answered, "I wouldn't be helping her out. She's dead. I'd be helping you out." Kelleher then says the rep matter-of-factly added, "That's really not the way to look at it. I know that if it were my mother, I'd pay it. That's why we're in the banking crisis we're in, banks having to write off defaulted loans." Kelleher added he thought the rep sounded like she was reading this crazy claim that the unpaid credit card debts of dead people caused the meltdown. He said it sounded like Bank of America policy. And TPM Muckraker found an ex–B of A collections unit guy who said it sure was. Class all the way.

Number one: Andy Card is a fool–gate. We mentioned yesterday this claim that by appearing in shirtsleeves in the Oval Office, President Obama was, Card said, damaging "the Constitution, the hopes and dreams and I'm going to say democracy, and that the president, any president should always wear a jacket in the Oval Office, the way President Bush always wore a jacket in the Oval Office."

Mr. Card, perhaps one photograph will refresh your memory. Aha! January 22, 2001, two days after his inauguration, the guy on the right—I don't know if you remember him—it's President Bush in shirtsleeves. Mr. Card, you can apologize to President Obama anytime you'd like. I'd suggest you include the phrase "I am a buffoon," but use your own judgment, if any.

In a Station at the Bill-O

FEBRUARY 12, 2009

The bronze to the Manatee [Sean Hannity]. On Tuesday, the Senate Republican Communications Center issued a press release incorrectly tracking the growth of the stimulus plan. A Fox Noise meat puppet read it almost verbatim on the air, complete with a typo, from the press release. Now Hannity has done the same thing on the radio and claimed he discovered it. Discovered it in the pile of propaganda they pass through him everyday like fois gras through a goose.

The runner-up is Bill-O the Clown, Bill-O the Scared Clown, apparently, rattled enough by the backlash to his having compared correspondent Helen Thomas to a witch to open his show last night with an elaborate self-defense of his snotty remarks about her, and then do two more segments on it later. The Bill O'Reilly show about Bill O'Reilly.

Tuesday he said of Thomas's question at the presidential news conference, "It is like the Wicked Witch of the East. If I were Obama, I would have poured water on her and she would have dissolved. What is her name, the old lady? Helen Thomas."

Wednesday he said of what he had said about her Tuesday, "I didn't call her a witch. I said her voice sounded like—and I did the voice. That was clear."

Three segments of him saying this again and again. Bill, you are saying you were only comparing Helen Thomas's voice to the voice of the Wicked Witch of the East in the movie *The Wizard of Oz*? You do realize that in the movie, we never hear the voice of the Wicked Witch of the East, right? She is the one who got squashed when Dorothy's house landed on her. Nice try, Billy.

But our winner . . .
Bernard Goldberg, gradually devolving from shrill critic to fomenter of violence. Responding to the critics of Bill-O's jokes about Helen Thomas, he lost it. "Screw them. Screw them," he said. "They are unimportant people. They are throwing spitballs at battleships." O'Reilly said he wanted to send a cake to his critics. Bernard Goldberg then said, "You should send them flowers, black, dead roses."

It would seem as if Mr. Goldberg would be well taken to tamp down the references to violence and battles and death right now. Just this week, the letter left by murderer Jim David Atkinson, intended as a suicide note, was released by the authorities. Atkinson is the man who burst into a Tennessee church last year during the kids' musical and started shooting. He killed a 60-year-old man and a 61-year-old woman.

He explained he was there to kill liberals. In the previously unrevealed note, Atkinson had written, in part, "This was a symbolic killing. Who I wanted to kill was every Democrat in the Senate and House, the 100 people in Bernard Goldberg's book."

The book came out four years ago and was called *The 100 People Who Are Screwing Up America*. Goldberg included Jimmy Carter, Al Gore, Anna Nicole Smith, Ken Lay, Michael Savage, and Phil Donahue. This hateful man read what Goldberg wrote and decided to kill innocent people as proxies, because he couldn't kill "the 100 people in Bernard Goldberg's book."

None of us at any end of the political spectrum can be responsible for what the hateful or the deranged wrongly infer from our work. But the same week it is revealed that this terrorist was partially inspired by Bernard Goldberg, maybe Mr. Goldberg could skip the lines about screw them or the reference to dead roses, or the one last week where he said, "I would probably have gotten a baseball bat and gone down to the *New York Times* with it and found the person that wrote the editorial, but that's me."

Wait until Monday until you give the next Jim David Atkinson something to work with, sir. Bernard Goldberg, today's worst person in the world!

Worst Person in the World

Hannity's Bull-ion
FEBRUARY 19, 2009

The bronze: Good old Sarah Palin. She has been advised by the state of Alaska that she owes an additional $17,000 in personal income taxes. That the money she got from filing expense reports counts as income. Her expense reports for the last two months of 2008 have thus become part of the public record, and parts are astounding. Anytime she did what she considered work for the state while at her home in Wasilla she put in for per diem. Phone conversation at her house with Senator Elizabeth Dole, that's $60 in meal and incidental expenses Alaska owes her. The interview with the right-wing lunatic Web site Human Events, $60. Photos taken with the University of Anchorage basketball team, $60 per diem. November 9 appearance from Wasilla on Fixed News, another big six-o.

Runner-up: Comedian Rush Limbaugh. He has authored a fiery op-ed as yet unpublished for the *Wall Street Journal*. Subject, his opposition to the old radio Fairness Doctrine. Problem? Yesterday the Obama White House reiterated yet again the president's opposition to reinstatement of the old radio Fairness Doctrine.

He is still foaming. Told that the press spokesman for the White House, Ben LaBolt, said, "Obama does not believe it should be reinstated," Comedian basically called the president a liar.

"At the next break, I'm going to fire off a note to the people at the *Journal* because there is an expiration date on every Obama statement. He can say today he doesn't believe in it and then an emergency will come up in a day or two or a week and force him to change his mind."

So now the *Journal* has an outdated useless Limbaugh column, as if there could be any other kind, and Limbaugh's mortal enemy, the Fairness Doctrine, turns out to be a figment of his paranoia.

Comedian doesn't understand what the Fairness Doctrine was. Relax, Rush, if it did come back, it wouldn't force you to be fair. Thus your livelihood is still secure.

But our winner...
The Manatee. You've heard of the latest Bernie Madoff wannabe, Allen Stanford, the billionaire, certificate-of-deposit guru who fled after trying to defraud 50,000 of his clients out of $8 billion. They found him tonight. One of his scams is the Stanford Financial Group, and one of *its* scams is Stanford Coins and Bullion. And guess who one of Sean Hannity's biggest radio sponsors is? He even reads the ads himself:

"I have been buying gold. As a matter of fact, two weeks ago I ordered some gold from our friends at Stanford Coins and Bullion. Call Stanford Coins and Bullion, mention my name, and get a free guidebook of U.S. coins free with purchase. Or go to the Web, Stanfordcoins.com/hannity."

Mention my name and get your pocket picked personally by Allen Stanford. And if you order now, he will come to your house and vacuum the gold from your teeth. You wait, before the economic scandals finish shaking out, Sean Hannity's company will be left applying for a bailout from the Obama administration. Maybe he can melt down his statuette for being tonight's "Worst Person in the World."

You Have Always Been My Unsafe Home

FEBRUARY 26, 2009

Number three: Katrina-gate. With 68 percent of the $6 billion promised by the president to rebuild the Gulf remaining unspent, maybe we all should have guessed this. CBS reported last night it appears the FEMA office in downtown New Orleans appears to be dragging its feet so its senior managers will keep their jobs there. Employees speaking out anonymously out of fear have been told to expect the office to remain open for 15 years. Managers not only make $100,000 a year, plus benefits, but, CBS reported, they are living like the Wild West in there; 80 complaints of sexual or racial harassment have been filed in that one FEMA office since last month.

Number two: Under cover of darkness–gate. A senior official at the Pentagon has told NBC News that Defense Secretary Robert Gates has decided to lift the automatic ban on media coverage of the return of the U.S. war dead to Dover Air Force Base in Delaware. Most sensibly, the new policy will neither be no coverage, nor coverage of every casket. Media coverage will now be the decision of the families.

Remember the origin of this ban? It came on December 21, 1989. That was the day that live coverage on CNN, ABC, and

CBS of the *first* President Bush's not exactly solemn news conference at the White House was suddenly put on a split screen with live coverage of caskets arriving at Dover containing the first war fatalities after he ordered our invasion of Panama.

Number one: Anthrax-gate. As you know, under Mr. Bush, the FBI closed the case, saying that army scientist Bruce Ivins made them a flask of anthrax at Fort Detrick, in Maryland, flask number RMR-1029, and then he killed himself. Maybe not. The magazine *Nature* now reports that at a recent biodefense conference, a scientist from Sandia National Laboratories in Albuquerque presented analysis of three anthrax letters, the ones sent to Senator Tom Daschle, Senator Patrick Leahy, and the *New York Post*. They show anthrax mixed with silicon, oxygen, iron, and tin.

Bruce Ivins's flask at Fort Detrick, good old number RMR-1029, contained anthrax, no silicone, no oxygen, no iron, and no tin. In fact, Ivins's entire lab at Fort Detrick showed anthrax, silicone, and oxygen, but no iron and no tin. The analysts cautioned that the iron and tin could have worked their way into the anthrax between its time in a flask, somebody's flask, and its time in those envelopes.

You remember the anthrax attacks. Killed five Americans, sickened seventeen more, from September 19, 2001, until November 21, 2001, thus falling into that time period after 9/11, the time when George Bush and his apologists still insist he kept us safe.

There He Went

MARCH 2, 2009

The bronze to right-wing documentarian, failed sportscaster, and Sarah Palin would-be groupie John Ziegler, a guy who once scared her by showing her a picture of me. Speaking at the conservatives' coven, he unloaded on conservatives who criticized Palin or each other. In his words: "A lot of us end up selling out to the other side for a guest spot on *Meet the Press* or *Larry King Live*, because they know that a conservative saying something bad about another conservative is automatically going to be newsworthy and get them a higher profile. Well, those people ought to be ostracized and punished. This goes far deeper than those who are traitors for a spot on *Meet the Press*. This goes throughout the entire organizational structure of the conservative movement. They do not take this issue seriously. They do not protect their own."

By the way, Bobby Jindal is going on *Larry King* this week. Well, good! Stay off *Meet the Press* and CNN, isolate yourselves even further. Bigger than that, you are calling conservatives who criticize conservatives traitors. Didn't you just criticize conservatives?

Our runner-up: Mary Matalin, who went on the *Today Show* and got Governor Bobby "Let Me Tell You a Story" Jindal in more hot water. "He's the greatest public policy innovator in the country today," she said. "Bobby Jindal has made more progress in Louisiana in the shortest period of time in the history of the state, probably in the country. Education reform, ethics reform; everything that put Louisiana down in scale is now one of the top states in the country."

The annual report card on education in the states by *Education Week* for 2007 puts Louisiana at 21st best. The annual report card on education in the states by *Education Week* in 2008 has Louisiana at 35th best. This comes from a press release issued in January by the Louisiana Department of Education.

But our winner . . .
Bill-O the Clown, once again getting a well-meaning charity into trouble. In 2007, it was the Naples, Florida, branch of the National Center for Missing and Exploited Children, which had invited O'Reilly to be its keynote speaker at a fund-raiser, just weeks after he claimed that when 11-year-old Sean Hornbeck was kidnapped by a pizzeria manager and held captive for two years, "the situation here for this kid looks to me to be a lot more fun than what he had under his old parents. He didn't have to go to school. He could run around, do what he wanted. I . . . what it all comes down, what is going to happen is there was an element here that

this kid liked about his circumstances." This kid was repeatedly raped and abused by his abductor for two years. After a few weeks, the Center for Missing and Exploited Children quietly announced that there had been a scheduling conflict, and Mr. O'Reilly would no longer be appearing at its event. Now it has happened to the It Happened to Alexa Foundation, which has invited O'Reilly to speak at its upcoming fund-raiser in Palm Beach, Florida. It is a group that supports rape survivors.

On August 2, 2006, on the air, O'Reilly blamed a rape and murder victim for her own terrible death. "So anyway," he said, "these two girls come in from the suburbs and they get bombed and their car is towed, because they are moronic and, you know, they don't have a car. Jennifer Moore, 18, on her way to college, she was five feet two, 105 pounds, wearing a miniskirt and a halter top with a bare midriff. Now again, there you go. So every predator in the world is going to pick that up at two in the morning."

Translation, she was asking for it. The assumption is that the It Happened to Alexa Foundation was not aware of O'Reilly's attitude that the victim is sometimes to blame or they would not possibly have extended the invitation. One assumes it will quietly announce another scheduling conflict before the March 19 event.

There's one person who knew about O'Reilly's attitude. And if he had a soul, he would have had the decency not to expose this group to his bitter hypocrisy.

That, of course, is Bill O'Reilly, today's worst person in the world!

Worst Person in the World

Snow Jobs

MARCH 3, 2009

The bronze: Bill-O. He is still planning to address a fund-raiser this month for the It Happened to Alexa Foundation. This is a group doing the best possible work, supporting rape victims, especially during trials. Nearly three years ago, O'Reilly called a murdered rape victim moronic and suggested that by the way she was dressed, she was asking for it. He, of course, never apologized. Today comes word from the group's executive director, Ellen Augello, who told us, "Bill O'Reilly is still speaking at the fund-raiser. We are aware of his comments. We don't have any comment about it. I don't feel as if it would be productive." How productive is it to have a man who blames rape victims speak to a group supporting rape victims?

Runner-up: Newt Gingrich, on Twitter. It may be new technology, but he's the same old liar. His Tweet was that as they flew in to Santa Barbara, California, he and his wife pointed out you could see the oil rigs offshore. Ironically, they have had no spill since 1969. True, other than one two weeks ago from Exxon's rig, a mile long and ten feet wide. And other than the one three months ago Sunday from Platform A, 1,100 gallons right into the Santa Barbara Channel.

But our winners . . .
The Manatee and former Notre Dame football coach Lou Holtz. Hannity's topic with Holtz and with one of John McCain's campaign spokespeople—global warming. Global warming? You're talking global warming with Lou Holtz? Lou Holtz barely makes sense talking Notre Dame football.

"I'm walking over here. I don't have a coat on. I'm freezing. Thank God for global warming or I would be really cold," Hannity said. "Maybe it's just a coincidence that nearly every global warming protest occurs on the exact same day we have a major snowstorm. Or maybe the big guy up there is trying to send a message to these people."

You mean Limbaugh? Hannity also repeated the only point he's been able to conjure up from that slow-moving brain of his, that there couldn't be global warming because it still gets cold here in the winter. "Nancy Pelosi couldn't make it because of the snow!"

Don't you get this, even after it's been explained slowly to you using small words? The snowstorm Sunday is not proof there isn't global warming. Just like when it hit 68 degrees here three days after Christmas, that was not proof that there is global warming. If global warming already had enough immediate impact to reverse the normal weather patterns, to prevent all snowstorms in the winter, we'd all be preparing to die within five years anyway!

Sean Hannity and Lou Holtz, today's worst persons in the world!

He Ought Not to Be in Fox's House

MARCH 4, 2009

The bronze to Bill-O. There is now a petition online asking the rape victim support group It Happened to Alexa Foundation to withdraw its invitation to O'Reilly to speak at its Florida fund-raiser two weeks from tomorrow. It was O'Reilly, of course, who three years ago declared a dead New Jersey rape victim a "moronic" girl and proceeded to describe how she was dressed before she was brutally and fatally attacked. The petition, from what is apparently an ad hoc group called Concerned Citizens Against Sexual Violence, includes a new statement from the people at the Alexa Foundation, who told us yesterday that they knew of O'Reilly's blame-the-victim comments but still wanted him at their support-the-victim event.

The new statement makes even less sense. An administrator at the foundation is quoted thusly online: "Bill is speaking about his new book, not rape victims." First it was a blame-the-victim person addressing a group of support-the-victim people. Now it's a blame-the-victim person trying to sell a product to a group of support-the-victim people.

The silver shared by Fox Noise new actress Megyn Kelly and Republican congressman Trent Franks of Arizona. The right-wing talking point Bobby Jindal spat out a week ago last night apparently did not stick, that $8 billion of stimulus money is to be spent on a magnetic levitation line from Las Vegas to Disneyland, a prospect that seemed to terrify the governor.

So now it's not from Disneyland to Las Vegas, it's now the whore train. "It's a super-railroad of sorts," Miss Kelly claims. "A line that will deliver customers straight from Disney, we kid you not, to the doorstep of the Moonlight Bunny Ranch Brothel in Nevada." If only all you were doing was kidding us, Miss Kelly. "The majority leader of the U.S. Senate, Harry Reid, has fought for this publicly and is committed to this project," Congressman Franks then parroted.

Truth be told, Senator Reid *has* been hoping to refurbish a historic train line that ends in Carson City, Nevada, indeed, not seven miles from the doorstep of that brothel. But the train does not go to Disneyland. It goes to Gold Hill, Nevada, 14 miles away. Honestly, Fox, you can do better than this.

But our winner . . .

The Manatee. In defense of Boss Limbaugh, arguing with Lanny Davis's son, Seth, "Did Harry Reid want Bush to win the war?" Hannity blustered. "Of course, he wanted Bush to win the war," answered Davis the younger. "He didn't think that Bush was winning the war. You think Harry Reid wants American servicemen and women to die and be wounded and lose limbs?"

That's when Hannity crossed the line: "Yes," he yelled, "yes!" That, sadly, is a passive accusation of treason against the majority leader. Mr. Reid should sue Mr. Hannity's ass off, because, to paraphrase one of Hannity's predecessors, "If Mr. Reid is giving comfort to our enemies, he ought not be in the House." If, on the other hand, Mr. Hannity is giving comfort to our enemies, he ought not be brought into the homes of millions of Americans by News Corp. The original version of that quote was from Senator Joe McCarthy, who is probably very proud at this moment in hell of Sean Hannity, today's worst person in the world!

Can't Win for Losing

MARCH 11, 2009

Number three: Poison-gate. The *Michigan Messenger* reports that flooding from a river contaminated with dioxin has left the toxic chemical in the soil at West Michigan Park in the Saginaw Township. For years, the Environmental Protection Agency has known that dioxin causes cancer, damages endocrine and immune systems, and can affect fetal development. So last year, the Government Accountability Office suggested Mr. Bush's EPA ought to hurry up its dioxin report, so it could start enforcing laws against dioxin.

Mr. Bush said no. This week, President Obama said yes, after last week having frozen the cleanup negotiations with Dow Chemical, talks that had been criticized for their secrecy under Mr. Bush. Dow now says it will clean up the dioxin at West Michigan Park.

Number two: Representative democracy–gate. President Bush won the presidential election of 2000, despite losing the popular vote, thanks not only to the Republican-leaning Supreme Court but also to the suppression of Democratic votes, most notably in Florida. Despite that scandal, Mr. Bush won again in 2004 in another election marred by voter-access irregularities, most notably in the decisive state that year, Ohio.

But at least we managed to fix this democracy by 2008, right? A new study concluded that at least four million Americans did not vote last year due to registration or absentee ballot problems. Approximately the same number of voters who encountered such problems in 2000.

And number one: Taliban-gate. The Associated Press reports that a Taliban operations chief named Mullah Abdullah Zakir has been put in charge of countering Obama's surge of troops to Afghanistan. Zakir had been captured back in 2001 by the

Northern Alliance and turned over to U.S. forces. How is he now free to plan the death of American military servicepeople? Mr. Bush set him free. In December 2007, President Bush handed Zakir and a dozen other Guantanamo detainees over to the Afghan government, which promptly released them, which means one of two things: either Mr. Bush tossed an innocent man into Guantanamo, thus creating a terrorist who will likely have American blood on his hands all too soon, or Mr. Bush had an actual terrorist in his hands and, even free from legal restraints and free from Miranda and due process, free from any deadlines at all, he still could not succeed at prosecuting, let alone convicting, a terrorist who may well have American blood on his hands all too soon.

Worst Person in the World

The Ministry Network of Love

MARCH 13, 2009

The bronze to the Manatee for putting his sadism before his religion. "If we capture an enemy combatant in the battlefield or we can use Osama bin Laden, who may have information about a pending attack, you know what? I don't have any problem taking his head, sticking it underwater, and scaring the living daylights out of him and making him think we're drowning him. And I'm a Christian."

No, no, you are not.

I'm not saying you don't think you're a Christian, but if you actually think Christ would endorse torture, Sean Hannity, it has probably never dawned on you just what event that little crucifix thing is supposed to represent.

The silver: Congresswoman Michele Bachmann telling the Fox Out-of-Business Channel that she believes someday we will have an earmark-free spending bill.

"I took a pledge in my own district. I have not taken earmarks in the last three years that I have been in Congress because the system is so corrupt. It is possible to make that pledge."

It's possible to make that pledge, but if you are a raging hypocrite like Bachmann, it's not possible to keep it. The Web site Legistorm.com says Bachmann put in for seven earmarks for fiscal 2008 alone.

She asked for an earmark for $94,000 for a sheriff's youth program, another earmark for $335,000 for equipment acquisition for a medical center, and another earmark of $803,000 for the replacement of the small buses for the St. Cloud, Minnesota, bus line.

Bachmann's personal earmark total for 2008: $3,767,600.

And, oh, by the way, while she did sign the no-earmark pledge sponsored by the Club for Growth for 2008, without evidently knowing what a pledge is, she did not sign it for 2009.

But our winner . . .
Glenn Beck of Fixed News.

This week a man named Michael McClendon killed ten people during a rampage in Alabama. Slowly, subtly, perniciously, Beck defended this mass murderer.

"As I'm listening to him, I'm thinking about the American people that feel disenfranchised right now. They feel like nobody is hearing their voice. The government is not hearing their voice. Even if you call, they don't listen to you on both sides.

"If you are a conservative, you are called a 'racist.' You want to starve children. And every time they do speak out, they are shut down by political correctness.

"How do you not have those people turn into that guy?"

Well, you could give them a show on Fox. That seemed to work for you, Glenn.

Glenn Beck, rationalizer of the murder of ten people, today's worst person in the world!

Enough!

MARCH 19, 2009

Regarding the latest atrocity from the banks, those vast, engorged, gluttonous multinational corporations whose sneezes can be fatal to our jobs, whose mistakes can turn us into the homeless, whose accounting errors can be so panoramic that they can make our economy tremble and force us to hand them billions after billions in a blackmail scheme that has come to be known as "bailout."

Five weeks ago, Vikram Pandit, the chief executive officer of Citigroup, went back to Congress, tail seemingly between his legs, and, with entreaty dripping from his voice, announced, "I get the new reality and I'll make sure Citi gets it as well."

In point of fact, as Bloomberg News reports today, what Mr. Pandit "got" was a new $10 million executive suite for himself and his key associates.

This is the same Mr. Pandit who said he would show his leadership by accepting compensation from Citigroup of one dollar a year. In fact, he then accepted a total compensation package for 2008 of $38 million.

Enough!

Mr. Pandit, you're probably just a good actor and a damned liar and a con man. But I'll give you the benefit of the doubt and assume instead that you just can't tell the difference between one dollar and 38 million of them. That would certainly explain the maelstrom into which you, your colleagues at Citi, and your counterparts elsewhere have gotten us, including the vast majority of us who are just innocent bystanders.

Your bank says your new $10 million office is part of a global strategy of space reduction that will ultimately save billions, consolidating two floors of offices into one. You know this does not need to cost more than about $50 in boxes.

It seems entirely appropriate to remind everyone, sir, that this promise could be fulfilled by Citi saving two dollars a year for a billion years.

God knows you guys have pulled off every other accounting trick ever dreamt up by immoral man. You, sir, and the other corporate pirates like you, you who have been rescued by the taxpayer after your obsessive spending and your greed and your self-aggrandizement, you who then pretend to atone, who then publicly promise good behavior, and who then revert immediately to the rapaciousness that is your only skill; you, sir, all of you, need to be fired.

Enough!

Mr. Pandit's corporation should be cut up into little pieces. And when he and the other ultramillionaires wonder what hit them, we should make sure they are easily reminded. Our representatives should title the legislation that ends their immoral Ponzi schemes the "Punish Vikram Pandit Act of 2009."

The Far Right in this country, without the slightest provocation or justification, screams "socialism," and the sheep who follow that Far Right, and who do not know what the word means and do not know it is only being used because "communism" now rings laughably hollow—in this cry of fire in a crowded unemployment line, there is outrage, to be sure.

But there is also license. They think this is socialism? There are a million miles of reform left to go before we hit actual socialism. But if they're going to call us names, whether they apply or not, let's give them real reform.

Break up the banks. Regulate the financial industries to within an inch of their existences. Roll back corporate legal protections. Make liable the officers of corporations for their debts and for their deeds. Resurrect the rallying cry of a hundred years past: Bust the trusts!

AIG gives "failure bonuses" to those cretins whose dalliances in derivatives brought the company and part of the nation to her knees? Well, spin off the division those traders are owed the $165 million in bonuses from, underfund it, and cause it to go bankrupt.

Enough!

Let those with bonuses owed stand in line before a bankruptcy referee or judge, and wind up, just as you and I would, with half a cent on the dollar. Northern Trust fires 450 employees in December, then takes $1.6 billion in bailout money. Then sponsors a golf tournament. Then flies hundreds of clients to Southern California for private Oscar parties, including the renting of an airplane hangar and the hiring of the group Earth, Wind & Fire?

Enough!

Fire those executives. And fire up the Justice Department to figure out just how much fraud was involved in asking for $1.6 billion in bailout money when Northern Trust said nothing as the checks were being written, even though it knew in advance that millions could be saved by simply cutting the fluff and the trumpery.

Thirteen more companies that took bailouts and signed the mandatory documents that said they owed no back taxes, lied. Turned out, per Congressman John Lewis of Ways and Means today, they *lied*. They owe, just among those thirteen firms, $220 million in back taxes.

Enough!

Have the IRS take these companies, immediately, to the tax courts to which the rest of us are liable. And strip those ancient, outdated laws of incorporation, so that the officers of the corporation are personally liable for their companies' debts, just as you or I would be. And if the monopolies of radio or television rear up to support the corporate structure, to say a contract is a contract, even though that isn't true for a union these days, only for an AIG trader, take the invisible, unused Sword of Damocles they still fatuously insist is hanging over their heads, and make it real.

Enough!

Make sure both sides are heard. Reregulate the radio and television industries to limit station ownership and demand diversity of management and product. Reinstate the old rules that denied one man all the voices in a public square. End all waivers of multiple ownership of television stations and networks and newspapers in the same market.

And, yes, if a voice of the privileged classes unfairly uses his cable platform to call our neighbors, who are the victims of this, "losers," and to insist that he alone speaks for the real people, or if another indicts without equal time for defense a particular elected official, and then offers himself as a candidate for that very official's seat, in violation of all canons of good, or even fair, broadcasting, then tell the cable industry that the free ride is over and it is time that it too be regulated by the FCC.

Enough!

To all of you in the corporate boardrooms, stop viewing the public's reaction to this naked, unhindered robbery of the public coffers, and your audacious, immeasurable sense of proprietorship and entitlement, stop viewing our anger as some kind of brief impediment, some traffic delay that keeps you from your God-given corporate ballpark sponsorships, and perpetually remodeled offices, and the divine right of $38 million "compensation packages."

You, gentlemen and ladies, and not the good and long-suffering average people of this country, you are fomenting rage in this nation. You are the losers in this equation, and the people are the generous ones; they have not assembled in the streets with pitchforks and flaming torches. You are the ones perceived—understood in a visceral and even transcendent way—as the committers of what is becoming class economic rape.

And heed this one word before these people grow weary of forgiving you, and instead decide to bring the "good life," which you have built on their backs, crashing down on top of your heads; when the next boardroom needs remodeling, or the next bonus paid, or the next jet purchased, remember that one word: *Enough!*

Worst of Bush

In Texas They Call That Hospitality

MARCH 25, 2009

Number three: Torture-gate. Two former top administration figures have written in the *Washington Post* that a presidential commission on torture is critical to American security. They eloquently advance the now standard argument about formal review of the Bush torture policies that "detainee mistreatment flies in the face of

American ideals. It strengthens the case of those who fight against us. These methods yield suspect information. They put our troops and, indeed, all Americans at greater risk of torture and abuse if they are captured by our enemies."

What is news here is who cowrote that: Thomas Pickering, the elder George Bush's ambassador to the UN, and William Sessions, the FBI director under the first Bush and under Ronald Reagan.

Number two: Iraq-gate. The thing that made it look like the surge worked when maybe it really didn't may be unraveling. Thomas Ricks blogs at ForeignPolicy.com that the so-called Sunni awakening, the 100,000 politically and militarily active Iraqis who suddenly switched to our side in 2006 and 2007, have had another one of its members attacked just west of Baghdad.

Mr. Ricks also notes a report from yesterday's *New York Times* that the promises to members of the awakening that they would get permanent jobs in the Iraqi security forces have gone almost entirely unfulfilled, that only 5 percent of them have gotten those jobs. If the Sunnis now lose patience, change sides again, or strike back, we are screwed. Thank you, President Bush.

Number one: Gitmo Jr.–gate. Imagine the Bush government having instituted a system of near gulags and other detention centers so vast that it can hold not a couple hundred people, but rather 400,000 foreigners and even Americans of foreign birth. They don't get to see lawyers. They don't get their detentions individually reviewed by judges. They don't get minimum standards of jail, cleanliness, or hygiene. They don't get out for at least 10 months. And 10 months is considered lightning fast.

Some new piece of nightmare reporting by Seymour Hersh? Some fantasy of the Far Left? No. These are the ICE [Immigration and Customs Enforcement] facilities, courtesy of George W. Bush. Amnesty International is out with its report on immigration detention centers in this country, in which are stored thousands of human beings, many of them Americans pulled off the streets, who, because they did not have their naturalization papers with them, stayed in there for months. The report contains stories of people as innocent as a Tibetan monk fleeing the Chinese, tortured twice by the Chinese, arriving in New York, seeking political asylum, and instead being sent straight to an ICE detention facility, even with a lawyer and an affidavit, and a pledge from co-religionists that he had a place to stay with them.

ICE failed to respond to any legal attempts to free the man for ten months. The report cites falsification of records by the Bush appointees still running ICE in 2008, including a claim that the average detention is just 37 days. But a new study has shown that about 10,000 people are, or were, detained for longer than that claimed average, the most recent comprehensive study from 2003 saying the average is, in fact, 10 months.

The most startling fact about Amnesty's report: nobody at Immigration, nobody at the horrifically acronymed ICE, and nobody hearing the details of this American gulag is denying anything.

What Can Brown Do to Bill?

MARCH 27, 2009

The bronze to House Minority Whip Eric Cantor of Virginia. Although he was supposedly overruled when he had the common sense to suggest that his party not release an alternate budget proposal with no numbers, no math, no digits of any kind, he still did put his foot into it on Fixed News. Rocket scientist Gretchen Carlson said, "I found it interesting that it was only 19 pages, compared to the 142 pages of the Obama budget. Was there symbolism in that?"

Congressman Cantor replied, "I think, Gretchen and Steve, you can take some symbolism in that." Yes, you can. History proves that no matter how much BS you think you have in your hands, you can never, ever, ever write a paper for school, for college, or even for national politics that actually makes it to the full 20 pages.

The runner-up: Blogger Michelle Malkin, responding to a proposal by Senator Ben Cardin of Maryland that the newspaper industry, which is bleeding to death, should be permitted to opt for tax-exempt status, nonprofit status, the way public TV and radio stations can, perhaps preserving an entire industry. Malkin thinks this could mean a bailout of newspapers and, therefore, the government controlling what is printed in newspapers. Gee, Michelle, you spent the last decade telling us that the Democrats already control what is printed in the newspapers. Either you were full of it then or you're complaining about the threat of something that's already happened now.

But our winner . . .
Bill-O the Sad Clown, who just lost an advertiser. You could have left it alone. You could have just said nothing when you got called out for addressing a rape victims' support fund-raiser, after at least twice blaming rape victims, one of whom was then murdered. No, you had to go send your stalker producer to hunt down the managing editor of ThinkProgress.org, Amanda Terkel, to follow her for two hours while she was on vacation, as she checked into a hotel on vacation, to ambush her.

Tonight begins the comeuppance. ThinkProgress.org contacted the sponsors of O'Reilly's TV program asking not if they supported his right-wing stances, his hypocrisy, his racism, his misogyny, his fact-optional approach, but if they could stomach him, time after time, stalking people who had dared to criticize him in print or online. Tonight, UPS has said, "Enough." Its e-mail to Think Progress: "Thank you for sending an e-mail expressing concern about UPS advertising during the Bill O'Reilly show on Fox News. We do consider such comments when we consider ad placement decisions, which involve a variety of news, entertainment and sports programming. At this time, we have no plans to continue advertising during this show."

To paraphrase the famous phrase from church, Bill, here beginneth the lesson. Bill "What Can Brown Do for You" O'Reilly, today's worst person in the world!

Having His Big, Fat Say

MARCH 30, 2009

The bronze to Charles E. F. Millard, the Bush administration's director of the Pension Benefit Guaranty Corporation. Just months before the economy hit the wall last year, he took most of the $64 billion in the government pension fund, the fund from which more than a million Americans get pension checks and which guarantees the pensions of another 43 million of us, and he moved it out of bonds and into stocks, foreign market stocks, real estate company stocks, stocks tied to private equity funds.

The funds' stocks promptly dropped 23 percent, as of last September 30. Pension Benefit Guaranty will not say how much its stocks have dropped since last September 30. Mr. Millard is a former managing director of Lehman Brothers. I'm not sure, but I think he is now the CEO of the hot dog cart over on Sixth Avenue.

The silver: The disgraced ex–*New York Times* columnist William Kristol. A caller to C-Span pointed out how he and so much of the right-wing echo chamber had hyped the president's phony claim—the *former* president's phony claim—that Iraq had WMD. And the caller asked, will you personally apologize to those folks right now? Simple yes or no, thank you. Kristol did as asked. "No, I think the war was right. I think we've succeeded in the war. I think those lives—we should honor those soldiers who gave their lives and fought so hard and also were wounded for what they did. Also in Afghanistan—"

It must be great when faced with criticism of the greatest mistake of your life, the only time you utterly failed in the very limited demands made on you by your nation, the time you prevaricated, and Americans died as a result, Bill, it must be nice to be questioned about that and then just be able to change the topic. "And also in Afghanistan—"

But our winner . . .

Glenn Beck, getting more publicity out of this transparent, holier-than-thou, hypocritical 9/12 project, which the *New York Times* today described as "an initiative to reclaim the values and principles that he said were evident on the day after the September 11, 2001, terrorist attacks. On a special broadcast, he asks, whatever happened to the country that loved the underdog and stood up for the little guy? What happened to the voice of the forgotten man?"

Well, what happened to it was people like Glenn Beck killed it out of selfishness and prejudice and the hatred that boils in their souls. Two days before the fourth anniversary of 9/11, Glenn Beck, Mr. Spirit of 9/12, went on the radio and said, "You know, it took me about a year to start hating the 9/11 victims' families. It took me about a year. And when I see a 9/11 victim's family on television or whatever, I'm just like, oh shut up. I'm so sick of them because they're always complaining. We did our best for them."

To Beck's credit, he noted to the *Times*, "If you take what I say as gospel, you are an idiot." Did you ever see *The Music Man*, where the con artist walks into River City and sells the rubes band instrument after band instrument that they can't possibly afford? Harold Hill, or, as he now calls himself, Glenn Beck, today's worst person in the world!

Worst Person in the World

Shouting Fire

APRIL 7, 2009

The bronze to the Manatee, who opened his hour of delusion by saying, "Welcome to day number 77 of the age of Obama. And it is looking dangerous. That is our headline this Monday night. So it starts out with the president of the United States telling the rest of the world that America is an arrogant country, and then seemingly apologizing for our engagement in the war on terror, the war on terror that *THE 9/11 COMMISSION REPORT* said was being waged on us, that we weren't paying attention to."

Wait. So bin Laden was also waging a war on terror? That went south quickly. As to Hannity, what set him off, apparently, was Obama's statement that the United States is not, and will never be, at war with Islam, because Hannity does not realize there is a difference between Islam and terrorism, or because he doesn't *want* to realize it. Just a coincidence that the Hannity show begins with an illustration of a giant balloon filled with hot air.

Runner-up: The unidentified sellers of this "Hitler Gave Great Speeches, Too" T-shirt. They told the *Washington Independent* that they had sold out three boxes of the shirts by three o'clock Saturday afternoon at the Nob Creek Machine Gun Shoot outside Louisville. The gun shoot, at which new members were being recruited by the National Rifle Association. This message to the NRA, if you do not want your organization to become synonymous with racism, treason, hatred, paranoia, and political assassination fantasies, you better do something and fast. Oh, and murdering policemen. I forgot. If you don't want your organization to become synonymous with murdering policemen—

Bringing us to our winner . . .
Harold Hill—I'm sorry, Glenn Beck. Richard Poplawski killed three Pittsburgh policemen on Saturday because he was afraid of, a friend said, "the Obama gun ban that's on the way." He "didn't like our rights being infringed upon." When several Web sites correctly pointed out that this sounded awfully like one of Beck's hysterical rantings or maybe his interview last month with the head of the NRA, Beck immediately went back to his normal speed—high, stupid, dudgeon. "Blaming anyone except that nut job for what happened in Pittsburgh is crazy. Police officers over the weekend were killed by a crazy with a gun. And blaming anyone else besides him is like blaming the flight attendant after a terrorist takes down a plane. Giving passengers a nice little safety talk to prepare them doesn't mean you are responsible should a terrorist actually make that worst-case scenario happen."

Here is where you go wrong. You are not the flight attendant on the plane. Thanks for invoking that image again. You, Beck, are one of the cowards, safely on the ground, telling the nut job on the plane it is time to "rise up." You remember March 19, right? You probably don't. "The Second Amendment is under fire. We knew that they were going to try to bring the assault weapon ban back. Now they are blaming it on Mexico. The 9/12 Project is kind of a grassroots thing where you can go meet other people who think like you and think about values and principles and want to do something to take your country back."

And then you proceeded to read a letter from a woman who said that since the election, she had gone out and bought a handgun and joined the NRA. So when you talk about taking your country back, and then you read letters from people who are stockpiling guns, do you think these things are unconnected? That people even crazier than you, who you are encouraging to do something to take your country back, that they have bought these guns as paperweights? They bought them to shoot other people with.

You, Glenn Beck, you personally are encouraging Americans to shoot other Americans. Maybe, especially if you are right about your religion, maybe not this psychotic in Pittsburgh. Maybe he is not your fault. I hope not. What about the next one, Glenn? You want to cry about something on television. Cry about the next one. Beg him to ignore you. Beg the kids that the next one orphans to forgive you.

Glenn Beck, today's worst person in the world!

Not Since Coolidge

APRIL 14, 2009

Number three: Cooking the books–gate. The inspector general at Homeland Security has finally ruled on a little oopsy from the days when Mr. Bush's people were still trying to make the draconian airport-screening process seem effective. The FAA had scheduled a secret test of security at 12 major airports for late April 2006. Oddly enough, just before that test, somebody in the Transportation Security Administration sent out an e-mail warning that at Jacksonville Airport the FAA might conduct a secret test, and that this is what the officials would look like, and this is how they would be dressed. So TSA officials should make sure every passenger and ID matched.

In other words, Homeland Security made sure Homeland Security would pass the test.

Number two: George Bush, worldwide distributor of democracy–gate. The new president of Pakistan, Mr. Zardari, has, in an effort to reduce violence and tension between his government and extremists in the area, just signed a law permitting the Taliban to impose Sharia law in the northwestern part of his country. That would be the same Taliban that led village elders in southwestern Afghanistan to debate for two days the case of a 14-year-old girl and her 17-year-old boyfriend, who tried to break her engagement to somebody else by eloping to Iran. Half the town council there wanted to find a way to let the couple marry. So the Taliban stepped in and executed the teenagers.

Number one: Tax the poor–gate. Former Bush press secretary Ari Fleischer is still fighting mental health. This time writing in the pages of the *Murdoch Street Journal* under this bizarre headline, "Everyone should pay income taxes; it's bad for our democracy to exempt half the country." He wrote: "It's what's called redistribution of income and it's getting out of hand. A very small number of taxpayers, the 10 percent of the country that makes more than $92,400 a year, pays 72.4 percent of the nation's income taxes. Their burden keeps getting heavier."

You know, Ari Fleischer is right. That poor 10 percent of this country paying nearly three-quarters of all the taxes, it's just not fair to—wait a minute. Mr. Fleischer has left out some details here about himself and me and other top income makers. According to statistics from 2005, for the top 1 percent of the country's wage earners, our share of the total income is about 22 percent. That's a level not seen since the days of President Calvin Coolidge. The top 10 percent, which in 2005, by the way, still consisted of people making a hundred grand or more, not 92 grand, make 48.5 percent of all the reported income in this country.

In other words, the top 300,000 American earners make as much as the bottom 150 million American earners. Individually, we make 440 times what they make individually. Wait, Ari says, the top 10 percent earns 48.5 percent of all the income, but pays 72.4 percent of all the tax? That's not fair. Actually, it's not. It's more than fair. Because a lot of that bottom 90 percent, they make nothing at all. And if we raise their taxes, guess what, Ari, they still won't be paying anything.

Take it from me, the rich are making out like bandits. And to complain about the relative tax burden is not just offensive and embarrassing, but it taxes something else—credulity.

Worst of Bush

Headslappers

APRIL 15, 2009

Number three: Torture-gate. The *Murdoch Street Journal* now says President Obama is leaning toward the lifers at CIA, the ones who keep secret the specifics about the agency's crimes of torture and domestic spying. These are the follow-up Justice Department rationalization memos we were told were to be released but have not been. Nothing in them, mind you, just, the *Journal* reports, details like how President Bush was told it was legal to bang a detainee's head against the wall as long as the head was being held and the force of the banging was controlled by the interrogator.

Let's try that on a volunteer. John Yoo? John Yoo in the audience?

The point of the *Journal's* article and the leak of a detail like that might seem inscrutable, but it isn't. Just listen to this part of the article: "People familiar with the matter said some senior intelligence advisers to the president raised fear that releasing the two most sensitive memos could cause the Obama administration to be alienated from the CIA's rank and file as happened during the Bush administration when Porter Goss, who was unpopular among CIA officers, headed the agency."

You got it now? It's a warning, via a leak through the *Wall Street Journal*, from the CIA to Obama and new director Panetta. Keep the secrets secret, or we'll leave you hanging.

Number two: Exporting democracy–gate. Mr. Bush's triumph in Afghanistan keeps getting better and better. First, his president there, Mr. Karzai, unilaterally approved legislation that effectively legalizes marital rape. Now, Afghan women have protested, 300 of them. They were met by, today, 1,000 male counterprotesters, who, like the CIA with the *Wall Street Journal*, spoke mostly in symbols. They threw stones at the women who were protesting the legalized rape. But small stones, this time.

And number one: Tea bag–gate. As handfuls of sheep are herded into made-for-TV protests of taxation with representation, the U.S. Public Interest Research Group has now analyzed a Senate report from last year that showed just how much we lose as a nation in tax revenues hidden by corporations in places like the Cayman Islands. The opportunities to do so are growing immeasurably under the Bush administration.

The total figure is up to $800 billion a year. But U.S. Public Interest has now figured it out state by state. Texas would be losing $8 billion a year, $8 billion its ordinary citizens have to pay in taxes. So is New York State at that amount. Residents of California have to make up $11 billion lost to Tax Dodge Island. The District of Columbia, $713 million. Even Alaska—Alaska, $174 million that Alaskans have to pay because Alaskan corporations do not.

So where are your Tea Bag protests about that? Where is the Fox Out-of-Business network on this corporate piracy? Where is Neil Cavuto explaining to the simpletons in Sacramento that they're getting ripped off by international outfits like News Corp? Where is Captain Tea Bag himself, Glenn Beck? Why don't you take credit for this idea from someone else? Get up there and weep about U.S. corporations making us—all of us, rich and poor—pay $100 billion of their taxes so we get the privilege of getting to buy their products and bail out their failures?

Get up there and do that, and I'll march with you. Until then, you're just a bunch of greedy, water-carrying corporate-slave hypocrites defending the rich against the poor.

This Nightmare, the Torture Memos
APRIL 16, 2009

This president has gone where few before him dared. The dirty laundry, illegal, un-American, self-defeating, self-destructive is out for all to see.

Mr. Obama deserves our praise and our thanks for that. And yet he has gone but halfway, and in this case, in far too many respects, half the distance is worse than standing still.

Today, Mr. President, in acknowledging the science fiction–like documents, you said that "this was a time for reflection, not retribution. I respect the strong views and emotions that these issues evoke. We have been through a dark and painful chapter in our history. But at a time of great challenges and disturbing disunity, nothing will be gained by spending our time and energy laying blame for the past."

Mr. President, you're wrong. What you describe would be not spent energy, but catharsis; not blame laid, but responsibility ascribed.

You continued: "Our national greatness is embedded in America's ability to right its course in concert with our core values, and to move forward with confidence. That is why we must resist the forces that divide us, and instead come together on behalf of our common future."

Indeed we must, Mr. President. In the forces of which you speak are the ones lingering with pervasive stench from the previous administration. Far more than a criminal stench, sir, an immoral one—one we cannot let be re-created in this nation. One, President Obama, it is your responsibility to make sure cannot be recreated.

Forgive me for quoting from a comment I offered the night before the inauguration, but this goes to the core of the president's commendable but wholly naive intention here. This country has never moved forward with confidence without first cleansing itself of its mistaken past. In point of fact, every effort to merely draw a line in the sand and declare the past dead has served only to keep the past alive and often to strengthen it.

We moved forward with slavery in the Declaration of Independence and the Constitution. And four score and nine years later, we had buried 600,000 of our sons and brothers in a civil war. After that war ended, we moved forward without the social restructuring and without the protection of the rights of minorities in the South. And a century later, we had not only not resolved anything, but black leaders were still being assassinated in our southern cities.

We moved forward with Germany in the reconstruction of Europe after the First World War. Nobody even arrested the German kaiser, let alone conducted war crimes trials then. And 19 years later, there was an indescribably more evil Germany and a more heartrending Second World War.

We moved forward with the trusts of the early 1900s, and today, we are at the mercy of corporations which are too big to fail. We moved forward with the Palmer Raids and got McCarthyism. And we moved forward with McCarthyism and got Watergate. We moved forward with Watergate, and junior members of the Ford administration realized how little was ultimately at risk. They grew up to be Paul Wolfowitz and Donald Rumsfeld—and Dick Cheney.

But, Mr. President, when you say we must come together on behalf of our common future, you are entirely correct. We must focus on getting things right in the future as opposed to looking at what we got wrong in the past. That means prosecuting all those involved in the Bush administration's torture of prisoners, even if the results are nominal punishments or merely new laws.

Your only other option is to let this sit and fester indefinitely—because, sir, someday, there will be another Republican president, or even a Democrat just as blind as Mr. Bush, to ethics and this country's moral force. And he will look back to what you did about Mr. Bush, or what you did not do. And he will see precedent, or as Mr. Cheney saw, he will see how not to get caught the next time.

Prosecute, Mr. President. Even if you get not one conviction, you will still have accomplished good for generations unborn. Merely by acting, you will prevent this construction from someday entering the history books: Torture was legal. It worked. It saved the country, the end.

This must not be.

"It is our intention," you said today, "to assure those who carried out their duties relying in good faith upon legal advice from the Department of Justice that they will not be subject to prosecution."

Mr. President, you are making history's easiest, most often made, most dangerous mistake. You are accepting the defense that somebody was just following orders.

At the end of his first year in office, Mr. Lincoln tried to contextualize the Civil War for those who still wanted to compromise with the evils of secession and slavery. "The struggle of today," Lincoln wrote, "it's not altogether for today—it is for a vast future also."

Mr. President, you have now been handed the beginning of that vast future. Use it to protect our children and our distant descendants from anything like this ever happening again, by showing them that those who did this were neither unfairly scapegoated nor absolved. It is good to say we won't do it again. It is not, however, enough.

Worst Person in the World

Cluster-Fox

APRIL 22, 2009

The bronze to Mike Kilburn, county commissioner of Warren County, Ohio. You remember Warren County, part of the still unexplained terror-threat lockdown on election night 2004. The commissioners there are rejecting $373,000 in stimulus money for three new buses and vans meant to get the county's rural residents to health care and educational opportunities. Kilburn said, "I'll let Warren County go broke before taking any of Obama's filthy money. I'm tired of paying for people who don't have. As Reagan said, 'Government is not the answer, it's the problem.'" Commissioner Kilburn, Reagan's dead and he was a lousy president.

Our runner-up: Bill-O the Clown; his vendetta against NBC and GE has now gotten so desperate that he is talking to people from the Fox Out-of-Business Channel about an article in the *Wall Street Journal* and pretending nobody will notice that they all work for Rupert Murdoch. O'Reilly said, "The *Wall Street Journal* headlined GE's latest income statement this way: 'GE's net tumbles 35 percent through finance woes.' Here is how the überliberal *New York Times* headlined GE's trouble: 'GE's first quarter net tops analysts' estimates.' Quite a difference from the *Journal*, wouldn't you say?"

Yes, yes, I would. And clearly it has nothing to do with the fact that your boss also owns the *Wall Street Journal*. What is the journal going to say about *Broadcasting & Cable*'s story today, Billy? That Fox will shortly report network ad sales down by 20 percent, station ad sales down by 45 percent, Fox News ad sales down, for the first time ever, by 4 percent, to go with company stock down 56 percent in one year?

"President Obama recently appointed GE Chairman Jeffrey Immelt to be one of his economic advisers, even though the man has run GE into the ground. That appointment was payback for allowing NBC News to openly support Obama for president."

Hey, bully boy, you care to try to prove that? Or was that just something God whispered to you?

"So now we have powerful corporations not only intruding on electoral politics, but also attacking Americans like, the Tea Party protesters. That is the situation all Americans should condemn."

Seriously? You and the other Fox talking points readers mocked every antiwar protester, every critic of the last administration, every defender of the Constitution, and your boss sent instructions to President Bush in the White House. You have the nerve to criticize actual critical coverage of poorly intended News Corp–sponsored cluster Fox?

Bill, you know nothing about news. Your company doesn't have the journalistic chops of *Scholastic* magazine.

But our winner . . .

Democratic Senator Ben Nelson of Nebraska. "Too many Americans," he said in a speech in Lincoln, "get their news from entertainers who tell them what to be angry about today." Entertainers, he says, like Jon Stewart, Rush Limbaugh, Bill O'Reilly, Glenn Beck, Sean Hannity, Keith Olbermann, and Rachel Maddow.

"Responding to the talking points of either extreme is not the way to enact good public policy. There is a lot of inaccurate and incomplete information out there, thanks to talk shows from either the Left or the Right. Facts often get in the way of a good rant."

You'd know, Senator. Thanks for the opportunity to tell you you don't know what the hell you're talking about. I am fed up with this equating of what we do here to circus performers like Limbaugh and the Fox crowd. We don't make up stuff like Beck does. We don't stalk people like O'Reilly does. We don't support racism and encourage violence like Limbaugh does. We don't recite talking points like Hannity does.

Not from anybody, Senator Nelson. Rachel caught you out to lunch on the stimulus and called you on it. And I slammed a Democratic president last week. We believe first, Senator, in right and wrong over here, not Right and Left. Let me know when you start believing in something, besides reelection.

Democratic Senator Ben Nelson of Nebraska, today's worst person in the world!

Worst Person in the World

Mao-Maoing the Flack Catchers

APRIL 23, 2009

The bronze to Congressman John Shimkus of Illinois, clearly unhappy that he ranks no better than fourth among our insane representatives, behind Michele Bachmann and the two Kings

[Pete and Steve]. This is the guy who said global warming was much worse during the time of the dinosaurs than it is now, forgetting that the dinosaurs became extinct. He also was the one who said we didn't have to worry about global warming, because "the earth will end only when God declares it's time to be over. A man will not destroy this earth. This earth will not be destroyed by flood."

Apparently Congressman Shimkus has lost his groove. He doesn't like the Obama energy plan. "I think this is the largest assault on democracy and freedom in this country that I have experienced. I've lived through some tough times in Congress, impeachment, two wars, terrorist attacks. I fear this more than all of the above activities that have happened."

It's worse than Afghanistan or Iraq or Bill Clinton or 9/11? Obama's energy plan is worse than 9/11? Congressman, I wouldn't even say that *you* were worse than 9/11. Anyway, if somehow you are right, won't God defeat the Obama energy plan?

Our runner-up: Little Jesse, Bill-O the Clown's stalker producer, bought some shares of GE stock, giving him access to the shareholders meeting. During the open-questions part of the event, he and at least one other person affiliated with Fox proceeded to exercise their right to ask. Little Jesse's question was about Janeane Garofalo's visit here last week, when she suggested that the Tea Party crowd was made up largely of racists. He was complaining that Olbermann didn't bother to challenge her, according to another GE shareholder, who was quoted in several news accounts.

O'Reilly portrayed this as some kind of uprising against GE about, well, me. But now he says it's also about GE making money off cap and trade. So I got Obama elected by attacking Bill. Besides that paranoid delusion, there are several problems with this today. Little Jesse never identified himself as a Fox News employee when he asked his question, nor did he identify himself as representing Fox News as he tried to interview other GE stockholders in the parking lot afterward. He simply wore a sticker badge reading "share owner."

He also claimed his microphone had been cut off. It was not. Every GE share owner who wanted to talk got to, some multiple times. Also, Little Jesse recorded the question-and-answer session, in violation of corporation rules. And when caught recording it, he lied about whether or not he was recording it.

Also, two facts completely left out of Fox's reporting: Not one GE shareholder, not even Little Jesse, complained about the $200 million or whatever it is MSNBC made for the corporation last year. And as the whole event was summed up in the last sentence in the Reuters story about Wednesday's uprising, "Shares of GE rose 10 cents Wednesday to close at 11.80."

Went up another eight cents today. Thanks, Bill.

But our winner . . .

Bill-O the historian, the man who made the Americans the war criminals at Malmedy, the man who evidently cut most of his history classes, gets into a debate with Alan Colmes about the propriety of Obama meeting Hugo Chavez. "Do these people have a problem with Mao and Nixon?" Colmes asks. "Of course, you worked for Richard Nixon. I mean, Nixon goes to China. Do you have a problem with—"

Bill-O interrupts, "It was Zhou and Nixon. Mao was not involved." Colmes: "There was—" Bill-O interrupts again, "Yes, Zhou. All right, but okay—all those points are valid, as long as you realize it was Zhou Enlai, not Mao Zedong." Colmes, flustered, says, "Zhou Enlai, okay."

So Bill is saying that when Nixon made his historic trip to China in 1972, he never met with Chairman Mao? He only met with the premier, Zhou Enlai? Do we have that film?

So, in the famous film taken at the summit in China in 1972, who was that guy Nixon was shaking hands with, Bill? Alfred Hitchcock?

Geez! Bill, help me out here. I'm supposed to take you seriously?

Bill, who are you gonna believe about Mao, me or your lying archival footage, O'Reilly, today's worst person—get a history book—in the world!

Made Us Think

APRIL 24, 2009

The bronze to Bill-O. Remember that catchphrase from *Rocky and Bullwinkle*, "I put bomb in squirrel's briefcase and who gets blown up? Me."

You will recall Bill-O's latest conspiracy theory, that I got Barack Obama elected president by attacking Bill-O and Fixed News so GE could make money off green energy. "This is obviously a major story. When a powerful corporation which controls a major part of the American media may be using its power on the air waves to influence politics in order to make money from government contracts. That kind of corruption would make Watergate look small. We hope it is not true."

Powerful corporation controls a major part of the American media, influences politics in order to make money. That phrasing made many of us think about 1995, when the Republicans in the House changed federal law so that Rupert Murdoch could make money by owning multiple TV stations in one city while also owning a newspaper in the same city. And then it made us think of 1996, when Republican mayor Rudy Giuliani ordered that Murdoch's new Fox News Channel be carried on one of the TV stations the city of New York then owned.

And then Giuliani threatened cable operators who refused to run Fox News. Made us think then of 2003, when the Republican Congress changed the law again to increase how many stations Murdoch could personally own. I don't know, Rupe, I think your boy Bill-O said your corrupt actions would make Watergate look small.

Our runner-up: Congresswoman Michele Bachmann of Minnesota. I tried to read this, but it's been a long night. I could not get through this without bursting into laughter. Here is the representative from Mars, climate change denier, on the actual floor of the House:

"Carbon dioxide, Mr. Speaker, is a natural by-product of nature. Carbon dioxide is natural. It occurs in Earth.

"Carbon dioxide is portrayed as harmful. But there isn't even one study that can be produced that shows that carbon dioxide is a harmful gas. There isn't one such study because carbon dioxide is not a harmful gas. It is a harmless gas.

"But carbon dioxide is perhaps three percent of the total atmosphere that's in the Earth."

No, no, no, no. It's 0.04 percent. It's not 3 percent. If it was 3 percent, we would all be unconscious or we would have gills. Also, this point that carbon dioxide is natural, so it's harmless. You know what else is a natural product of nature, Congresswoman? Disease, anthrax, fatal lightning strikes, being eaten by wolves, and stupidity.

But our winner . . .

Debbie Marco, the property manager of CCRT Properties, which runs the Cambridge on the Lake Apartments in Kenosha, Wisconsin. Local news reports there say she has notified Colin Byars's mother, Danielle Eckert, that Mr. Byars broke his lease without giving the required 30 days' notice, and, thus, as his mother, she owes them his rent for March and April, $2,060. Miss Marco says she has contacted her lawyers.

Colin Byars broke that lease in February because on the 24th of that month, the middle-school teacher came to the aid of several women being harassed by three men outside a bar. One of the men killed him, and his landlord is now threatening to sue his mother because he didn't give his 30 days' notice as he was being murdered.

Debbie Marco of CCRT Properties of Wisconsin, today's worst person in the world!

Foxx News

APRIL 29, 2009

The bronze to Congresswoman Michele Bachmann. We're all laughing at her historical gaffe yesterday about Jimmy Carter and swine flu. It turned out she topped herself on the floor of the House.

The Carter gaffe first: "I find it interesting that it was back in the 1970s that the swine flu broke out then under a Democrat president Jimmy Carter. And I'm not blaming this on President Obama. I just think it is an interesting coincidence."

The swine outbreak was in February 1976, when Republican Gerald Ford was president, 11 months before Carter was inaugurated. But on the same day, she pulled this whopper: "FDR applied the opposite formula, the Hoot-Smawley Act, which was a tremendous burden on tariff restrictions and then, of course, trade barriers and the regulatory burden and taxpayers. That's what we saw happen under FDR. The American people suffered for almost 10 years under that kind of thinking."

Seriously, Congresswoman, you are a buffoon. *Smoot-Hawley*, not *Hoot-Smawley*. It was the Smoot-Hawley Tariff Act. And not only was it passed in 1930, three years before Franklin Roosevelt became president, but it was written by two Republicans, Senator Reed Smoot and Congressman Willis Hawley. It was signed into law by a Republican president, Herbert Hoover, over the pleading of all the economists and big bankers, even the head of J. P. Morgan, and it was repealed under FDR in 1934.

I know, I know, Congresswoman. You weren't paying attention in history class in high school. You were too busy going to the movies. But it was in the movies, in *Ferris Bueller's Day Off*, where Ben Stein, the economics teacher, asked his class, "Anyone? Anyone?" where anyone who knew the answer was asked to raise or lower his hand. He was asking about the Smoot-Hawley Act. Hoot-Smawley. Hoot-Smawley.

We let this woman vote on actual pieces of legislation. But it's worse that that. We let her drive a car. Hoot-Smawley.

Runner-up: Rupert Murdoch. The Audit Bureau of Circulations reports the average American daily newspaper lost just over 7 percent of its circulation during the past six months compared to a year ago. Some did better, some did worse. The circulation of the *Los Angeles Times* dropped 6.6 percent. That of the *New York Times* dropped 3.6 percent.

But the biggest loss in the top 25 markets: Murdoch's *New York Post*. Circulation is down 20.5 percent. This other piece of the Murdoch empire, the cornerstone of the reactionary, the knee-jerk, half-fiction racist, xenophobic, retaliatory conservative media, and one out of every five readers has vanished, three times as fast as *New York Times* readers.

How can the stockholders of News Corp continue to indulge Rupert Murdoch's personal political agenda, vanity press? How can the folks not stand up and say, "Rupert, you owe me money"?

But our winner . . .

And this is the most despicable thing said on the floor of the House in decades. Here is Congresswoman Virginia Foxx from the fifth district of North Carolina, in Winston-Salem, arguing against the Matthew Shepard hate crimes bill:

"The hate crimes bill that is called the Matthew Shepard Bill is named after a very unfortunate incident that happened where a young man was killed. But we know that that young man was killed in the commitment of a robbery. It wasn't because he was gay. The bill was named for him. The hate crimes bill was named for him. But it is really a hoax that continues to be used as an excuse for passing these bills."

Congresswoman Foxx, you are the only hoax here. One of Matthew Shepard's killers admitted under oath that he knew he was gay, that they lured him from a bar by pretending to be gay themselves. Then they robbed him, pistol-whipped him, fractured his skull, tortured him with sharp implements, and then tied him to a fence post in rural Wyoming. He was not found for 18 hours.

There is no excuse for Congresswoman Foxx's remarks. She is, at best, callous, insensitive, criminally misinformed. At worst, she is a bold-faced liar. And if there is a spark of a human being in there somewhere, she should either immediately retract and apologize for her stupid and hurtful words, or she should resign her seat in the House.

She is not worthy to represent this country nor any of its parties nor any of its peoples. She is our shame. And adding to our shame, she said all that as Matthew Shepard's mother sat in the House gallery.

Congresswoman Virginia Foxx, Fifth District of North Carolina, today's worst person in the world!

Worst Person in the World

Wearing Out the Shovel

APRIL 30, 2009

The bronze to Bill-O the Clown. In a webcast I mentioned earlier—a gold mine. No makeup, comb-over not reinforced, nobody reining him in. Fabulous, thank you, Bill. Here is Bill on the first 100 days of the Obama presidency:

"He wants to give health care to people who can't afford it, for whatever reason. Some of these people could afford it if they'd stop drinking, you know, a quart of gin every day."

There it is, what Bill-O really thinks of the folks.

Our runner-up: Karl Rove, another op-ed in the *Murdoch Street Journal*, during which Rove pulls off the most dishonest thing you can do in a newspaper, or, since Murdoch also did this on Fox, on television. "Now Mr. Obama," Rove writes, "is asking, as he did in a town hall meeting last month, why not do a universal health care system, like the European countries? Maybe because he was elected by intimating that would be extreme?"

Except Mr. Obama did not ask that. Richard in California asked it. In the online town hall meeting on March 26, Obama read it and answered it, pointed to it, and read it and answered it:

"Now, the question is, If you're going to fix it, why not do a universal health care system like the European countries?"

Obama then answered the guy's question by saying we can't do it like the European countries. Congratulations, Mr. Rove. Anybody can be a scum of the earth in one thing like politics, but it takes a man of super genius to be the scum of the earth of politics and then in journalism.

But our winner, again . . .

Congresswoman Virginia Foxx of North Carolina. She is now blaming her remarks, before the passage of the Matthew Shepard Hate Crimes Bill by the House, on ABC News. She had called the story that Shepard was beaten, his skull fractured, then tied to a fence post for 18 hours and left to die, because his murderers knew he was gay, a "hoax."

The congresswoman now calls that choice of words poor and offers the standard insincere apology. In her words, "I am especially sorry if his grieving family was offended by my statement." You are either sorry or not, Congresswoman. The burden does not depend on whether somebody else was offended. "I was referring to a 2004 ABC News *20/20* report on Mr. Shepard's death.

"ABC's *20/20* report questioned the motivation of those responsible for Mr. Shepard's death. Referencing this media account may have been a mistake, but it was a mistake based on what I believed were reliable accounts."

The girlfriends of the two murderers testified at their trials that the men had plotted beforehand to rob a gay man and were not under the influence of drugs at the time. In the ABC report, though, one of the women said she had lied under oath just to enhance the murderers' gay panic defense. Also, the murderers suddenly claimed they had been high on meth for a week.

However, several interviewees also insisted to ABC that one of the murderers had known Matthew Shepard socially and known he was gay. Congresswoman Foxx apparently didn't see that part of the report.

Congresswoman, you are digging yourself in deeper. Apologize, sincerely this time, or resign. Get out and take your myopic view of the world with you.

Congresswoman Virginia Foxx, today's worst person in the world!

The New Emperor Has Clothes

MAY 8, 2009

Number three: False idols–gate. This is back in 2006. This program, *Countdown*, revealed that the former number two man in Bush's Office of Faith-Based Initiatives was about to publish a book blowing the whistle on the administration's exploitation of the Christian right. The office did not really do anything to advance the supposed causes of religious charities; it just specialized in paying lip service while stroking egos of Christian right-wingers with trinkets and symbols.

So what do they want now that Obama is in office? More symbols. After President Obama did not mark the National Day of Prayer yesterday with a formal event, Fox News and the Christian Right screamed that Obama had broken tradition, not noting that Mr. Bush had only established the tradition by holding events for the first time during his presidency.

In other words, they don't mind being duped on the substantive stuff; they just want their parties back.

Number two: "Change Who Can Believe In?"–gate. After President Obama this week announced his plan to cut 121 government programs, for an estimated savings of $17 billion, Mr. Obama's move was praised as "a serious first step toward changing the culture in Washington."

What raving liberal lunatic would damn Mr. Bush with that comparison? Senator Tom Coburn of Oklahoma, a Republican described by Politico.com as "a hard-line fiscal conservative."

Coburn even said, "Many presidents have proposed specific spending cuts, but nearly all have failed to carry through."

Somewhere in Dallas, somebody's ears are burning.

Number one: "Keeping Us Safe"–gate. First Mr. Bush allowed Osama bin Laden to escape, and instead of attacking bin Laden, he diverted U.S. resources to Iraq. Then he helped prop up Pervez Musharraf with money and political backing while Musharraf did nothing to get Al Qaeda. Mr. Bush even signed off on a truce that allowed Islamic extremists who were harboring Al Qaeda to live their lives in peace, ostensibly, while planning future attacks on us.

Now, less than four months after Mr. Bush left office, Mr. Bush's days of appeasement are over. Last night, the prime minister of Pakistan went on national television there, and almost eight years after September 11, finally declared war on the Taliban, in part because of U.S. pressure.

Pakistan's government has the support of its people in this, finally, in part because of the U.S. pressure on a top opposition leader, a religious conservative. But also because the Taliban have become so successful in recent years in capturing new territory and spreading their brand of violent Islamic extremism that it has genuinely threatened the average Pakistani. And that peril is thanks to the appeasement by President Bush.

WTF?

The Carrie Prejean Experience

MAY 8, 2009

It is not that she is wrong on the issue, though she is; one thing all sides can agree on, there are many who are wrong on the issue of gay marriage. Also, there is one fact that has completely vanished from the Carrie Prejean experience. She was asked. She didn't just stand up there at the Miss USA pageant and cut off Perez Hilton in the middle of a question about breast implants or nuclear fission and start shouting, "I only believe in opposite-sex marriage." She was asked.

But this is no longer about her opinion. It's about her. It's about the amazing holier-than-thou, know-it-all-ism that she has exuded from the moment the question was asked, right through every complaint about how she was being unfairly paraded on the public stage as the evildoers foisted news conference after news conference onto her and the anti–gay marriage group she joined, and as the evil left-wing media forced her to do interview after interview with the likes of Dr. James Dobson.

She said: "I felt as though Satan was trying to tempt me in asking me this question. And then God was in my head and in my heart saying, Carrie, do not compromise this. You know, I—you need to stand up for me. You need to share with all these people—if there were 95 percent of the people in the audience that were gay, you need to witness to them."

God and Satan, battling it out for the future of freedom of speech inside the head of St. Carrie of La Jolla. Where exactly, Carrie, were God and Satan when the Miss California people came to you and offered to pay for you to alter your God-given body with breast implants, so you stood a better chance of getting what amounts a better job inside the Donald Trump Miss Whatever company?

Where exactly, St. Carrie, were God and Satan when you posed in only your panties as a teenager, and didn't know the photographer with the camera and all the lights might be, I don't know, a photographer?

Where exactly, St. Carrie, were God and Satan when, incredibly enough, the same exact thing happened again, and another evil photographer took hidden surveillance photos of you without your consent and without the express written consent of the commissioner of baseball?

Prejean explained: "While I don't know who released the photos from this morning, I do know who released the photos that were actually just released as of a few hours ago. And I find it appalling that a professional photographer would violate my trust by releasing an unauthorized and inappropriate image taken in between posed shots on a windy day, which I was unaware of."

Which were you unaware of, the windy day or the photographs or the photographer? Imagine this, somebody in the modeling business violating somebody else's trust. And St. Carrie in the unauthorized and inappropriate image taken in between posed shots, you're looking right at the camera, twice.

And exactly what was up with that wind? Windy enough to get a reaction from part of your body, but not windy enough to move your hair significantly? That's some kind of wind. Satan's winds.

Your grandfather fought against that wind at the Battle of the Bulge.

As Prejean reminded us: "My grandfather served under General Patton during World War II. He never spoke about the Battle of the Bulge that he participated in as a rifleman. On April 19, on that stage, I exercised my freedom of speech. And I was punished for doing so.

"This should not happen in America. It undermines the Constitutional rights which my grandfather fought for."

Ahh, thank you for bringing us back to the two cruxes here. First, you were not exercising your freedom of speech during the Miss USA Pageant. Your freedom of speech, my freedom of speech, has nothing to do with something as crassly commercial as a beauty pageant, nor as crassly commercial as Donald Trump. On April 19, you were an employee of USA Inc., or Donald Trump Inc. Unless you have a written contract guaranteeing you carte blanche, and nobody does, the pageant people also have the right to take that right away from you at any moment, just as MSNBC, NBC, or GE could take away this industrial version of free speech I'm utilizing right now.

Uh, by the way, about that, don't.

This, St. Carrie of La Jolla, is exactly what your freedom of speech, what my freedom of speech, consists of in its entirety: "Congress shall make no law respecting an establishment of religion or prohibiting the free exercise thereof; or abridging the freedom of speech, or of the press, or of the right of the people peaceably to assemble and to petition the government for a redress of grievances."

No more, no less. I'm sorry, but your grandfather did not fight to protect your right to answer a question during a network television soft-porn special without consequences or fallout. And he did not fight to protect my right to criticize you on TV, either.

He fought to protect you from having the government stop us from speaking our minds. If you want to extend that to protecting you from having your employer stop you from speaking your mind, I advise you to join an entirely different political action committee, because if your National Organization for Marriage suddenly decides that people with breast implants also shouldn't be allowed to get married, and for some reason you disagree with them, they won't have to honor your freedom of speech, either.

Now, the other part. Let's take a look at the second half of that last answer again: "On April 19, on that stage, I exercised my freedom of speech and I was punished for doing so."

First of all, crying in a beauty pageant, there's no crying in beauty pageants. How exactly were you punished? The Miss California people say you entered into that contest under false pretenses. They claim you are in breach of contract, that you posed seminude and more seminude, while claiming you hadn't. They say you violated the rules by joining a political organization. And they say you have not been showing up for your contractually obligated appearances as Miss California.

So, naturally, you got fired. Wait, she—she didn't get fired?

Instead, Donald Trump announced: "Carrie will remain Miss California, very importantly."

After all this, Donald Trump, who never compromised a dollar for the sake of a principle, did not suddenly kick this publicity-generating machine to the curb. Still she thinks she got punished.

Oh, she assumed she didn't win the pageant because of her answer. So? That wasn't an election. It was a business decision made by a bunch of employees about another bunch of employees. They weren't electing a new pope over there. They were just expressing their corporate freedom of speech, Carrie.

What the—?

Stones from Water

MAY 13, 2009

Number three: Sleep-gate. After waterboarding, what was the CIA inspector general's second-biggest complaint about interrogation techniques when he first blew the whistle on torture in 2004? Sleep deprivation. So reports the *LA Times*, saying interrogators thought you could keep a man awake for 180 hours without injuring him. The prisoners had their feet shackled to the floor and their hands cuffed close to their chins, according to the Justice Department memos. A prisoner who started to drift off to sleep would tilt over and be caught by his chains.

Apart from scars, there was psychological damage. But the Justice Department, of course, issued a memo in 2005 saying there were no lasting aftereffects from sleep deprivation. When the Obama administration banned sleep deprivation, it got a frantic call from Mr. Bush's last CIA chief, Michael Hayden, who was still pumping the party line that sleep deprivation was not serious. "Are you telling me that under all conditions of threat, you will never interfere with the sleep cycle of detainees?" Hayden asked.

Number two: Shut up–gate. Dick Cheney should heed this development between his self-rationalizations Sunday and yesterday. A U.S. senator decided he had had enough. In his words, "No, we're not less safe. I suppose that's the short answer and probably as good as I can give. I disagree with some of the things the administration has done. Even in the closing of Guantanamo, they're being very methodical at this point. Our guard is up. On balance, we remain as safe as we can possibly be in a world in which there is Islamic extremists who want to attack us."

Who has gotten off the Dick Cheney team? Who did the former vice president yak, yak, yak back to reality? Senator Joseph Lieberman.

But number one: Water-gate. Channel 11 in Houston reporting from Iraq that our soldiers there are not getting enough water—in Iraq, where temperatures can hit 130 degrees. "We were rationed two bottles of water a day," the station quoted Army Staff Sergeant Dustin Robey, now back from his tour. That would be 3 liters in a climate where you can lose 15 liters a day just walking around. Sometimes the water, most of it supposed to be supplied by the Halliburton spin-off KBR, was overtreated with chemicals. So Roby and his men would get nauseous. So they stopped drinking it.

So then Roby and his men would get kidney stones. So they would instead drink the local water. That's when they got dysentery. Sergeant Roby says he now takes 26 different kinds of pills per day. He's been forced to retire at a fraction of his pay because of what all that insufficient water supply has done to him. His family is now facing foreclosure.

Private Bryan Hannah recalled to the TV station that two years ago his platoon ran out of water, ran *out*. The sergeant then said go find some, which meant going to the civilian contracting facility and stealing water. This is how the Bush administration cared for the troops. Send them to Iraq without water. This, not what Dick Cheney says, not what Mr. Bush tries to get recorded in his library—this is his legacy.

WTF?

The Democrat Socialist Party

MAY 13, 2009

As Roger Simon of Politico.com reported, the Republican National Committee, at a special committee meeting next week, is expected to adopt a resolution requiring its membership to refer to the other guys as the "Democrat Socialist Party." This on the heels of their brilliant success in trying to rebrand the Democratic Party as the Democrat Party in 2001, which not only did not keep the

Democrats out of the White House, but which still hasn't achieved 100 percent success inside the Republican Party.

The Democrat Socialist Party—since the election, the Republicans seem to be doing whatever has just popped into one of their leaders' heads. The idea-generating talent of Donald Trump, say, combined with the thorough planning and foresight of the Octomom.

The Democrat Socialist Party—there are apparently 55 countries right now with parties with names that are some combination of Democrat, Democratic, Social, and Socialist. From Afghanistan to Azerbaijan, from Great Britain to Gibraltar. From the Hong Kong League of Social Democrats to the Party of Bulgarian Social Democrats.

And all 55, in English, or in their English translations, are known in that order, Social Democrats. The RNC does not want that built-in advantage of familiarity. They want Democrat Socialists. Genius, I tells you, genius.

And this just gets better and better. A Pew Research survey last month indicated a dramatic increase in the number of people for whom the word "socialist" was sticking to President Obama. Last September, it was 6. In February, it was 13. Last month, it was 20. Twenty percent of Americans are using the word "socialist" to describe Obama? No wonder the Republicans are doing this. It's genius. Genius, I tells you.

No, not percent, 20 *people*. Let's look at the survey again, how often people describe Obama with the word "socialist." Last September, it was 6 people out of 629 polled. In February, it was 13 out of 620. Last month, it was 20 people out of 742—20 people, 2.7 percent. Brilliant.

The Democrat Socialist Party; the choice of nearly 3 out of every 100 Americans.

Wait, it gets worse still. Rasmussen, polling done by the people who founded, then bailed out early on, ESPN; Rasmussen polling, now done generally for and shaped by Rupert Murdoch; Rasmussen actually asked Americans early last month what they thought of socialism. Oh, for God's sake, only 53 percent say capitalism is better than socialism; 20 percent prefer socialism; 27 percent aren't sure which.

And the younger voters, adults under 30, favor capitalism, but only by 37 percent to 33 percent, with 30 percent undecided.

A question for Michael Steele or Shelby Steele or Steely Dan or whoever is running the GOP this week: Do you guys read these polls? I mean, we got them off the Internet for free. The word "socialist" is not sticking. And even when it does, extraordinarily large numbers of Americans think it's a compliment.

Younger voters, including the people who may still be voting in the presidential election of 2072, think it's a toss-up. So of course, try to portray your opponents as the Democrat Socialist Party.

Well, this is what this is about, of course. The Hugo Chavez handshake. The effort to portray Obama as foreign, un-American, sympathetic to strange cultures and ideas, the one the Republicans rolled out during the campaign, the reason that at this moment John McCain is the president of the—oops.

Anyway, you've seen the Chavez poll numbers, right? CNN polling at the end of last month: Republican Party, 39 percent favorability in this country. The unfavorable score for the Republicans in this country, 55.

CNN polling, beginning of last month: Venezuela, 42 percent favorability in this country. Their unfavorable score is 54. Venezuela, home of an actual socialist strong man, is more popular in the United States than the opposition party in the United States is popular in the United States.

The Democrat Socialist Party. I am beginning to think I understand what's happening here. It is a story of political intrigue, even scandal, that is unmatched, if it's correct, in our nation's long history. The Republicans have gotten so turned around that Pete Hoekstra and Lamar Alexander are now trying to bait the Democrats into a full-scale investigation of torture, the kind the Democrats wouldn't dare do without Republican support.

The Republicans blast Obama's stimulus plan. John Boehner presents their own version. There are no numbers in it. Arlen Specter bailed out of the GOP. Joe the Plumber bailed out of the GOP. Their last vice presidential candidate couldn't define the Bush doctrine. And her daughter, an unmarried teenage mother, who, after giving birth and splitting with the father, is now trying to convince people that abstinence works, even though it appears in her case to desperately not have worked.

There's a congresswoman who can't stop talking, who called the Smoot-Hawley Tariff Act the Hoot-Smawley Tariff Act. There's a nut bag on TV who uses a teleprompter, who ripped the president for using a teleprompter, apparently unaware of the irony therein that that means they both use teleprompters.

The chairman of the party had to grovel for forgiveness from a radio announcer. A congressman from Georgia had to grovel for forgiveness from a radio announcer while on the radio announcer's show. The radio announcer is trying to expel John McCain, John McCain's daughter, Colin Powell, and countless others from the party. And the Republican governor of Texas and Republicans in dozens of other states are actually proposing secession as a rallying point for the party.

In other words, the GOP could take back America by leaving it.

And now they want to rename the Democrats the Democrat Socialists. It's genius. Genius, I tells you. This mass madness, this cascade of rookie mistakes, this seemingly deliberate narrowing of the Republicans to a third party, this can all have only one possible explanation: they're all Democratic agents.

You heard me. Cheney, a Democrat. Boehner, Democrat. Palin, Democrat. Steele, Democrat. Bachmann, Democrat. Limbaugh, big fat Democrat.

You got another explanation? Steele said even when he seems to be making a gaffe, there's a secret strategy behind it. Of course there is.

I mean, maybe they're not Democrats. Maybe they think they can simply get the Republican Party absorbed by the Democrats in a kind of Trojan horse deal, and then take over from the inside. But even that would be too complicated. Compared to their recent uninterrupted sequence of bone-headed brainstorms, it would be too good.

They're moles, turncoats, spies, sellouts, political traitors. They have to be. They can't be that stupid. The Democrat Socialist Party.

What the—?

The Human Equation

MAY 14, 2009

Most of you know that my mother passed away suddenly on April 4. Many of you were kind enough to express your condolences at the time and since. And it is truly the case that such condolences are an invaluable and sustaining thing, and I thank you again for them.

Today, my mother's death was turned into a sleazy gossip item online. The proprietor of the Web site did not contact me for comment before posting and did not try to contact our MSNBC media people until virtually the very moment he did post. He has resisted all entreaties to remove the item. And it has already been linked around the Net.

My mother's illness, her diagnosis with terminal cancer, and her death came all in a span of just two weeks. I did what a lot of us do in such circumstances, full speed ahead, with occasional hours or days off to see her and my family. We had the memorial on April 9. We had a family gathering planned for the next weekend. My sister and nephew were coming down from their home upstate, so he could see his first games at the new Yankee Stadium during his spring vacation, which began on the 18th.

I went to the opener of the ballpark the preceding Thursday, the 16th. Then I went downtown to do this show. And somewhere during that day, I hit an emotional wall about my mother's passing. So on short notice, I asked my bosses to extend my long weekend, which was originally Saturday to Tuesday of the following week, to Friday to Tuesday. And they generously agreed.

That Friday the 17th proved especially therapeutic. Saw the Yankees in the afternoon and the Mets at night. Some people meditate. I go watch baseball.

I hit another kind of wall over that weekend, and by Monday I was in bed with flu or something like it. Monday's game was rained out, much to my nephew's dismay. But the next night, you will remember, was the game in which a player's bat flew into the

89

stands and my nephew got to keep it. A player wearing the same number, oddly enough, that Chuck Knoblauch had worn when his throw hit my mother in our seats at the ballpark back in 2000.

By Wednesday morning, I was feeling better, good enough to take Jacob to a matinee on a rainy day in the Bronx and then return here to do the show.

I've gone into such excruciating detail because this afternoon I discovered this posted on a Web site called City File. Quote: "If you regularly tune into *Countdown* with Keith Olbermann on MSNBC, you may remember that Olbermann was mysteriously absent from the show for three days at the end of April. But Olbermann didn't just have the night off, as David Shuster, his fill-in, said on the air three evenings in a row. According to a source inside MSNBC, it was a bizarre temper tantrum on Olbermann's part that led him to storm off the set in protest. Olbermann was not scheduled to take a vacation at the end of April, but he ended up missing three shows, Friday April 17, Monday April 20, and Tuesday April 21."

This message, from a parallel universe, posted by somebody named Remy Stern, went on to explain that I had a fight with Rachel Maddow over the booking of Ben Affleck as a guest. In fact, Ben Affleck had been tentatively booked for *Countdown*, then wound up on Rachel's show due to some really shoddy work by a fill-in publicist for his latest movie.

This double-booking stuff happens. It was resolved internally and quickly, and the only thing it had to do with the weekend of mourning was that it happened more or less contemporaneously, if I remember correctly.

The irony in this is even the gossip idiot recognizes the story he printed does not hold together. "The biggest question—and no one can really answer except for Olbermann himself—is why having Ben Affleck on his show meant so much to him in the first place. The two have a past. Affleck spoofed the MSNBC host late last year. Although Olbermann seemed to find the imitation flattering, . . . it's much more likely that Affleck's role in this latest bit of drama didn't matter all that much, and this was just Olbermann attempting to once again force MSNBC to give in to his demands and satiate his ego. In which case, it was just another day at MSNBC."

Yes, there's the problem with your pretend reporting right there. It wasn't about Ben Affleck. My mother died. Mr. Stern claims a reliable source that he published before he could receive the denial which would have deflated most of his delusions, which are pretty standard stuff about me circa 2003. He also brings Dan Abrams into this epic, which from both Mr. Abrams's and Mr. Stern's points of view, is rather unfortunate, because considering Mr. Abrams's irrelevance to the rest of the story, and indeed now to MSNBC, it does rather point a finger toward a small group that could be the source of this sad and sadly out-of-touch gossip.

The site refused to remove the false story, refused to apologize for treading on a weekend of mourning, refused to recognize its extraordinary failure and irresponsibility. It merely printed my protest and then a really embarrassing, defiant retort.

Their response: "We were saddened to hear of Olbermann's loss and found his tribute to his mother deeply moving. But if that was the reason Olbermann took time off two weeks later, we can't imagine why Olbermann wouldn't have simply said as much. Furthermore, we find it hard to believe one of his colleagues at MSNBC, a respected journalist no less, would have attributed his absence to the flu/allergy season if Olbermann had made the perfectly understandable decision, take a few days off to mourn his mother's passing."

When didn't I say as much and to whom? To you? The journalist to whom the fellow refers, David Shuster, was told why I was out, told also that I was under the weather, was told that my return might be Wednesday, might be Thursday. So he was on standby. He had to clear this with you before you decided whether or not it was believable?

The Web site has since called me a liar because I went to baseball games after my mother died. The first site to link off this and swallow it whole was, sadly, Wonkette. Advised of its mistake, its editor, Ken Layne, who apparently doesn't understand that laughing all the time about everything is not wit, but more likely a serious medical condition, wrote:

"Keith Olbermann denies this one particular instance of jackassery. Whoo hoo. Does this mean Wonkette is now beneath contempt in Keith Olbermann's mind? Self important much?"

Yes. My dead mother is, in fact, more important than your lousy Web site. Again, I'm sorry this has been in such detail. But I think it serves a purpose in reminding us about both the Internet—and I know how strange this will sound coming from me—and about remembering the human equation.

Even in the heat of public discourse—which is why I objected on air to Wanda Sykes's two jokes about Rush Limbaugh at the White House Correspondents' Dinner—political dispute is one thing. But let's leave everybody's kidneys, their possible roles as the 20th 9/11 hijacker, and their mothers out of it.

As I mentioned, I was going to do this segment tonight on John McCain's mother's comments about Limbaugh and Michael Steele and me. But as this nonsense broke around me this afternoon, it struck me just how absurd that idea was. She was just a mother sticking up for her son. My mom would have appreciated that.

Finally, and just for the record, I also mysteriously took off Monday, May 4, and was seen at the Yankees game that night with my friends Jason Bateman and David Cross. Stay tuned to City File or Wonkette or Gawker or a *Boston Globe* blog, because maybe, maybe, I really had a fist fight with Brian Williams in the NBC commissary earlier in the day. Or maybe I had gone to Westchester that afternoon to place the urn containing my mother's ashes in her final resting place.

You know what they say. We report, you decide. To which we can add . . .

What the—?

WTF?

Not Since Calhoun

MAY 15, 2009

An elected governor of an American state continues to flirt with treason. Rick Perry of Texas, who probably would advocate stoning the heathen in Valverde if it would win him 37 extra votes, has once again refused the opportunity to step back from the stupidity that is secession.

He said: "We live in a great country. America is—Texas is a very unique state inside that great country. And there's no reason for us to be even talking at seceding.

"But if Washington continues to force these programs on the states, if Washington continues to disregard the Tenth Amendment, you know, who knows what happens. There may be people standing up all over the country in tea parties saying, enough. All right."

How about them standing up in Texas and saying enough, all right, Governor Ass Hat? Recent polling suggests more than a third of all Texans believe the place would be better off independent of the United States. It is a split among Republicans. But when you reduce it to just the bully's threat to take his ball and go home, 51 percent of all Texas Republicans approve of the suggestion that Texas may need to leave the United States.

You know what the South Carolina politician James Lewis Pettigrew said of his state, just before the Civil War—too small for a republic and too big for an insane asylum.

Governor, have you or your separatist friends considered what would happen if you actually seceded? Assuming the rest of the country did not decide it was a rebellion, and didn't send in federal troops, and didn't try to capture you and hang you, and, in a bitter irony, did not suspend habeas corpus in the rebellious territory, so that former president George W. Bush could be detained without charge and without access to attorneys?

I'm talking about what would happen if we all just sat back and said bye, have fun storming the castle.

Let's start internally. Your taxes would shoot through the roof. FEMA alone has sent $3,449,000,000 to Texas since 2001. Other agencies sent you another billion just for Hurricane Ike in 2008.

When NASA pulls out of Houston, that's 26,000 jobs, another $2.5 billion you just lost from your economy. We'd obviously move everybody out of Fort Hood, Texas, whose financial impact on your new kingdom is another $6 billion.

Your own country—get your own damn forts and your own damn air force, army, and navy. What is that, $10 billion a year,

$100 billion, a trillion? You'll need some form of welfare and Social Security. You'll have to get your own FDA, CDC, FDC, FEC, FBI, CIA, NSA, and Post Office. You'll need a lot of new investments after the Americans—I'm sorry, the Gringos—pull out. You've got four nuclear power plants there. Good for you. Where were you going to put all, the nuclear waste? The Alamo?

Remember, these are all the start-up costs. I lost track at about $500 billion, and we haven't even gotten to annual maintenance or expansion or improvements. Pell Grants, I forgot Pell Grants. The U.S. gave Texas students a billion dollars in Pell Grants for the academic year 2006–2007. Good luck with that.

What are you going do about your sports franchises? The Cowboys just spent a billion on that new stadium. America's team. That's funny, the Cowboys, north Texas's team.

Now, no American network is going to want to televise their games, because the ratings in Texas will no longer count in America. You'll be Canada with something of a twang. Do you think it's a coincidence that half the Canadian baseball teams went Out-of-Business because of TV revenues and other reasons, and half of the Canadian basketball teams?

So take your choice, Astros or Rangers. One of them is going to move to Charlotte. Who exactly do you think your University of Texas football team is going to play now? USC? Oklahoma? Try Sul Ross or San Jacinto JC or the new big rivalry with Tom DeLay Exterminator University.

Now, security. You'll need your own Gitmo. Starting wars is optional, of course. See your Mr. Bush about that. And since you'll be surrounded by the United States and Mexico, presumably the U.S. will continue this knuckleheaded border fence you guys started, only it won't be on your southern border anymore. Now it will be on your northern one, because the rest of us here, we can't risk the economic impact of hordes of illegal aliens fleeing the chaos of the United State of Texas, or the Texican nation, or Texaco, or whatever you're going to call yourselves.

So you'll have to put up your own fence at your own expense.

We'll talk politics for a second, too. Let's look at what your departure will mean back here in the northern 49. Congratulations to the Democrats and their filibuster-proof 60 seats in the

98-seat, Texas-free Senate. And thanks from the Dems in California, New York, Florida, Illinois, and Michigan, which will take the lion's portion of those Texas electoral college seats, 13. Eleven more would go to other blue states. The other red states would, of course, get the leftovers, 10.

Per Nate Silver's calculation, if Texas had left last year, Obama would have won the electoral college by 242 votes, not by 192. And also speaking of politics, remember, sovereign republic of Texas, you've got your big political nightmare coming up 11 years from now. The big political nightmare, you know, when the Mexican Texans get the ballot initiative passed on whether or not Texas should become part of Mexico.

Right now, Texas is 48 percent Anglo, 36 percent Hispanic. With no major change in population, just progressing things outward, by 2020, every projection has Anglos being outnumbered by Hispanics in Texas. That's in 2020. By 2040, the Anglos will compose barely a fourth of the population of Texas. I don't happen to have an issue with that, but a lot of Governor Perry's crowd seems to, there in Texas.

I'm sorry, in "Tay-has," the Texas state in Mexico. Hasta la vista, baby.

Don't let Oklahoma hit you on the backside on the way out. Secession: what the—?

A Small Mind on Small Business

MAY 18, 2009

Chairman Michael Steele of the Republican National Committee says his party can retool its message and sell it to a broader base by recasting its culture war issues as lessons in pocketbook economy. For instance, he now says the Republicans should paint gay marriage as an attack on small business, suggesting that businesses would have to pay more for health care, because all those gay partners would suddenly be gay husbands and gay wives, and legally designated gay beneficiaries. "Now, all of a sudden," Steele warns, "I've got someone who wasn't a spouse before that I had no responsibility for, who's now getting claimed as a spouse that I now have financial responsibility for. So how do I pay for that? Who pays for that? You just cost me money."

You want to sell opposition to gay marriage on economic grounds as a kind of drag on small business? Um, Mr. Steele, in this country, weddings are a $70-billion-dollar-a-year industry, B, *billion*, as in *Bridezilla*, $70 billion—most of it spread among local florists, local jewelers, local caterers, local photographers, local hotels, local restaurants, local bridal stores.

Admittedly, the number of wedding gowns ordered when two men get married is usually zero. But think of the all-women weddings, with two gowns and two sets of bridesmaids.

Seriously, legalizing gay marriage is, in fact, a really simple-to-understand gold mine, especially in terms of jump-starting a lousy economy like, say, the one you Republicans gave us, the one that is doing a lot more harm to small businesses right now than would a minor increase in spousal benefits.

There is a reason that a lot of conservatives in California opposed Prop 8 last year. Before the rights of same-sex couples were repealed there, UCLA had published a study calculating that just in California, the wedding business in the state was going to explode by $684 million over three years. Same-sex marriage would have created 2,200 jobs just in California. Same-sex marriage would have created $64 million in additional state tax revenues just in California.

Same-sex marriage would have created $9 million just in lousy county marriage license fees just in California.

Five years ago, *Forbes* did an amazing set of extrapolations as to what nationwide same-sex marriages would mean to the economy, based on the calculation that there would be 464,000 additional hitchings. Receptions, catering, and wedding planning would be up by $4.7 billion, $153 million of that just to the wedding planners. Wedding gift purchases, $3.94 billion; honeymoons, $1.7 billion; engagement rings, $1.66 billion; wedding gowns and other apparel, $1.3 billion; photography and video, an even billion; flora and decor, another $816 million; music and entertainment, $659 million; wedding bands, $604 million; invitations and stationery, $217 million; cakes, $197 million.

Total increase in our gross national wedding product: $16.8 billion. My God, Steele, it's a stimulus package.

Not only am I surprised that you are trying to kill it as a drain on small businesses. But at these rates, I'm shocked you Republicans didn't try to make it mandatory.

As usual, he is Michael "Hey I Just Thought of This" Steele. And he is so wrong as to be laughable.

The stationers of America, as we move further and further away from the printed page, are dropping like flies. You're going to sell them on the new revitalized GOP by explaining to them how great banning same-sex marriage is for small business. By the way, they can't have the $217 million more a year that same-sex weddings would bring them?

It's genius, genius, I tells ya.

In fact, there is such a fabulous brain pulsing under that notable Steele skull, I'm sure this is just the start of social issues which he can camouflage as economics without thinking the whole thing through 100 percent of the way. Well, thinking it through 75 percent—50—at all.

For instance, we in the Republican Party should oppose increased spending on education because if you have a better-educated American kid, think how much more hiring him will cost America's small-business people in the future. We in the GOP say, keep them stupid. They cost less that way. I mean, McDonald's must be doing something right.

We cannot engage Iran or these other evildoers, of course. My goodness, don't you understand, without war there are no military procurement contracts. How then do you expect small business to thrive in this country if the small-business owners cannot dream of becoming somebody like the next Halliburton or Blackwater USA guy?

Think of the savings if we just eliminated government altogether— no taxes, no fees of any kind. Ehhh, maybe a parking permit, a little tag you could wear on your trunks for the municipal swimming pool. Imagine if everybody got to keep 99.9 percent of their income. Now, admittedly, the power grid would collapse within hours, and crime would quadruple by midnight. And we'd be invaded by every nation up to and including Liechtenstein before Friday.

You don't think a zero-tolerance policy on government would do wonders for the Republicans at the polls?

Lastly, of course, there is the one specious argument Mr. Steele seems to be making without trying: Why bother to spend money searching for thoughtful leaders or candidates for the Republican Party? I mean, sure, there are disadvantages to shrinking the GOP to the dimensions and the geographic scope of the American Independent Party that George Wallace led 40 years ago. But think of the savings.

This wouldn't be one of those silly Karl Rove permanent-Republican-majority promises, ludicrous and never to be fulfilled. For the Michael Steele permanent-Republican minority, all you need is to get rid of all those expensive real Republican leaders and get some egomaniacal clowns who would do it for peanuts, just for the publicity, to lead the way like, you know, Rush Limbaugh, Newt Gingrich, Dick Cheney, and Michael Steele.

Oh, yes, you're doing that already. They'd be worth $16.8 billion a year to the economy. But same-sex marriage would hurt small business.

What the—?

What's the Co-pay at Gitmo?

MAY 19, 2009

A United States senator from Nevada has just returned from a visit to our gulag at Guantanamo Bay, Cuba, insisted that all of those entered there should abandon hope and be kept there forever, compared them to Charles Manson, even though they have been convicted of, and often charged with, nothing, and repeated all the half-Republican, half-totalitarian talking points, rationalizing the repudiation of due process and the Constitution.

Then Senator John Ensign, having been hit by some sort of an interstellar asteroid of honesty, added, in one of the truest things ever said by man, that the detainees "get better health care than the average American citizen does."

What the—?

The men we have locked up without charge or trial, some of whom have been tortured, psychologically or physically, all of whom have been, at a minimum, traumatized, and at least some of whom, just by the laws of statistical probability—even the most rabid of right-wingers will admit this—at least some of whom must be innocent, and *they* have better health care than the average American citizen.

Torture at Gitmo, punishments at the drugstore. You certainly nailed that one, Senator. For the past eight years, the Republican Party has been far more concerned with breaking the health of the average Gitmo prisoner than it has been with improving the health of the average resident in this country. And no one, nowhere, at no time has boiled it down with the economy of words, the startling presages, of John Ensign. "The detainees get better health care than the average American citizen."

The Bush administration and those Republicans now following it, like the guys with the brooms who have to follow the parade of elephants, have turned this nation's priorities on their collective head. Throw out the rights we were born with, which we have assiduously granted even the worst of our enemies for 233 years, and prevent the extension of the obvious, necessary, urgent right of every American to even just the bare minimum of health care.

But no, if you argue for closing Gitmo, John Ensign and his pals will call you a Nazi appeaser. Then if you argue against torturing people, they will call you a fascist. If you demand prosecution of those who tortured, they will call you un-American. They will claim with the same level of insight and memorization available from a parrot that we only waterboarded people who planned the attacks on September 11 that killed 3,000 Americans.

And then if you argue for better health care, they will call you a socialist.

Congratulations, you're a liberal, Nazi-appeasing, un-American, fascist socialist.

Meanwhile, they will wrap themselves in the flag and insist they kept us safe. Senator Ensign, I've never heard this question asked, let alone answered before. Who exactly is the *us* in that sentence? The average American who, as you suddenly blurted out, is not getting health care as good as the guys at Gitmo? Is that the *us* you protected? Or is it the various health care industries, the drug manufacturers and HMO chains, and the insurance industry, and the rest?

Is that it, Senator? You made the world safe for pharmacy?

Besides his Freudian slip, Senator Ensign said much else of note. The detainees "are like having Charles Manson times whatever factor. These people are so dangerous."

How do you know that, Senator? Your visit there lasted less than a day. Did you look into their souls while you were there? Were you briefed? By the way, did anybody mention we tried Charles Manson, and he is still in prison? The evil, crazy, without any sense of the sanctity of life, trying to kill as many people as he could, and our quiet little quaint old justice system worked like a charm on him.

"It is permissible to hold people until the military conflict is over. Does anybody think this global war on terror is over? It's not even close. If these people get out, they are coming back to kill Americans."

Sounds like you just defined these people as prisoners of war, Senator. Indefinite detention is legal, provided there is a formal declaration of war. Do you recall the Senate ever legally declaring war on anybody? I mean, you were there, you should have noticed—oh, who am I kidding?

Anyway, there it is, in the proverbial nutshell, nearly a decade's worth of twisting this country's heritage inside out, of doing half of what any terrorist could ever dream of doing to this country for him—let's put this up on huge stone tablets like the Ten Commandments outside that courthouse in Alabama, only these would go outside the U.S. Senate, and outside every CVS, Rite-Aid, emergency room, and medical office building in the land, a statue of Senator John Ensign of Nevada, a contribution check from big pharma in one hand and a waterboard in the other, and his words beneath him, because they certainly should have been beneath him.

"The detainees at Gitmo, they get better health care than the average American citizen does."

What the—?

Rush, We Believe You Suck

MAY 20, 2009

In a span of 24 hours, two of the titans of knee-jerk, right-wing, brains-free, racist, xenophobic, delusional, greedy, unfeeling, inept, indifferent, self-inflating, and unconscionably profitable voices of the lunatic right wing have self-destructed.

Even more titanic than Glenn Beck's sad end—pecked to death, carcass consumed, nothing left but the veneers from his teeth, and swallowed whole in only six minutes by the hosts of *The View*—Rush Limbaugh's startling admission that he cannot take it anymore, that this network's coverage of him has not only gotten to him, but gotten him to a point perhaps never reached before by any other megalomaniac. He's suddenly gone all Greta Garbo on us. He wants to be left alone.

He has surrendered. He cannot say it that way, of course. Were he to, the entire edifice that is Rush Limbaugh would come crashing down, and then we'd have to get one of those rescue squads from ski resorts to go and look for survivors. No, suddenly the impact of being accurately called out day after day, hour after hour as a faux populist, press-release-regurgitating lackey of repressive and regressive political flunky, that has hit bone, finally. Took awhile.

In sum, Rush Limbaugh, who told me in person years ago that his dream of dreams was to be on television, to be on ESPN, perhaps to sit next to me on *SportsCenter*, an utter television failure who yearns to somehow undo that permanent label, Rush Limbaugh does not want to be on TV anymore.

He declared: "It seems that the liberalism that is MSNBC isn't selling as well as they would like, because they cannot, from the Scarborough show in the morning all the way into the night, they cannot go any appreciable length of time without showing video of me, the CPAC speech, or excerpts from this radio show, or having a bunch of hack guests on to discuss me.

"So my challenge is this. To MSNBC, let's see if you can run your little TV network for 30 days. Let's see if you can do Rush withdrawal. Let's see if you can run your little TV network for 30 days without doing a single story on me. And then let's take a look at your ratings during those 30 days. And see what happens."

F you. You're in charge of this? You're not in charge of this. You put your bile out into the public airwaves for three hours a day and you get to decide how people react to it? The hell you do.

There are rules about how we can and cannot react to the peril to this nation? There are no rules. You built this little world. Either man up and live through the bad press, or get out.

He also said: "Obviously MSNBC thinks they cannot get numbers without focusing on me."

To the degree that the numbers we are getting have anything to do with Rush Limbaugh, it's like the numbers we got after Hurricane Katrina. There was a blight upon the land. There was a huge campaign to BS the American public that the problems were actually the solutions. We told the truth about it, and people watched.

Rush, you are the radio equivalent of "Heck of a job, Brownie," and the Bush flyover, and the refugees in the Superdome. You are a human federal disaster area.

And he went on: "It is clear to me that MSNBC is hoping to build its ratings on my back."

This is where he would say, of somebody else, "But there's so much room back there." Instead I will go here. This man, this publicity addict, this fame junkie, this victim of the unquenchable thirst for attention, all of a sudden he's afraid of being criticized on a television network which he believes has no viewers, no reach, and no impact.

He went on and on: "See if you can do it. You know, stand on your own two feet. Stand on liberalism. Stand on what you believe."

Rush, this is in part what we believe. This isn't a bid for ratings. We believe you suck. We believe you have contributed to the coarsening and deadening of the political dialogue in this nation. And I'm saying that as a guy who just said, "F you."

We believe your fixation on Bill Clinton's sex life lessened the chances that everybody in this country could have begun a serious discussion of terrorism before terrorism hit.

We believe that you used chicanery, trickery, and outright lies to influence gullible people, whose entire understanding of complex issues vital to their own happiness and survival is then reduced to a bunch of your catchphrases, and they don't even understand the catchphrases.

We believe that the day you stop doing your show, even if you're replaced by one of those buffoons who fill in for you, that the collective intelligence of this nation will jump by at least one IQ point simply because you shut up.

We believe that as you boast that you are listened to by 14 million Americans a week, you cannot see the forest for the ratings trees. All the rest of us, the crushing majority of the other 292 million Americans, we divide into three groups: those who are hating you, those who are laughing at you, and those who will go blissfully through their lives not having any earthly clue who the hell you are. Or were.

And he concluded: "So I challenge you, MSNBC, 30 days without anything mentioning me. No video of me, no guests commenting on me."

No video, you say? You mentioned the CPAC video, where you forgot the first rule that guys like you and me, the hefty of this world, are supposed to remember. Never undulate. You don't like us showing it. I can understand that.

You got it. How is this? This matrix of 64 separate shots of you undulating at CPAC? You know, if you look at this long enough, it's got a strange, soothing effect. Kind of a lava lamp of hate speech and condescension and subconscious reminder to everybody to check your support columns under your front porch. Do it today.

The video, let's just make that permanent. All right? Dear viewer, this is our new logo.

So, Mr. Limbaugh, your challenge, with all this yet, am I still up for negotiation? It's one of the problems with having a liberal heart. When the wounded animal, no matter how venomous, no matter how much at fault, begs to be left alone, I still listen. I will go 30 days on this program without referencing what has been done or said or boasted about by Rush Limbaugh, provided you go 30 days on your program without mentioning what has been done or said or boasted about by Rush Limbaugh.

Hannity would last longer on the waterboard.

What the—?

The Weakness the Terrorists See

MAY 21, 2009

Neurotic, paranoid, false to fact and false to reason, forever self-rationalizing his inner rage at his own impotence, and failure dripping from every word, and as irrational, as separated from the real world, as dishonest, as insane as any terrorist—the former vice president has today humiliated himself beyond redemption.

The delusional claims he has made this day could be proved by documentation and firsthand testimony to be the literal and absolute truth, and he still, himself, would be wrong because the America he sought to impose upon the world and upon its own citizens, the dark, hateful place of Dick Cheney's own soul, the place he to this hour defends, and to this day prefers, is a repudiation of all that our ancestors, all that for which our brave troops of two years ago and two minutes ago, have sacrificed and fought.

I do have to congratulate you, sir. No man, living or dead, could have passed the buck more often that than you did in 35 minutes this morning. It's not your fault that we waterboarded people, you said. It isn't torture, you said, even though it is, based on 111 years of American military prosecutions.

It was in the Constitution that you could do it, even if our laws told you you could not. It was in the language of the 2001 Military Authorization you force-fed the Congress that you could do it. Even if our international treaties told you you could not.

It produced valuable information, you said. Even though the firsthand witnesses, the interrogators of these "beasts," said the information preceded the torture and ended when it began.

It was authorized, you said, by careful legal opinion, even though the legal opinions were dictated by you and your cronies. And, oh, by the way, the torture began before the legal opinions were even written.

It was authorized, you said. And you imply that even if it really wasn't, it was done only to detainees of the highest intelligence value. It was more necessary, you said, because of the revelation of another program by the real villains of our time: the *New York Times*. Even though that revelation was possible because the program was detailed on the front page of the Web site of a Defense Department subcontractor.

It was all the fault of your predecessor, you said, who tried to treat terror as a law enforcement problem before you came to the office and rode to the rescue, after you totally ignored terrorism for the first 20 percent of your first term and the worst attack on this nation in its history unfolded on your watch.

"9/11 caused everyone to take a serious second look at threats that had been gathering for a while," you said today, "and enemies whose plans were getting bolder and more sophisticated."

Gee, thanks for being motivated by the deaths of nearly 3,000 Americans to go so far as to take a serious second look. And thank you, sir, for admitting, obviously inadvertently, that you did not take a serious first look in the 7 months and 23 days between your inauguration and 9/11.

For that attack, sir, you are culpable, morally, ethically. At best, you are guilty of malfeasance and eternally lasting stupidity. At worst, sir, in the deaths of 9/11, you are negligent.

The circular logic and the self-righteous sophistry falls from a copy of Mr. Cheney's speech like bugs from a book on a moldy shelf. He still believes in "dictators like Saddam Hussein with ties to Middle East terrorists." He still assumes everyone we capture is guilty without charge or trial, but that to prosecute lawbreaking by government officials is "to have an incoming administration criminalize the policy decisions of its predecessors."

And most sleazy of all, while calling the CIA's torturers honorable, he insists the grunts at Abu Ghraib were "sadistic prison guards who abused inmates in violation of law, military regulations and simple decency." Even though, and maybe he does not know we know this—even though there is documentary proof now that those guards were acting on the orders originating in the office of Secretary of Defense Rumsfeld.

It is, in short, madness. Madness, sir, Mr. Cheney, your speech was almost entirely about you. There are only five or six other people even mentioned. And only two quoted at any length. And why would you have quoted, as you did, the man who said this: "I know that this program saved lives. I know we've disrupted plots. I know this program alone is worth more than the FBI, the Central Intelligence Agency, and the National Security Agency put together have been able to tell us."

As you know, sir, you were quoting former CIA director George Tenet. That would be the George Tenet who told Congress on February 11, 2003, "Iraq is harboring senior members of a terrorist network led by Abu Musab al-Zarqawi, a close associate of Al Qaeda."

Mr. Tenet, sir, then went into elaborate detail about the Iraq/Al Qaeda connection. None of it was true. This is your source, as he was your boss's source. "George, how confident are you?" President Bush asked Tenet about Saddam Hussein's weapons of mass destruction, just before the Iraq war, according to Bob Woodward's book *Plan of Attack*.

"Don't worry," Tenet answers. "It's a slam dunk."

That is your independent authority on how well torture worked. Next time you see him, Mr. Cheney, you might as well ask Mr. Tenet if he thinks he is Napoleon. I don't want to know who you think you are.

"Those are the basic facts on enhanced interrogations," you concluded. "And to call this a program of torture is to libel the dedicated professionals who saved American lives, and to cast terrorists and murderers as innocent victims."

You saved no one, sir. If the classified documents you seek to have released really did detail plots other than those manufactured by drowning men in order to get it to stop, or if they truly did know plans beyond the laughable ones you and President Bush have already revealed—hijackers without passports, targeting a building whose name Mr. Bush could not remember; clowns who thought they could destroy airports by dropping matches in fuel pipelines 30 miles away; men who planned to attack a military base dressed as pizza delivery boys, forgetting that every man there was armed; and today, the four would-be synagogue bombers, one of whom turns out to keep bottles of urine in his apartment and is on schizophrenia medicine.

If those documents contain anything of value, you would have leaked those already, as you leaked those revenge fantasies of the Library Tower and the JFK Bomber and the Fort Dix Six.

"When they"—meaning terrorists—"see the American government caught up in arguments about interrogations, or whether foreign terrorists have Constitutional rights, they don't stand back in awe of our legal system and wonder whether they had misjudged us all along," you said. "Instead, the terrorists see just what they were hoping for, our unity gone, our resolve shaken, our leaders distracted. In short, they see weakness and opportunity."

The weakness the terrorists see, sir, is the weakness of blind rage replacing essential cold logic. The weakness the terrorists see, sir, is the weakness of judgment suspended in favor of self-fulfilling prophecy. The weakness the terrorists see, sir, is the weakness of moral force supplanted by violence and revenge fantasies.

The weakness the terrorists see, sir, is the weakness of Dick Cheney.

And yet still, ceaselessly, indefatigably, you moralize and lie to us.

"I might add," someone said today, "that people who consistently distort the truth in this way are in no position to lecture anyone about values." Very apt. The quote, of course, is from your speech. Your speech, which was in essence about your fantasy that you and Mr. Bush were not negligent. Not your pigheaded certainty, but first these attacks were impossible; then they were a good excuse for a war you already planned in Iraq; and finally, they were to be imminently repeated and only you knew when the next threat would come.

You saved no one, Mr. Cheney. All you did was help kill Americans. You were negligent before 9/11. Your response to your complicity by omission on 9/11 was panic and shame and insanity, and lying this country into a war that has done nothing but kill 4,299 more of us so far.

We will take no further instructions from you, sir. And let me again quote Oliver Cromwell to you, Mr. Cheney. "You have sat too long for any good you have been doing lately. Depart, I say, and let us have done with you. In the name of God, go."

WTF?

Putting the Mental in Fundamental

MAY 27, 2009

If on the subject of your opposition to same-sex marriage you come across as less generous than David Brooks, less nuanced than Pat Buchanan, and less informed than Carrie Prejean, you may still get yourself elected to Congress and reelected, and re-reelected—five times, in fact. But when asked about this opposition to same-sex marriage, if your answer makes David Brooks and Pat Buchanan and Carrie Prejean all say, WTF, you, sir, have transcended the born, achieved, thrust-upon-them equation, and moved directly to all of the above.

Meet Congressman John Culberson of the Seventh District of Texas. We have heard him before say goofy stuff, but nothing that would make him a first-teamer. He is the guy who announced that the stimulus package was "a Trojan horse that liberals are using to ultimately turn America into France."

But that's nothing like the work of the true all-stars: Steve King of Iowa; John Shimkus of Illinois, the one who occasionally has ecstatic religious visions in the middle of his hearings; and, of course, legendary team captain Michele Bachmann.

But now, Mr. Culberson has elevated his game. He went on C-Span, which always seems like a good idea until you find yourself in the terminal stages of an answer so labyrinthine, so filled with double entendres, that you can't remember a time when you were not on C-Span lost in your own sentences.

Mr. Culberson was asked a pretty straightforward question by a female caller: "You said a lot about how the federal government shouldn't be in our house. My question is about gay marriage. So do you really think the federal government should be in our house or the government shouldn't? I know gay marriage is—it's the state government that controls that. So what do you think on that?"

One assumes he thought he was giving a pretty straightforward answer: "Well, under the Tenth Amendment, the state has a first responsibility for providing for public safety, public health, public morality, all issues that just affect the people within that state. It's up to the states. And you either follow the Constitution or you don't."

Okay. We haven't gotten to the crazy yet. I just wanted to interject that the Tenth Amendment reads as follows: "The powers not delegated to the United States by the Constitution, nor prohibited by it to the states, are reserved to the states respectively, or to the people."

That's it. That is the whole can of Cheez Whiz. It doesn't say a damn thing in there, Mr. Culberson, suggesting that the states have a first responsibility for morality in public. Maybe he was thinking of that when he went off like this:

"Now, personally, I think that—it's just I think also self-evident that you've got to have a marriage between a man and a woman or society's not going to make it. You're not going to have a fruitful, productive, growing civilization unless marriage is between a man and a woman.

"That's just history. History will show you that. But it is a person's private business. Their private life is their private business. I'm fundamentally libertarian at heart. And I do believe in the Tenth Amendment. I don't want to hear about somebody's private behavior."

Then I don't want to hear you keep referencing parts of the Tenth Amendment that you and only you can see:

"Think about this, you cannot—if we provide civil rights protection to somebody based on private sexual behavior, well, the

Constitution, the Fourteenth Amendment, says we have to provide equal protection."

Congressman, hello, you're talking about private sexual behavior and providing protection. Hello.

He continued: "Federal law cannot permit—if one state, Vermont, wants to do that, you can't let that cross state lines. You've got to let, frankly—frankly, a lot of these issues have to be up to the states. But the federal government cannot permit—the federal government has a legitimate role in interstate commerce."

Interstate commerce? Where the hell did interstate commerce come from, Congressman? Oh, yes, we have to ship all that protection for the private sexual behavior.

He concluded: "And that's where the federal government's role comes in. I think the federal government shouldn't recognize it. It's just a—it's just a—it's just a bad idea. And—but fundamentally the right of privacy is fundamental."

Well, there you have it. "Fundamentally, the right of privacy is fundamental." If Congressman Culberson sounds at all familiar to you, I suspect this is why.

As one man said: "Hell, I was born here and I was raised, and, dad gum it, I'm gonna die here. And ain't no side-winding, bushwhacking, horn-swaggling cricker-croaker is going to rouin me bishen cutter."

And another replied: "Now, who can argue with that?"

Congressman John Culberson, Seventh District of Texas, where the answer to every question is either the Tenth Amendment, or fundamentally, the right of privacy is fundamental, or the government has to provide protection for private sexual behavior.

Possibly, to harken back to the congressman's remark about the stimulus plan, possibly protection involving a Trojan . . . horse.

What the—?

Engineered Horribly

MAY 28, 2009

According to the right-wing paranoia sphere, militant Democrats are out to destroy Republican car dealerships in this country.

It's true. The *Washington Examiner*, which is like the *Washington Times*, only with fewer Moonies, has breathlessly reported that "evidence appears to be mounting that the Obama administration has systematically targeted for closing Chrysler dealers who contributed to Republicans. What started earlier this week as mainly a rumbling on the right side of the blogosphere has gathered some steam today with revelations that among the dealers being shut down are a GOP congressman and the competitors to a dealership partly owned by former Clinton White House chief of staff Matt McLarty."

Oh, this gets better and better. Obama's car czar, Steven Rattner, is married to the former national finance chairman of the Democratic National Committee. And what's worse, he used to be a reporter for the *New York Times*, as recently as 1982! 1982? The chip implanted in his brain to make him act all liberal and anti-American must still be running on its original battery, 1982.

He worked for the *New York Times* when Reagan was president. Of course, he's leading a Democratic plot to destroy Republican car dealers.

Then there's the real victim here: "Florida Representative Vern Buchanan learned from a House colleague that his Venice, Florida, dealership is on the hit list. Buchanan also has a Nissan franchise paired with the Chrysler dealer in Venice. 'It's an outrage. It's not about me. I'm going to be fine,' said Buchanan, the dealership's majority owner. 'You're talking taking over 100,000 jobs. We're supposed to be in the business of creating jobs, not killing jobs.'"

Before we get back to the vast right-turn-on-red conspiracy to wreak revenge on Republicans by closing their car dealerships, an important note about the GOP stance on this auto bailout that is keeping three-quarters of all Chrysler dealerships open: they all voted against it.

Last December, before Obama became president, the Republicans, from McCain to Bunning, from Bachmann to Cantor, preferred seeing the whole industry go under, all the jobs, not just the 100,000 Congressman Buchanan just mentioned, but all the car dealerships—Republican, Democrat, socialist, communist, used. Thirty-one Republican senators voted against the auto bailout, 151 Republican congressmen, including, in the height of chutzpah, considering that he is now alleging a political conspiracy to close his car dealership, Congressman Vern Buchanan of Florida. He voted against the auto bailout.

If he'd had it his way, it wouldn't have been his Chrysler dealership closed. It would have been everybody's Chrysler dealership being closed, all of them. Chowderhead.

This has been fun, this specter of Republicans who insisted we should let Detroit dry up and blow away. With it, all the parts manufacturers and all the repair shops and all the dealerships—Chrysler, Ford, GM, the people who told an entire industry and all its satellite industries to go to hell. Suddenly these hypocrites are getting all riled up because only about one-quarter of just the Chrysler dealerships are being closed.

But this misses the basic issue. "The basic issue raised here is this," concludes the *Washington Examiner* guy. "How do we account for the fact millions of dollars were contributed to GOP candidates by Chrysler [dealers] who are being closed by the government, but only one has been found so far that is being closed that contributed to the Obama campaign in 2008?"

Da-da-daaa. Of course, actual journalists would try to answer that question before posting their rage-inducing, conspiracy-theory-feeding, paranoia-producing tattle in a semi-newspaper and not afterward. Then again, journalism for these guys means sticking your byline on the tape, and then writing down what Mr. Bouncy-Bouncy says:

"Nobody can figure out exactly why certain dealerships are being targeted to be closed. There are some people looking into it, but the evidence is sketchy. All we know is that a whole lot of really successful dealerships are being shut down. Some of them happen to be owned by people who contributed lots of money to Republicans."

Oh, yes, about the really successful car dealerships that aren't being shut down. Turns out some of them happen to be owned by people who contributed lots of money to Republicans, too. I'm not being honest when I say that. Nearly all of the really successful Chrysler dealerships that aren't being shut down happen to be owned by people who contributed lots of money to Republicans, because nearly all car dealers who donate money to either party donate it to the Republicans.

Who else but Nate Silver did the math here? He used *Huffington Post*'s wonderful search engine Fund Race and pulled down "auto dealer" from the occupation menu. Result: Donations by auto dealers to the GOP total over 8.5 times more than donations by auto dealers to the Democrats; 8.6 to 1.

If you list yourself as a "car dealer," it is a little closer. Maybe that includes used car dealers, I don't know. Donations to the GOP are only triple the donations to the Democrats there.

There were other variations that Nate found. For example, "automobile dealers" give 10 times as much to Republicans as to Democrats. Among "automotive dealers"—I'm guessing those are the ones who sell the Stanley Steamers and fleets of Cadillacs—there is about a 16-to-1 Republican edge.

Put them all together, as Nate did, and, as he writes, 88 percent of the contributions from car dealers went to Republican candidates, and just 12 percent to Democratic candidates. Another reality-based analyst using a different data source puts the number at 92 percent.

The gist of this is inescapable. The reason it was nearly impossible to find a Chrysler dealership that gave to the Democrats and was just ordered closed is not that there aren't any that were ordered closed, it's that there aren't any, period.

In their haste to scapegoat Obama for everything and anything, Limbaugh and his wimp followers neglected to look at the larger picture: this evil, Democrat, socialist, racist, bomb-throwing, White Sox fan has secretly enacted a plan that makes sure that nearly 8 out of every 10 Chrysler dealers who donated to the

Republicans are forced to keep their property, stay in business, stay open, and continue to make money. The bastard!

A conspiracy to eliminate Republican automobile dealers. What the—?

She Looks Even Wiser by Comparison

JUNE 1, 2009

The bronze to William Kristol of the *Weekly Standard* and Fixed News. Back with another great idea after his push for the invasion of Iraq and the bombing of Iran. "You know," he says, "it might be worth doing some targeted air strikes to show the North Koreans—instead of always talking about, gee, there could be consequences—to show that they can't simply keep going down this path."

And then what happens? You thought about that, right? When Kim Jong Il says, "Thank you very much, stupid American," and sends 400,000 troops over the border into South Korea?

Our runner-up: Senate Minority Leader Mitch McConnell. After the wave of bizarre racism charges and hints against Judge Sonia Sotomayor last week by the likes of Senator Jim Inhofe and Congressman Lamar Smith and former Speaker Newt Gingrich and Rush Limbaugh, the ones denounced by even Senator John Cornyn, Senator McConnell was asked if people were making it a lot harder by using language like that. His reply: "Look, I've got a big job to do dealing with forty Senate Republicans and trying to advance a nation's agenda. I've got better things to do than to be the speech police over people who are going to have their views about a very important appointment."

No, you don't. Plus, thanks for acknowledging that there are only 40 Senate Republicans, not 41, now that Norm Coleman is now in the alumni association.

But our winner . . .

Boss Limbaugh. Last week, he compared Judge Sotomayor to ex-Klansman David Duke. He's now been paddled by David Duke. "Limbaugh," he writes, "a recent addict to illegal drugs, has no business making personal attacks against me for my past." Duke's Web site also says he criticized Judge Sotomayor as an activist in the primarily Mexican organization La Raza, which literally means "the race."

About that, it actually means race or family or branch of a family or clan or lineage or generation or quality of cloth or ray of light or a cleft in the foot of a horse.

Anyway, Duke's Web site also explains that Sotomayor's appointment was part of the vast Jewish conspiracy.

And even that nutbag trashed Boss Limbaugh, today's worst person in the world!

WTF?

Republicans Whigging Out
JUNE 2, 2009

No person alive has seen what has happened, or seen what might be happening right now, in American politics. I might be wrong about that. There might be some 167-year-old out there who is lying about his age, who has a clear memory of this country's Whig Party disintegrating between 1852 and 1856, and who could tell us, yes, what the Republicans are doing right now, that is how it started for those poor Whigs.

This story takes us to Marathon County, Wisconsin, and a man named Kevin Stephenson. A little more than two months ago, the local newspaper, the *Wassau Daily Herald*, printed his regular guest column in which he criticized Boss Limbaugh. "Sadly," he wrote, "today's politics is full of self-interest. Rush Limbaugh is not a politician. He does believe in conservatism and has a forum to express his views. You must admit that he has a large and loyal following, but so does Rachel Maddow as an extreme liberal. Both of these people need to shock to keep their ratings high. They are entertainers who earn their living by what they say, not what they accomplish.

"Republicans do not agree with all of the president's policies, but no one wants him to fail as president. That's because when leaders fail, so do their followers. No good citizen wants the United States to fail. Some may think that he will fail, but this is far different from wanting him to fail."

Last week, because of that article, Mr. Stephenson lost his job. This is not some instance of external revenge by Limbaugh, or Rachel, some back-channel retribution from Limbaugh's corporate masters, Clear Channel Communications. This isn't a freedom of the press issue. You can put down your calendar. You do not have to meet at the barricades. This has nothing with violations of Mr. Stephenson's First Amendment rights to free speech.

That is all true, because the job from which Mr. Stephenson was fired was that of spokesman for the Marathon County, Wisconsin, Republican Party. Last Thursday, when that county party met, it, to quote Mr. Stephenson, "got hostile and it got personal."

"They felt I was too moderate in what I was speaking and printing." The Marathon County Republicans, for reasons known only to themselves, dismissed their spokesman on a technicality about where he lived. And then the former county president, and still local Republican treasurer, blew the lid off that excuse.

"If the leadership had wanted a more moderate position, we would have let him continue," said Kevin Hermening to the local paper.

"This is just part of what you are seeing nationwide," the fired Mr. Stephenson concluded. "Party members know that I don't agree with Rush Limbaugh. Rush Limbaugh is hurting more than helping us."

The more you hear from Mr. Stephenson, the more apparent it becomes that he is exactly the kind of guy whom 20 years ago the Republicans would have embraced. Upon his firing, he issued this statement: "The most imminent danger facing the Republican Party comes from within. A growing party embraces its differences and uses the strength of its differences in a positive manner.

Differences should not be feared but embraced, as we as Americans are a mixture of diverse cultures with a rich history. The Republican Party is at a crossroads. Purging people who have differences from its ranks will ensure it remains a minority party well into the future. The direction the Republican Party chooses, not the Democratic Party, will determine its fate."

Purging—an ugly word, but the correct one. If you don't agree with the extremism of Limbaugh, you are out. Ask Arlen Specter, Michael Steele, Congressman Phil Gingrey, John McCain, Roberta McCain, or Meghan McCain. And if you point out that it is extremism, one of the guys escorting you out the door will shout, "Extremism in defense of liberty is no vice." The odds are pretty good that the screamer will know that is Barry Goldwater he is quoting. The odds are also pretty good that the screamer will never have made that great intellectual leap to the realization that 110 days after Barry Goldwater uttered that immortal manifesto, he lost the election by 16 million votes, and 434 of them in the electoral college.

The problem is, then and now, if you keep showing people the door, sooner or later, there will be more people outside the door than inside it with you.

This brings us back to the hypothetical 167-year-old viewer who is saying, "I warned Daniel Webster about this in 1852, and he didn't listen to me, either." The Whig Party was half of the American two-party system. It rose to prominence by being the party of no, in fierce opposition to the then-dominant Democrats. The Whigs managed to elect William Henry Harrison president, and then Zachary Taylor. The party included them and Daniel Webster, and the famous senator Henry Clay, and former and future presidents like John Quincy Adams, John Tyler, and Millard Fillmore.

As the 1850s began, the Whigs had an incredible advantage as well. The Democrats were descending into a proslavery position. Whereupon the proslavery faction in the Whig Party started to expel the antislavery Whigs. Then they put the squeeze on the Whigs who were merely neutral or moderate about slavery. It was a purge, a cleansing of those who were not conservative enough to be Whigs.

So the local Whig Party leader in Illinois quit the party. In fact, he quit politics. He went back to being a lawyer. His name was Abraham Lincoln. But the Whigs kept their party pure. Extremism in the defense of what they believed was liberty was no vice. And by 1860, the Whigs had no candidates. They didn't even hold a convention.

Kevin Stephenson is not Abraham Lincoln. And ultraconservative rage of today is not about the issue of slavery. And the Republicans are not the Whigs—not yet, anyway. But no organization, political or otherwise, collapses only from the top. Just as you have to screw it up nationally, so too do you have to unravel down to the grass roots. As the firing of Mr. Stephenson by the Marathon County GOP suggests, the one area in which Republicans are firing on all cylinders is in firing moderate Republicans.

What the—?

WTF?

The Man Who Read Too Much

JUNE 3, 2009

Until Dick Cheney eclipsed it with his own tour of the CYA [cover your ass] variety, the most prominent public effort by the Republicans this year had been the George W. Bush presidential legacy tour. Even if underpublicized at the moment, it is still continuing. But now it has hit a huge land mine, a fact about George Bush's presidency that may overwhelm every other symbol of it.

It is, with great irony, about reading. It is that the previous president had enough time to read one or two books per week.

Apparently, this is the current president's behind-the-scenes interview week. He did one of those unprecedented access performances with Britain's BBC. So this quote comes from yesterday.

Justin Webb: "Reading anything at the moment?"

President Obama: "You know, I'm reading a book called *Netherland*, by Joseph O'Neill, almost finished, excellent novel."

Justin Webb: "We'll let you get back to it. I'm sure you have other things to do."

Before you wonder just how stoked Mr. O'Neill is at the presidential plug, consider this from our friend Howard Fineman, who published it online for MSNBC on May 6: "Here's a small but revealing sliver of news concerning our cool, hard to fathom president: according to his closest adviser David Axelrod, Barack Obama really likes the novel he's reading right now. In fact, he likes it a lot. It is the first nonbusiness reading he's allowed himself since Inauguration Day. The first novel by the First Reader, revealed by David Leonhardt in the *New York Times* is *Netherland* by Joseph O'Neill."

Revealed by David Leonhardt of the *New York Times*, you say. That would have been on April 28, but it referred to an interview he had with Mr. Obama two weeks earlier on the 14th. "At the end of our conversation, when I asked him if he was reading anything good, he said he had become sick enough of briefing books to begin reading a novel in the evenings, *Netherland*, by Joseph O'Neill."

Oh, began reading it on April 14 and he's nearly finished, you say?

One suspects this is no indictment of the quality of the prose or the plot. He is the president of the United States. He's busy. He can't spend all his time reading books or watching, say, cable chatter on television. Frankly, I don't want the president to have more time to read books than I do. This is where we double back to Mr. Bush.

I don't read a lot of Karl Rove's columns in the *Wall Street Journal*, but frankly, even if I did, I don't think I know of anything I would like to read less than a Karl Rove column at Christmastime. Yet here, helpfully resurrected, is part of his Yuletide offering from last December 26. "With only five days left, my lead is insurmountable. The competition can't catch up. And for the third year in a row, I'll triumph. In second place will be the president of the United States. Our contest is not about sport or politics. It's about books. It all started on New Year's Eve in 2005. President Bush asked what my New Year's resolutions were. I told him that as a regular reader who had gotten out of the habit, by goal was to read a book a week in 2006. Three days later, we were in the

Oval Office when he fixed me in his sights and said, I'm on my second, where are you? Mr. Bush had turned my resolution into a contest," et cetera, et cetera.

Rove revealed that in 2006 he had read 110 books to Mr. Bush's 95. In 2007, it was 76 books to Bush's 51. And as of that last week of last year, 2008 was Rove 64, Bush 40.

Rove tells us that during the three years of the contest, Bush read a lot of history and biography—of course, biography is merely history made specific—about Lincoln, William Jennings Bryan, Genghis Khan, LBJ, Huey Long, Andrew Carnegie, Mark Twain, King Leopold, the English-speaking peoples, the manhunt for Lincoln's assassin, Khrushchev, Andrew Mellon, Dean Acheson, Vienna in 1814, FDR, the Spanish Civil War, and Babe Ruth.

The mind reels. For eight years, history ran hot and cold through every minute of George Bush's life. He was knee-deep in it, carried by it, reckless with it, desperate to influence it. Instead of staying focused on it, he preferred to read about it.

Unless he took Evelyn Woods's speed-reading course in his 20s, Mr. Bush clearly made some terrible choices during his presidency, reading about King Leopold instead of reading about the economy. Reading about Genghis Khan instead of reading about A. Q. Khan. Reading about the Spanish Civil War instead of reading about the Iraq civil war. Reading, reading, reading; at a pace that never got significantly below a book a week, and often approached two of them.

What anyone with, say, a full-time job could only dream of doing. So here is the true Bushian legacy finally evident: the man who read too much. Ironic, that, considering the infamy of his reading *My Pet Goat* on that Tuesday morning, so many Septembers ago. Ironic that, considering that a month earlier, in the most prime of reading venues, at the ranch, after a hard six months plus of not really doing anything yet as president, it was what he *didn't* read that made all the difference in the world. That day that they brought him the broad strokes of 9/11 in booklet form.

Too bad, Mr. Bush. Next time less Babe Ruth, more bin Laden determined to strike in the U.S.

What the—?

Media Fairness Circus

JUNE 4, 2009

The bronze to Congressman Lamar Smith of Texas, unveiling his new media fairness circus. I'm sorry, media fairness caucus. A dozen Republican congressmen, he said, will now point out unfair stories, meet with members of the media, and write op-eds and letters to the editor, because "the greatest threat to America is not necessarily a recession or even another terrorist attack. The greatest threat to America is a liberal media bias."

First off, if we really were running a liberal media, who in the world would be dumb enough to book Liz Cheney on every show except *Wheel of Fortune*? Secondly, liberal media bias a bigger threat than terrorism? Would you submit voluntarily to a Breathalyzer test, Congressman?

Thirdly, a dozen Republican congressmen are going to be the watchdogs for a grateful nation? Mr. Smith, don't you think you guys should focus first on trying to become actual congressmen, instead of lower-octane jokes?

A tie at the silver: Elisabeth Hasselbeck, and Michael Rubin of the *National Review* online. They didn't like what they said they didn't hear from the president today in Cairo. Ms. Hasselbeck said, "He stressed changing course and, also, he didn't mention the word democracy, which had some people kind of upset."

Mr. Rubin wrote this, under the headline "Obama Abandons Democracy": "Obama studiously avoids the word democracy."

One hopes there is no intermittent deafness afflicting either individual, because here is President Obama *not* mentioning the word democracy today four times in Cairo:

"The fourth issue that I will address is democracy."

"I know, I know there has been controversy about the promotion of democracy in recent years."

"There are some who advocate for democracy only when they're out of power."

121

"Elections alone do not make true democracy."

So, once again, a blatant falsehood about Obama is presented as fact, and an entire portion of the community, already inclined to believe that falsehood, with or without the slightest sliver of evidence, because of its own prejudices, swallows it whole. Look at Elisabeth.

But the winner . . .

Jill Stanek of the infamous *World Net Daily*, who did not get the point in the assassination of Dr. George Tiller that you can be complicit in such a crime even if you have never met the man or his assassin. Stanek has now posted photographs and addresses of the only two remaining physicians who will provide late-term abortions when the woman's life is in danger.

It's a very little switch, Ms. Stanek. You'll never understand in a just world, to tell a bunch of crazy people like your readers where they can find somebody and abuse, threaten, or kill them, that that should be enough of a crime to put you in jail for the rest of your life. So let's try this one out instead: you do realize that by posting online the addresses of these two doctors' clinics, you probably enabled some woman seeking their help to now find them and get an abortion. You, Jill Stanek, have just enabled an abortion.

Jill Stanek of *World Net Daily*, today's worst person in the world!

Worst of Bush

I Have to Punch You

JUNE 8, 2009

Number three: War profiteer–gate. A bipartisan commission charged with investigating waste and fraud in wartime spending in Iraq and Afghanistan has reached a conclusion startling even for those of us who already realized the primary reason for going to war in Iraq was so we could have a war in Iraq. The Bush Pentagon's oversight of private contractors, what we paid them, how they got their deals, what they did with the money, it was so lax that the government never established a central database just listing who they were. The Halliburton spin-off KBR was awarded a contract last September to remodel the dining hall at Camp Delta in Iraq. It was then discovered that the dining hall at Camp Delta had just been remodeled by KBR. Nobody had filed the paperwork. KBR got a contract to remodel the same dining hall twice.

Number two: The war against terror, or India-gate. A news agency in India reports that Pakistan received $7 billion from the Bush administration to fight terrorism, specifically the Taliban, especially along the Afghanistan border, and diverted untold portions of it, at least $660 million, to instead openly ordering new aircraft and missiles for its armed forces along the border with India, where the only thing being sneaked into Pakistan were Bollywood movies.

And number one: Gitmo-gate. Until now, Lakhdar Boumediene was just a name in a landmark lawsuit, the one that let those we kidnapped and stashed in Gitmo finally challenge their circumstances in court. Boumediene is back home in France after seven years of detention. He has talked to ABC. He was acquitted in Bosnia of charges of plotting to blow up the U.S. and British embassies in Sarajevo. But instead of being freed, he was turned over to the U.S. military.

From the day they got him to Gitmo, January 17, 2002, he says that not once did his interrogators ask him about that alleged plot, only about what he knew about Al Qaeda and Osama bin Laden. "If I tell my interrogator I am from Al Qaeda, I saw Osama bin Laden, he was my boss, I help them, they will tell me, oh, you are a good man. But if I refuse, I tell them I'm innocent. Never was I a terrorist. Never, never. They tell me, you are not cooperating. I have to punch you."

Boumediene says it was much more than punching. He said he was kept awake for 16 days straight. He said he was forced to run and to keep running, and if he stopped or fell, he would be dragged. He said his legs were shackled to a chair and then guards pulled him up from under his arms.

He said that during a hunger strike, our guards shoved his food IV up his nose and poked a hypodermic needle into the wrong part of his arm. "Over there," meaning Gitmo, he said, "you lose all the hopes. You lose all hope. Any good news they don't want you to be happy."

Boumediene says he worked for the Red Crescent, the term used by about one-fifth of the national Red Cross organizations worldwide. We, those acting in your name and mine, called Boumediene a terrorist. Two weeks after the Bosnians acquitted him of plotting to bomb our embassy there, then they handed him over to our military, then George Bush gave his first State of the Union Address. "Our soldiers," Bush said, "working with the Bosnian government, seized terrorists who were plotting to bomb our embassy."

Which one of those two men deserved to be in prison for seven years?

Worst Person in the World

But She Wouldn't Let Them Have Fries with That

JUNE 22, 2009

The bronze to the citizen patriots of Lancaster, Pennsylvania. It has 165 closed-circuit TV cameras trained on it, more than Boston or San Francisco. They're monitored not by the police but by a company to which the project was outsourced. The company turns out to have hired Lancaster's residents to do the monitoring and call police if they see something amiss. In other words, they're spying on one another.

The *LA Times* quotes a businessman, a beer and soft drink distributor, who calls it "a great thing" and adds, that there is nothing wrong with instilling fear. The beverage man's name is Jack Bauer.

The silver: Shared by Charles Krauthammer of the *Washington Post* and Bill Bennett of CNN, appalled that the president has referred to the chief ayatollah as the supreme leader of Iran. "Note the abject solicitousness with which the American president confers this honorific on a clerical dictator," says Krauthammer.

"We should be on the side of freedom, and not on the side of this supreme leader, as our president keeps referring to," whines Bennett. Later the same day, John McCain referred to this guy as the supreme leader.

In March, Senator Richard Lugar called him that four times in one hearing.

And even William Kristol called him that in a column.

It's a job title.

But our winner . . .

Cynthia Davis, who represents the 19th district in Missouri's State House of Representatives, the gold that is found off the beaten path. Representative Davis provides a few commentaries to a news release about the state's summer food program, which keeps feeding disadvantaged kids even while school is out. In short, Representative Davis does not get it. She writes, "Who's buying dinner? Who is getting paid to serve the meal? Churches and other nonprofits can do this at no cost to the taxpayer, if it is warranted. Bigger governmental programs take away our connectedness to the human family, our brotherhood and our need for one another. Anyone under 18 can be eligible? Can't they get a job during the summer by the time they are 16? Hunger can be a positive motivator. What is wrong with the idea of getting a job so you can get better meals? Tip: If you work for McDonald's, they will feed you for free during your break. It really is all about increasing government spending, which means an increase in taxes for us to buy more free lunches and breakfasts."

One in five kids in Missouri is already motivated by hunger, Ms. Davis. And last year, because the meals are offered at churches, the $9.5 million of federal money spent produced 3,700,000 meals at a cost of about $2.50 each. It is embarrassing enough that Cynthia "Let Them Eat McDonald's" Davis is a public servant paid by tax dollars, but she's also the chairwoman of the Missouri

House Special Standing Committee on Children and Families. It would seem that her advocacy of hunger would disqualify her from that job and that we'd be better off if she was working at a McDonald's.

Clearly, she has used, and is using, hunger as a positive motivator, because she seems to have been starving her brain of the recommended daily dosage of intelligence and humanity and oxygen.

Missouri State Representative Cynthia "Are There No Prisons, Are There No Workhouses" Davis, today's worst person in the world.

Worst Person in the World

Save the Date

JUNE 23, 2009

The bronze to Senator Judd Gregg of New Hampshire. He has proposed legislation which he has somewhat cumbersomely named the Ax the Stimulus Plaques Act. He said he doesn't want projects funded by the stim to have signs that reveal that they have been funded by the stim. Stimulus construction signs "are simply for political self-interest," says Senator Judd Gregg, who had no comment about his half-million-dollar earmark that led to the Judd Gregg Meteorology Institute at Plymouth State University, or the Judd Gregg Library, established by the National Police Athletic League, after he got it $150,000, or Gregg Hall at the University of New Hampshire, which followed Gregg's getting it $266 million in federal funds for the whole school.

Our runner-up: Newt Gingrich, who has inadvertently outed himself as America's least intelligent supergenius politician. He has launched a series of ads against Waxman-Markey, the clean energy reform bill in the House, claiming that the bill will push the economy to its breaking point. The ads are being produced by

Gingrich's 527 group, American Solutions for Winning the Future. The problem is that records show that the Gingrich 527 group received more than $250,000 in contributions last year from Peabody Energy, a giant coal company which would have to clean up its pollution if Waxman-Markey is passed. That's Newt Gingrich in the pocket of big coal.

But our winner . . .

Former president George W. Bush. Unlike, say, us, the British Parliament is beginning an investigation into how the nation it serves got conned into the phony war in Iraq. And one of the discoveries in the preliminary stages: another Manning memo, another document from Sir David Manning, who had been then–prime minister Tony Blair's foreign policy adviser, and whose notes constituted the infamous Downing Street Memo.

Not much to Downing Street, the sequel, except that on January 31, 2003, Blair and Bush met, acknowledged that it was increasingly clear that UN inspectors were not going to find any weapons of mass destruction in Iraq, and that would require a whole new rationale for the charade because, as Manning wrote in the second memo, Bush told Blair, "The start date for the military campaign was now penciled in for 10 March. This was when the bombing would begin."

This is when Bush proposed to "fly U2 reconnaissance aircraft painted in UN colors over Iraq with fighter cover" in hopes that Saddam Hussein would have his military shoot them down, giving the U.S. an excuse to invade. Failing that, Manning wrote, "Bush hoped the Iraqi defectors, one of them at least, might be brought out to give a show and tell on Saddam's WMD, and then we would have to go in because Saddam was still in charge. Or worse came to worst, maybe somebody would assassinate Saddam, and then we would have to go in because Saddam wasn't still in charge."

The bottom line here, ever more certain, ever more certainly to become this president's legacy: he wanted war in Iraq, and then he went excuse shopping.

Former president George Walker Bush, today's worst person in the world!

Are Not the Treadmill and the Poor Law in Full Vigor?

JUNE 24, 2009

The bronze to Congressman Randy Neugebauer, Republican extremist of Texas. He has signed on as one of the five—count them, five—co-sponsors of Florida loon Bill Posey's bill that would require birth certificates from presidential candidates. After he insisted on radio yesterday that the bill wouldn't apply to the Obama election, because it wouldn't be retroactive, Neugebauer was also asked, so you believe the president is a U.S. citizen? His answer: "You know, I don't know. I've never seen him produce documents that would say one way or the other."

Once again, *World Net Daily*, August 23, 2008, Drew Zahn: "A separate WND investigation into Obama's birth certificate, utilizing forgery experts, also found the document to be authentic." Read it, Congressman, if you know how to read. Also, the people who elected you are obviously idiots. That does not mean everybody else is. The bill wouldn't apply to Obama? You do realize that he is likely to run again in 2012, right?

The runner-up: Joyce E. Thomann, the president of the Republican Women of Anne Arundel County in Maryland. This pretty much speaks for itself. In her words: "Obama and Hitler have a great deal in common, in my view. Obama and Hitler use the blitzkrieg method to overwhelm their enemies. Fast carpet bombing, intent on destruction. Hitler's blitzkrieg bombing destroyed many European cities quickly and effectively. Obama is quickly and systematically destroying the American economy, and with it America."

Seriously, isn't comparing Obama to Hitler a little much even for the Republican party? Do you guys stand for anything? Why haven't you thrown this representative of your party out on her Anne Arundel?

But the winner . . .

State Representative Cynthia Davis of Missouri. When she first won this award, hands down, on Monday, we told you that Ms. Davis had attacked a series of what she called commentaries to report on the state's meal program for underprivileged kids while school was out for the summer, insisting these meals should be curtailed. Among her original observations, "Anyone under 18 can be eligible? Can't they get a job during the summer by the time they are 16? Hunger can be a positive motivator. What is wrong with the idea of getting a job so you can get better meals? Tip: If you work for McDonald's, they will feed you for free during your break."

Representative Davis has not apologized for, retracted, or clarified her remarks. She has blamed "an editorial that misrepresented my views," even though her views were in her editorials, which she wrote. She continues to believe that one-fifth of school-age children in Missouri who face hunger every day have somehow chosen to do that, that this is a family rights issue. As she said, "We all agree on the importance of feeding children, but we differ on who should do this. I believe this duty belongs to the parents. Instead of respecting this time honored jurisdiction of the family, the summer feeding program treats families like they do not exist."

You're wrong. It treats families like they don't have enough money to get meals for their kids, and they need our help. "When government takes over a family function like feeding children on a daily basis, we take a group of people who are capable and treat them like they are incapacitated. Look into your own heart and ask, what made a difference in my life as a child? Was it standing in a line for a cafeteria style meal at school or was it sitting around the kitchen table with others in your family?"

You're wrong. Gosh, Ms. Davis, I think more than either of these things, what would have made a difference in my life as a child was if one day there was no breakfast, and some idiot politician was trying to make sure I couldn't get one. And cafeteria-style meal at school? You're wrong. Missouri's summer meals are given out in churches. Your own state, and you don't even know the simple facts?

"My goal is not to replace parents, but to reinforce them. The solution is found in helping those near us, not in yet another gigantic, federally funded, mass market approach. Bigger government invites fraud and robs people of the dignity of personal human relationships."

You're wrong. Your goal here is to try to take an efficient program, providing needy kids millions of healthy meals at about two and a half bucks each, and turn it into another wedge weapon of paranoia to use on the buffoons who would vote for a political hack like yourself.

"My weekly Capitol Report is a way to have two-way communications with my constituents, and not a national manifesto for you to mock, distort, and be quoted out of context."

You're wrong. There was no distortion, no loss of context, and any mocking done here you have richly earned for today, for tomorrow, and for the rest of your tenure in public life, brief though the rest of us hope that might be.

"Yet to dare suggest there are alternatives for rational people to discuss any consequences of government taking over so much in people's lives is to be branded an inhuman monster."

Hey, on this we agree. Well-phrased. You're right. You're an inhuman monster. And you chair the state's Permanent Committee for Children? You're a positive menace to the health and well-being of the children of Missouri. Resign.

State Representative Cynthia Davis of Missouri, once again, today's worst person in the world, and not for the last time.

Worst Person in the World

203rd Trimester

JUNE 26, 2009

The bronze to Missouri State Representative Cynthia Davis. You know, the chairperson of that House's Children and Families Subcommittee, who was opposed to free meals for underprivileged schoolkids over the summer because she thinks hunger can be a positive motivator and that government is interfering with family mealtime by offering free meals to families who can't afford to feed their own kids.

When Representative Davis stuck to her guns Wednesday and suggested nobody had the right to criticize her, the State House Democratic leader, Paul LeVota, wrote to its Speaker, suggesting Davis's views on child hunger were "Dickensian" and that she should be removed as committee chair. There was also a spectacular postscript provided by a reader of the *Kansas City Star* Web site—can't verify this—posted by somebody identified only as "embarrassed": "Cynthia forgets how she takes multiple plates of food from committee and lobbyist dinners to feed her hungry children when she is in Jefferson City. She has been observed at receptions wrapping and stuffing food in her oversized hand bag. Maybe that's what other hungry children should have their poor working parents do, just steal food to bring home to them."

Our runner-up: Morton Kondracke of the *Weekly Standard*, pitying poor Governor Mark Sanford. "Multiple affairs did not stop Bill Clinton from being elected president. That's because the Democratic Party is a lot more tolerant of licentiousness than the Republican Party is. And that's the rub for poor old Mark Sanford here."

Right, that's why Governor Eliot Spitzer resigned and why Governor Jim McGreevey resigned, and why Gary Hart's presidential aspirations ended immediately, and why John Edwards could not get a free drink at a convention of John Edwards donors, and why John McCain and Rudy Giuliani ran for president last year, and Newt Gingrich will be unofficially running for president next year, and Senator John Ensign and Senator David Vitter and Governor Sanford are still in office this year, even though they now have six known public affairs and four divorces among them.

But our winner . . .
Coulter-geist. On the assassination of Dr. George Tiller: "I don't really like to think of it as a murder. It was terminating Tiller in the 203rd trimester. I am personally opposed to shooting abortionists, but I don't want to impose my moral values on others."

Ann? Annie? Over here, Ann. I know you think you're Dorothy Parker, but there are people even dumber than you are. I know it's hard to believe. As I was saying, there are people who are even dumber than you, who will not get the irony there. And they will decide they're now perfectly entitled to go shoot somebody they don't like, anybody in public, Annie. That includes me, and you.

Coulter-geist, today's worst person in the world.

Nuclear Fetish

JULY 7, 2009

The bronze to baseball's Manny Ramirez, just back from a 50-game suspension for using performance-enhancing drugs, with time off to play rehab games in the minor leagues. Nearly all players on such rehabs thank the minor leaguers with whom they have spent a few days by buying them a big postgame dinner. When Randy Johnson rehabbed in 2007, he bought his temporary teammates a meal that cost him three grand. Roger Clemens even bought one of his minor-league teams a new clubhouse.

A major-league pitcher named Joe Martinez, who makes the major-league minimum salary, bought his teammates in Modesto a full postgame meal. Not Ramirez. The newspaper the *Modesto Bee* reports that despite two games with Albuquerque and three with San Bernardino, despite the fact that his rehab got him back into shape after he shamed the sport and the Dodgers organization, Ramirez bought his new minor-league friends nothing. Ramirez's contract for this season was to pay him $23,854,494.

Our runner-up: Samuel "Joe the Plumber" Wurzelbacher, speaking at a rally in Houston. He stunned the crowd when he announced "I believe in making sure our country is safe first. I believe we need to spend a little more on illegal immigrants."

Did you get hit by lightning or something? Sadly, no. "Get them the hell out of our damn country and close the borders down. We can do it. We've got the greatest military in the world, and you're telling me we can't close our borders? That's just ridiculous."

Two points that racists like Wurzelbacher always forget: The official government estimate that there are between 12 million and 20 million undocumented immigrants in the United States. The official government estimate is that there are 3,385,000 members of the military, including the reserves, and including everybody stationed outside the country. So if 12 million immigrants don't want to leave, exactly how are you going to get them to?

Second point, and this a guy named Olbermann talking to a guy named Wurzelbacher: "I know my ancestors were not Native Americans. I'm pretty sure yours weren't, either. Do you have any records proving yours were not illegal immigrants?"

But our winners . . .

Former CIA analyst—ironically, in the bin Laden section in the '90s—Michael Scheuer and Glenn Beck of Fox News. A lot has been written online suggesting Scheuer merits a special comment. The man has some sort of perverse fetish about seeing part of this country destroyed by nuclear weapons. He came on this program in February 2007 and practically drooled at the prospect.

He deserves something, but not a special comment. As he said on Fox News last week, "The only chance we have as a country right now is for Osama bin Laden to deploy and detonate a major weapon in the United States, because it's going to take a grass-roots, bottom-up pressure, because these politicians prize their office, prize the praise of the media and the Europeans. It's an absurd situation again. Only Osama can execute an attack that will force Americans to demand that government protect them effectively, consistently and with as much violence as necessary."

Scheuer's interviewer, Glenn Beck of Fox News, did not attempt to correct him, did not scream at him, "What the hell do you mean the only chance we have as a country right now?" Beck did not accuse Scheuer of insanity, nor disloyalty, nor palling around with terrorists. Beck did not even burst into tears. The host merely nodded gravely, as if this made sense. "Which is why I was thinking," he said, "if I were him"—meaning bin Laden—"that would be the last thing I would do right now," agreeing with Scheuer and barely containing his disappointment as he did so.

We need bin Laden to destroy part of America in order to save America. You know, since that worked out so well for everybody on 9/11. Scheuer has already given comfort to the enemy. Now Scheuer adds the piquant touch of disingenuousness. Criticized online, Scheuer insisted he never said what he clearly had said.

"Far from wishing for another attack," he wrote, "I trust that Churchill's judgment that God looks out for drunks and the United States of America still holds good, and we remain safe. God better do the job, because no one in our elite is doing it."

Of course, here Mr. Scheuer is correct. No one in their elite is doing their job. Mr. Scheuer has issued a call for the head of Al Qaeda to "detonate a major weapon in the United States," and yet for some reason, to my knowledge at least, the Department of Homeland Security has not yet been to see him, nor been to see Mr. Beck, nor Fox News for having provided him a platform and passive assent, for approving of not just a terrorist attack which could kill Americans, but approving of one that might even kill Fox viewers.

If we're going to continue to prevent terrorism in this country, international or domestic, we have to legally stop the people who view terrorism as an acceptable means of effecting political change in this country, people like Michael Scheuer. And we have to legally stop the people like Glenn Beck, the enablers who simply nod gravely, as if the idea and the speaker were not treasonous.

Author Michael Scheuer and Glenn Beck of Fox News, today's worst persons in the world!

Worst Person in the World

Freepers Creepers

JULY 13, 2009

The bronze to Boss Limbaugh, feebly fading into the background lately, and thus begging for attention with even wackier stuff than usual, telling his audience during the Sotomayor hearing today: "So Russ Feingold, a couple words that Sonia Sotomayor said taken out of context, you mean like 'macaca'? George Allen saying 'macaca'? We heard about that for weeks and months. Sotomayor's comments are much worse than 'macaca,' and they're frequent."

A quick refresher: Senator George Allen called a dark-skinned blogger videotaping one of his speeches the racial epithet "macaca." To tie Allen on the racial slur level, the judge would have had to call somebody, like say Limbaugh, whitey. Worse than that, Ofay. As in hey, Limbaugh, yes you, you Ofay, you. Limbaugh says you're frequent. There you go.

The runner-up: Jim Thompson, the owner of the right-wing Web site Free Republic, which has moderated comments, meaning a grown-up is supposed to read them and delete the crazier ones. But Thompson's folks waited as long as three days before removing a comment thread devoted to the racist rage of a disturbingly large number of his posters, possibly some of the same people who had previously conducted polls on the site on how best to topple the freely elected government of the United States.

After President Obama's daughter appeared in a T-shirt with a peace sign on it at the G-8, a thread at the Free Republic was opened with another photo of the first lady, captioned, "to entertain her daughter, Michelle Obama loves to make monkey sounds."

Some of the posts describe the Obamas, individually and collectively, as "typical street whore," "bunch of ghetto thugs," "ghetto street trash," "dirt bags," "wonder when she'll get her first abortion," "they make me sick, the whole family, mammy, pappy, the free loading mammy-in-law, the misguided children, and especially little cousin."

No indication of how many of the racist attacks on Malia Obama were made by people who simultaneously were threatening anybody who even mentioned Sarah Palin's children. The most prominent response at Free Republic was not an apology, but rather the claim the comments were planted. This was, in turn, greeted by more racist comments by veterans of the site, and a call to action to flood the e-mail accounts of a list of the mainstream media people, people like Don Imus of MSNBC, the *CBS Evening News* with Dan Rather, and Paula Zahn, and Bill Hemmer, and Tucker Carlson, and Robert Novak of CNN.

Let me know if Dan Rather still answers his CBS e-mails, clowns.

But our winner . . .
Pastor Wiley Drake, the leader of the Buena Park Southern Baptist Church in California. He has confirmed that he does in fact pray for the death of President Obama. But he says that such petitions to God should only make up about 2 percent of your daily prayer diet. He says that the correct version of this is to pray that the Lord smite your opponent or bring him plagues or pestilence. Just stick to Scripture and then aim it in the proper direction, kind of like voodoo.

Pastor Drake says he does, indeed, pray for Obama's death, but he also prays, or has prayed, for the deaths of Presidents Clinton and George W. Bush and Pastor Rick Warren. Some sort of "I'm working this side of the street, bub," thing, I guess. I don't go for this praying for other people's deaths, myself. But if you do, this would seem to offer an unexpected opportunity for bipartisanship.

Combined, supporters of President Obama and supporters of President Bush and supporters of Pastor Warren—surely combined, they outnumber supporters of this Pastor Drake. I mean, certainly they can summon up more of these cumulative smites, plagues, pestilence, and death prayers than he can. Seems to be a simple question of math.

So at prayer time, remember the name Pastor Wiley Drake, today's, but possibly soon no longer to be eligible for a repeat victory, worst person in the world!

Worst Person in the World

Country First

JULY 14, 2009

The bronze to Newt Gingrich. He got a faceful last night on Al Jazeera, suggesting that the correct American policy toward Iran should be about special ops and midnight raids and sabotage.

Not exactly bombing Iran's oil refineries. In his words, "I called for sabotage, not bombing. Fundamental difference," he corrected interviewer Avi Lewis. "The only purpose of sabotaging them would be to create a gasoline-led crisis to try to replace the regime. I'm against using tactics that don't have any strategic meaning."

Whereupon Mr. Lewis said, "Which you could precipitate by provoking a gas crisis with black ops sabotage?" Which is when interviewer Lewis laughed at Gingrich. His justification for doing so was amplified when Gingrich suggested Iran has only the one gas refinery, which he and Rambo would have to sabotage. And somebody had to break it to him that it actually has nine refineries.

The runner-up: The right-wing media. A little bonus here: The South Carolina newspaper the *State* used a public records request to get e-mails sent to and from Governor Mark "the Raging Bull of a Pompous" Sanford, while he was hiking the old "Appalachian Trail." Among them were these from conservative news outlets, before they realized he was family values poison, as they tried to suck up to Sanford.

From a right-wing TV host: "Having known the governor for years, and even worked with him when he would host radio shows for me, I find this story and the media frenzy surrounding it to be absolutely ridiculous. Please give him my best."

From a staffer at the *Washington Times*, "If you all want to speak on this publicly, you're welcome to *Washington Times* Radio. You know that you will be on friendly ground here."

From Brendan Miniter, an opinion editor at the *Wall Street Journal*, "Someone at WSJ should be fired for today's story. Ridiculous."

Nice. Bury your own paper under the bus. Sadly, one more stroke job ended up in the e-mail trolling. "If the governor is looking for a friendly place to make light of what I think is a small story that got blown out of scale, I would be happy to have him on, in person, here, on the phone, or in South Carolina. Stay strong, signed Steven Colbert," who just barely gets away with this because he is a native South Carolinian and an old school gentleman who mistakenly thought hiking the old Appalachian Trail meant hiking the old Appalachian Trail.

But our winners . . .

Stefan Frederick Cook, major, U.S. Army Reserves, and his attorney Orly Taitz, who are seeking a federal court order in Georgia to delay, and ultimately prevent, his upcoming deployment to Afghanistan. Their premise, Major Cook believes, to quote McClatchy News, that President Barack Obama is not a natural-born citizen of the United States and therefore is ineligible to serve as commander in chief of U.S. armed forces.

The document itself says Cook believes he would "be acting in violation of international law by engaging in military actions outside of the United States under this president's command, simultaneously subjecting himself to possible prosecution as a war criminal by the faithful execution of these duties."

Lawyer Taitz is an Obama birther who has filed other delusional lawsuits about the president's birth certificate, a certificate which has even been validated by the Web site *World Net Daily*. Major Cook is reportedly a poster at the Web site we told you about yesterday, Free Republic.

When I was a kid in the '60s, thinking ahead toward possibly getting drafted, I thought, you know, if it comes to that, I'm not going to make up some political context or pretext. I'm not going to invent some sudden philosophical epiphany that I'm a conscientious objector. I'm just going to say, I really don't want to get shot and killed in Vietnam or anywhere else.

Too bad Major Cook doesn't have the guts to say that. Then he might be deserving of his rank, rather than an embarrassment to all those who have served without cowardice. Don't ask, don't tell, is still throwing out men and women who are willing to die for their country, but somehow we have room for this jackass Cook, and the skirts of this con woman Taitz behind which he hides.

Just remember their slogan from last year: "Country First."

Major Stefan Frederick Cook and his attorney Orly Taitz, today's worst persons in the world!

Birthers of a Nation

JULY 15, 2009

The bronze to Jake Tapper of ABC News. Following up on yesterday's revelation of suck-up e-mails to Governor Mark Sanford's office in hopes of getting an interview with him, Tapper on June 23: "NBC spot was slimy. For the record, I think the *Today Show* spot was pretty insulting."

Find cheek, plant kiss. Now it's gotten worse. First, an ABC News vice president said Tapper was "carrying some water for producers who know he had a relationship with the governor's office." Then Tapper got mighty defensive. On Twitter, "There was no story at the time, just mystery as to where he was. Only ones who knew about the affair: him, wife, mistress, and the *State*." The South Carolina newspaper, not the actual state.

Then also on Twitter, "The e-mail reflects a clumsy attempt to harm a competitor's chances of getting an interview, nothing else."

Then finally the sun broke through. An e-mail to *Politico*:

"Busted; in retrospect, the story I was referring to wasn't slimy enough. At that moment, the only ones who knew of the governor's affair were Sanford, his wife, his mistress and the *State* newspaper. But I shouldn't have said that. And I'll try to leave the media criticism to others from now on."

Good thinking, because what's slimy is for a news organization to offer to not cover some of the news as part of an agreement with a newsmaker or an agreement with another news organization or anybody, for that matter.

The runner-up: Boss Limbaugh. Just another half step away from reality, and the old living in glass houses things. "There's a show on MSNBC named after a horse, *The Ed Show*, a talking horse. I think they brought the horse out of retirement to host the show. And the horse, Mr. Ed, is talking to a former CIA officer."

So because Ed Schultz's first name is Ed, his show is named after a horse? Meaning that since Rush Limbaugh's first name is Rush, his show is named after a rush, like a drug rush?

But our winner . . .

Obama birther and general nut bag Orly Taitz, who has now gotten another Obama birther person fired. We told you yesterday that Stefan Frederick Cook, major, U.S. Army Reserves, had his attorney, Taitz, sue to get him out of assignment to Afghanistan. The claim was that Obama's not really the president, so he couldn't really order anybody to serve anywhere.

One thing Ms. Taitz never mentioned in publicizing the suit: Cook had volunteered for service in Afghanistan and then sued to stop it. But as a volunteer, he could simply change his mind, and the army could not send him there. Meaning, the suit was a transparent political stunt.

The army has already vacated Cook's orders. He's not going to Afghanistan. But what this dim bulb Taitz, and what increasingly looks like her sap of a victim Cook, did not consider was that in civilian life, Cook is a systems engineer for a Pentagon contractor. Naturally enough, the army, sued by a guy, has the right to say he is not welcome at Department of Defense facilities, which is exactly where Cook was working. Not anymore.

Major Cook, by now you must have gotten the hint that this obsession with a birth certificate already endorsed by one of your own whack job sites, *World Net Daily*, is clouding your judgment. It has become increasingly poor cover for your real issue with the Obama presidency. Steer out of the skid. See if you can give that advice to, if after costing you your job she hasn't gone into hiding, Orly Taitz, tonight's worst person in the world!

Special Comment

The Spirit of the American Corporation

AUGUST 3, 2009

Finally, tonight, as promised, a Special Comment on health care reform in this country, and, in particular, the "public insurance option."

In March of 1911, after a wave of minor factory fires in New York City, the city's fire commissioner issued emergency rules about fire prevention, protection, escape, sprinklers. The city's Manufacturers Association, in turn, called an emergency meeting to attack the fire commissioner and his "interference with commerce."

The new rules were delayed. Just days later, a fire broke out at the Triangle Shirtwaist Factory. The door to the fire escape had been bolted shut to keep the employees from leaving prematurely. One hundred and fifty of those employees died, many by jumping from the seventh-floor windows to avoid the flames.

Firefighters setting up their ladders literally had to dodge the falling, often burning, bodies of women.

This was the spirit of the American corporation then. It is the spirit of the American corporation now. It is what the corporation will do, when it is left alone, for a week.

You know the drill. We all know the drill.

You get something done at a doctor's, at a dentist's, at an emergency room, and the bills are in your hands before the pain medication wears off. And if you're one of the lucky ones, and you have insurance, you submit the endless paperwork, and no matter whether it's insurance through your company, or your union, or your nonprofit, or on your own dime, you then get your turn at the roulette wheel.

How much of it is the insurance company going to pay this time? How much of it is the insurance company—about which you have next to no choice, and against which you have virtually no appeal—how much is this giant corporation going to give you back? What small percentage of what they told you they were going to pay you will they actually pay you?

You know the answer. And you know the answer if you don't have insurance. But do you know why that's the answer?

Because the insurance industry owns the Republican Party. Not exclusively. Pharma owns part of it, too. Hospitals and HMOs, another part. Nursing homes, they have a share. You name a Republican, any Republican, and he is literally brought to you by campaign donations from the health sector.

Senator John Thune of South Dakota? You gave the Republican rebuttal to the president's weekly address day before yesterday.

You said the Democrats' plan was for "government-run health care that would disrupt our current system and force millions of Americans who currently enjoy their employer-based coverage into a new health care plan run by government bureaucrats."

That's a bald-faced lie, Senator. And you're a bald-faced liar, whose bald face happens to be covered by your own health care plan run by government bureaucrats.

Nobody would be forced into anything, and the public insurance option is no more a disruption than is letting the government sell you water, and not just Poland Spring and Sparkletts.

But, as corrupt hypocrites go, Senator, at least you're well paid. What was that one statement worth to you in contributions from the health sector, Senator Thune? Five thousand dollars? Ten?

We know what you are, sir; we're arguing about the price.

What about your other quote? "We can accomplish health care reform while keeping patients and their doctors in charge, not bureaucrats and politicians."

Wow, Senator, this illustrates how desperate you and the other Republicans are, right? Because Senator Thune, if you really think "bureaucrats and politicians" need to get out of the way of "patients and their doctors," then you support a woman patient's right to get an abortion. And you supported Michael Schiavo's right to take his wife off life support. And you oppose "bureaucrats and politicians" getting in the way. And we'll just mark you down on the pro-choice list.

That's a rare misstep for you, Senator Thune. No $12,000 pay-off for that statement!

I am not being hyperbolic, am I, Senator? About the money?

Senator Thune has thus far received from the health sector—and all these numbers tonight are from the Center for Responsive Politics—campaign contributions amounting to $1,206,176. So much for Senator Thune.How about Congresswoman Ginny Brown-Waite? Good evening, ma'am. You are the Florida representative who claimed on the floor that Democrats had "released a health care bill which essentially said to America's seniors: Drop dead."

Now those are strong, terrorizing, words. That's exactly what your insurance and medical overlords wanted to hear. But are you truly worth every dollar of the 369,255 of them you have received over the years from the health sector? Let's read the rest of the operative part of your speech, although your own rendition actually cannot be matched:

"Listen up, America, seniors have special needs. This bill ignores the—ignores the needs of Florida's health care system. We should be fixing what is broke, not disseminate—disseminating—decimating, the care of our senior population."

You can always tell, can't you, Congresswoman, when the hostage is reading her own ransom note, and when she is reading one written for her? So much for Congresswoman Brown-Waite.

There are so many other Republicans, bought and sold—like that unfortunate congresswoman there—by the health sector.

Minority Leader McConnell of the Senate?

You're worth $3.1 million to the health sector? A million and a half just for last year's election? And I'm supposed to think you aren't a sellout, a liar, a paid spokesman, a shill, a carnival barker? So much for Senator McConnell.

Congressman Joe Barton of Oklahoma: $2,660,000, Congressman? That's ten times what Senator Robert Byrd has accepted from the health sector. Congressman! What a guy! So much for Congressman Barton.

Senator McCain, $1.6 million?

To serve the hospitals, and serve the drug companies, and serve the nursing homes? And not to serve the retirement communities of Arizona? Or the cancer survivors? Or the veterans? So much for Senator McCain.

I could go on all night and never exaggerate in the slightest.

PBS pointed out that the health and insurance industries are spending more than $1.4 million a day just to destroy the "public option"—the truly nonprofit, wieldy, round-up and not round-down, government, from helping you pay your medical bills with about a billionth of the recklessness with which it is still paying Halliburton and its spin-offs to kill your kids.

And much of this money is going to, and through, Republicans.

But that's the real point tonight. Not all of it is going through Republicans. Because the evil truth is, the insurance industry, along with hospitals, HMOs, Big Pharma, nursing homes—it owns Democrats, too.

Not the whole party.

Candidate Barack Obama got more than $18 million from the health sector just last year. And you can bet somebody in the health trust, somebody responsible for buying influence, got fired over what Obama's done.

No, the Democrats are not wholly owned. Hundreds of Democrats have taken campaign money from the health sector without handing over their souls as receipts. But conveniently, the ones who are owned have made themselves easy to spot in a crowd.

They've called themselves Blue Dogs, and they are out there, hand in hand with the Republicans, whom they are happy to condemn day and night on everything else, throatily singing "Kumbaya" with the men and women who were bought and sold to defend this con game of an American health care system against the slightest encroachment.

Congressman Mike Ross of Arkansas, leader of the Blue Dogs in the House. You're the guy demanding a guarantee that reform will not add to the deficit. I'm guessing you forgot to demand that about, say, Iraq.

You're a Democrat, you say, Congressman? You saw what Sandy Barham said?

Sandy Barham is 62 years old. She's got a bad heart. She's hoping her valves will hold together for three more years until Medicare kicks in, because she can't afford insurance.

Not just for herself, mind you. For her employees. She needs the public option. So do those six people who work at that restaurant of hers, Congressman Ross.

And why should you give a crap? Because Sandy Barham's restaurant is the Broadway Railroad Cafe, and it is at 123 West First Street North in Prescott, Arkansas.

Prescott, Arkansas, Congressman Ross. Your hometown. You are Sandy Barham's congressman. Hers, sir. Not Blue Cross's and Blue Shield's, even if they do insure 75 percent of the state and they own you.

The top donor so far to Congressman Ross's bid for reelection next year? The Blue Dog PAC, $10,000. Second? Something called Invacare, $7,300. Oh, they make wheelchairs and rollers and slings. They're big in slings.

Tied for third? The American Dental Association, another grand or so, $5,000, as a matter of fact.

Your top donors by industry, Congressman Ross? Health professionals: $29,250. Then Pharma and health products: $12,250. And so far in your career, Congressman Ross, your total haul from the health sector is $921,000. That's 90th in the combined list of donations for the House and the Senate, sir, 90th out of 537.

You should be proud, Congressman!

Except for the fact that before you started living off the public dime, you owned a pharmacy. And your grandmother was a nurse. And it turns out you're not Sandy Barham's congressman, after all. You're Blue Cross's. So much for Congressman Ross.

Congressman Bart Gordon of Tennessee. Congressman? Undecided on the public option? At $1,173,000 in donations from the health sector, I'm surprised. You should have already said no, and loudly. The only thing you should be undecided about is whether or not you're really a Democrat. So much for Congressman Gordon.

Senator Max Baucus of Montana. Good evening, Senator.

So you're supposed to be negotiating all this out with the Republicans and the hesitant Democrats, to gain bipartisanship with a wholly owned subsidiary of the health sector? Bipartisanship that will get you, what? A total of no votes?

And your price has been, let's see, $414,000 in donations from hospitals, $667,000 in donations from the insurance companies, just over a million from Big Pharma, $1,300,000 from other health professionals, and $237,000 from nursing homes.

When you think of getting $237,000 in campaign contributions from nursing homes, Senator Baucus, do you ever think about whether they subtract that amount of money evenly from all the patients suffering and dying in the lousy nursing homes, or just from a few of the lousy ones?

So much for Senator Baucus.

Sadly, this list could go on almost all night, too.

I could ask Blue Dog congressman Democrat John Tanner of Tennessee if, since he's gotten $215,000 from hospitals over the years—if I and the appropriate number of my friends were willing to make it $216,000, if we could buy his vote, or would there still have to be an auction?

We could bring up Senator Kay Hagan, and Congressman Earl Pomeroy, who at $628,000 appears to represent the insurance industry and not North Dakota. I could bring up Senator Tom Carper and Senator Blanche Lincoln.

Senator Lincoln, by the way, considering how you're obstructing health care reform, how do you feel every time you actually see Senator Kennedy?

I could bring up all the other Democrats doing their masters' bidding in the House or the Senate, all the others who will get an extra thousand from somebody if they just postpone the vote another year, another month, another week, because right now, without the competition of a government-funded insurance company, in one hour, the health care industries can make so much money that they would kill you for that extra hour of profit.

I could call them all out by name. But I think you get the point. We don't need to call the Democrats holding this up Blue Dogs. That one word "Dogs" is perfectly sufficient.

But let me speak to them collectively, anyway. I warn you all. You were not elected to create a Democratic majority. You were elected to restore this country.

You were not elected to serve the corporations and the trusts whom the government has enabled for these last eight years.

You were elected to serve the people. And if you fail to pass or support this legislation, the full wrath of the progressive and the moderate movements in this country will come down on your heads.

Explain yourselves not to me but to them. They elected you. And in the blink of an eye, they will replace you.

If you will behave as if you are Republicans—as if you are the prostitutes of our system—you will be judged as such. And you will lose not merely our respect. You will lose your jobs!

Every poll, every analysis, every vote, every region of this country supports health care reform and the essential great leveling agent of a government-funded alternative to the unchecked duopoly of profiteering private insurance corporations.

Cross us all at your peril. Because, Congressman Ross, you are not the representative from Blue Cross.

And Mr. Baucus, you are not the senator from Schering-Plough Global Health Care, even if they have already given you $76,000 toward your reelection.

And Ms. Lincoln, you are not the Senator from DaVita Dialysis.

Because, ladies and gentlemen, President Lincoln did not promise that this nation shall have a new *death* of freedom and that government of the corporation, by the corporation, and for the corporation shall not perish from this earth.

False Witnesses

AUGUST 5, 2009

Number three: Attorneys-gate. Remember the name Rachel Paulose? She was the 33-year-old former office assistant to Alberto Gonzales, best friend of Monica Goodling, the theocrat with a law degree from box top university. Somehow Paulose wound up as the U.S. attorney for Minnesota, where she mishandled classified information and gave an employee enough ammunition for 96 discrimination lawsuits, by referring to that employee with terms like fat, black, ass, and lazy, and where four of her top lieutenants demoted themselves in protest.

Miss Paulose is working for us again. She has been hired by the Miami Regional Office of the Securities and Exchange Commission, and in her new job, she does not even have to use a mop.

Number two: Bush? Bush who–gate. At least eight former Bush administration staffers are now running for office, according to the *Hill*. At least one is running away from his past. Tim Nank, former Bush counterterrorism staffer, now running for the Virginia House of Delegates, says, "President Bush's popularity rating is obviously very low and I think the people in my district would probably not look favorably on that. I haven't had a lot of people ask me where I worked. They usually ask me where I work."

If it comes up, just say you were in some sort of witness relocation program. It'll sound better, and it's kind of true.

Number one: Bear false witness, win shoes–gate. Muhammad Jawad is the kid detained in Gitmo since 2002 who claims he was only 12 years old when we took him there. He was detained in Afghanistan for reportedly throwing a grenade at U.S. soldiers. Afghan officials threatened to kill him and his family if he did not confess.

That is not a wild story. Even the U.S. military investigated it, found it to be true, and threw out the confession. But Jawad remained at Gitmo. He might be 19 now. Maybe he's 25. Regardless, he's been there nearly seven years. Now comes an accusation filed by his U.S. military lawyers that may be as shocking as any charge of brutality or rendition or torture. The testimony that he threw the grenade comes from a series of witnesses whom Jawad's attorney, a Marine Corps major, has now been able to interview.

He says the witnesses have something odd in common. One was paid $400 by the U.S. government for cooperation. Another got a new pair of shoes. A third needed an operation and was transported to this country and got it. In short, when our ally threatened to kill him and the resulting fake confession didn't work, we sent Jawad to Gitmo and then tortured him. When that didn't work, we went out and bought witnesses to testify against him.

The Bush administration not only suborned perjury to find another scapegoat and cover up their own crimes, but they paid for it. *Paid*. Thanks to these men and women, we, you and I, are in the bribery business, and we are in the paying-to-break-the-Eighth-Commandment business. As if any of the phony Bible thumpers left over from that medieval period of American history would care about that.

We Must Not Be Enemies

AUGUST 10, 2009

"The America I know and love," the quitter governor of Alaska Sarah Palin began, "is not one in which my parents or my baby with Down syndrome will have to stand in front of Obama's 'death panel' so his bureaucrats can decide, based on a subjective judgment of their 'level of productivity in society,' whether they are worthy of health care. Such a system is downright evil."

Of course it is, Ms. Palin, and that is why it does not exist, has not existed, and would never, under this president, nor any other president, ever exist, in this country.

There is no "death panel." There is no judgment based on societal productivity. There is no worthiness test.

But there is downright evil, and Ms. Palin, you just served its cause. You shouted "Fire!" in a crowded theater—a hot one—and then today tried to roll it back with "No, no, sorry, not fire, I meant flashlights."

Too little, too late, too obvious. Madam, you are a clear and present danger to the safety and security of this nation. Whether the "death panel" is something you dreamed or something you dreamed up, whether it is the product of a low intellect and a fevered imagination or the product of a high intelligence and a sober ability to exploit people, you should be ashamed of yourself for having introduced it into the public discourse, and it should debar you, for all time, from any position of responsibility or trust in the governance of this nation or any of its states or municipalities.

But it will not. Because a percentage of America does not want explanations nor serious conversation. It wants panic and the guilty thrill of chaos and an excuse to bash skulls and hang people in effigy, as Maryland Democratic Rep. Frank Kratovil was last year at a rally in Salisbury, Maryland. Or not in effigy, as more than 4,700 people were by lynch mobs between 1882 and 1968?

Ms. Palin, what, in spirit, is the difference between the two: the indefensible smile of pride on the face of the idiot who held the effigy of Rep. Kratovil for a *Salisbury News* photographer and the expressions of the murderers in the mobs who, as in the famous *Life* photo of a 1930 lynching in Marion, Indiana, didn't even feel the need to hide their faces from the camera for fear of justice that would never come?

They are both, to use your phrase, "death panels." Ms. Palin, you might as well have declared that the government is being run by a coven of witches with fake Kenyan birth certificates.

And you might as well have told the vast unthinking throng that mistakes your ability to wink for leadership that they should start shooting at Democrats. There would be no need to tell them to bring guns. Others have done that. Somebody left his at an Arizona Town Hall.

And incidentally, madam, you have forfeited your right to be taken seriously the next time you claim offense at somebody mentioning your children. You have just exploited your youngest child, dangled him in front of a mindless mob, as surely as if you were Michael Jackson. You have used this innocent infant as an excuse to pander to the worst and least of us in this nation. You have used him to create the false image of "death panels."

The only "death panels," Ms. Palin, are the figurative ones you have inspired with such irresponsible, dangerous, facile, vile, hate speech. The death of common sense. The death of logic. The death, perhaps, of democracy, at the hands of mob rule.

If someone is hurt at one of these town halls, pro-reform, anti-reform, or, most likely, as these things tend to play out in the real life you know so little about, Ms. Palin—if the hurt befalls an innocent bystander, you will have contributed to that harm.

You might very well become, Ms. Palin, the very thing you have sought to create in the lurid imaginations of those spoiling for a fight, waiting for an excuse, looking for a rationalization of their own hatred, their own racism, their own unwillingness to accept democracy. You, Ms. Palin, may yet become the de facto chairman of a death panel. Your higher calling, Ms. Palin. God forgive you, Ms. Palin.

It is hardly all Sarah Palin. She is, in fact, a relative newcomer to the orgy of fantasized violence and imagined revolution, whose fires have been stoked, for weeks, for months, for years, by conservatives—but more often by mere mercenaries, men and women who believe nothing, who are in it for the game, or the profit, or the sheer kick of bending masses to their will.

Glenn Beck, who recoils when somebody actually readies for an attack on one of the "FEMA internment camps" he so cavalierly invented, who so cowers at the thought that he might get blamed, or might lose his precious and well-earned gold, that he actually has to plead with his viewers not to become new Timothy McVeighs.

Glenn Beck says that and then comes back three days later and jokes about poisoning the Speaker of the House.

It is irresistible to you, isn't it? It's the same thrill of irresponsibility, of caveman thought, of the drug addict who suddenly and joyously cares nothing about self-restraint. Sobered momentarily into realizing the prospective outline of the horrible shape on the horizon—soldiers wounded, shooter says she was liberating FEMA camp, says she saw Glenn Beck tell her to rise up and fight back—awakened to the idea that words you say on television have consequences which you cannot control, you plead, almost cry, for nonviolence.

And yet within 72 hours the thrill again rises up in your blood and you cannot resist it; you must fantasize about murder. And by the very action of speaking it aloud, you enable others to join you in this Neanderthalian ritual of violence to overcome the enemy— whether the enemy is real or imagined, or whether the enemy really isn't an enemy at all, just your neighbor with a different point of view who wants to talk about it, who wants to involve you in the decision even though it is his turn to steer and not yours, and even though you both know that someday our system will give you another turn to steer.

But ranting and crying and playing with toys on television does not work, if you are advocating compromise and dialogue and thought. It works only for a mountebank, making the promise of magic and power with the underlying inherent threat of carnage and chaos.

And now you add that you believe "death panels" are real. An idea so insane, which mainlines so directly back to the mercenary fantasies of the pathetic Betsy McCaughey, that even Sarah Palin backed quickly away from it.

But what a scare tactic! The big lie in the flesh. Your dream come true, which is probably why, Mr. Beck, we have not lately heard much of your 9/12 groups. Because there you had the germ of an idea, exploitative perhaps, but at its core beneficial, calming, unifying, thoughtful: restore the sense of September 12, 2001—not of dread or threat, but of collaboration, of meeting in the middle, of standing together under one flag and trying to improve the conditions of all Americans.

And then somebody from your 9/12 group told its members they should all go to the health care reform town hall in Tampa, and break it up, and shout down anybody who disagreed with them, and scuffle with the police, and demand not discourse but disaster. Your work, Mr. Beck. Your contribution to this. God forgive you.

There are other instigators free in the land, nearly all of them, in effect, un-true believers. Men intelligent enough to work their way up the political ladder in this country into the Senate of this nation, and yet suddenly foolish enough, or suddenly opportunistic enough, like Mr. John Cornyn of Texas, to float conspiracy theories about the White House using health care reform to try to compile an enemies list, one e-mail address at a time; when four years ago this same senator was saying that the previous White House's pernicious, warrantless, illegal consumption of everybody's e-mail address, and everybody's e-mail, and everybody's Web sites was defensible and justifiable because "none of your civil liberties matter much after you're dead."

And now pushing, is Mr. Cornyn, the supposedly independent analysis of the proposed health care reform by the Lewin Group that 119 million people would have to change their insurance. Mr. Cornyn not knowing, or being paid not to know, that the Lewin Group is wholly owned by an insurance company, the way the Lewin Group gave Mr. Boehner and Mr. Cantor $60,000 apiece. Wholly owned!

Then there are the birthers, laughable from the moment they opened their mouths, proffering a conspiracy that somehow began with the placement of birth notices in two Hawaiian newspapers 48 years ago this month.

But people who do not want this president to be president will believe anything. And that is meat for fading commentators like Lou Dobbs, whatever he actually believes.

Because the birther movement touches another essential part of the defective soul: the need for an excuse. For they need to convince themselves of an immense conspiracy and place that conviction as a barrier between their actions and the sad reality that they are not the victims of intricate machinations against freedom but are just garden-variety, ordinary, racists, that they can handle the most limited of integration only in theory.

They will take anything that will let them pretend that. When they burst into tears and cry that they want their America back, they are not asking for white power, not asking that somebody make the black man in the White House go away.

There are other instigators, of course, so obvious, so careless, knowing so well that anybody who desperately wants to believe lies will not even notice the truth standing next to them wearing a big red neon sign.

Like the "just a Mom from a few blocks away" at the Wisconsin town hall, who didn't think anybody might Google her name and find out she was really the ex-vice-chairman of the county GOP, and part of the campaign of the Republican who lost to the Democrat whose town hall she was at that moment helping to disrupt.

Or like the smooth-talking hospital corporate titan, spreading millions around to enable the hate, knowing that none of the haters will ever realize, nor care, that they have become prostitutes for the health care industries.

Like the people who propagated the widely cut-and-pasted "line by line analysis" of the Health Care Reform Act, one that saves right-wingers the trouble of actually reading the bill or thinking about it.

This is where the fictions come from: that it's funding ACORN, that it guarantees free health care for illegal immigrants, that it mandates abortions, demands euthanasia. If you read it without knowing the truth, you might shove the right-wingers out of the way at the town halls and start screaming yourself!

It seems to have been created by the Liberty Counsel, an offshoot of Jerry Falwell's Liberty University, an organization whose other big policy concern has been the attack on Christmas.

Maybe there is the most brazen of them all, that man at the town hall meeting in Connecticut, carrying the "We don't want government-run health care" sign, while still wearing his Anthem Blue Cross and Blue Shield shirt.

You might think it was because he was too stupid to wear something a little less corporate-slavish. But given what those around him have read, they not only wouldn't care, they might even take comfort from that logo; that he could boast, and that they could hate under the auspices of an actual caring, friendly, ruthless insurance company.

My words, of course, are nothing to Mr. Anthem or Mr. Cornyn or Mr. Dobbs or Ms. Blish or Mr. Scott or the others. This is a job to them. And since we have placed a price tag on everything in this country, there is no soul-searching involved.

You have a job. If it involves stirring up frightened people to defend the corporation against the citizen, well, you have a salary to earn and a family to feed. The same rationalization that enables Mob hit men to sleep at night.

But somewhere in those crowds of genuinely angry and scared people, people who listen to Cornyn or Dobbs, or fantasize with Beck about poisoning their way to a Democrat-free world, or salivate like Pavlovian dogs at the sound of the shrill whistle from Sarah "Death Panel" Palin—somewhere in those crowds are some actual people with some actual brains still working and thinking and evaluating.

For God's sake, trust your instinct to think.

There are no death panels. There could never be. Were there any steps taken toward them, I and 99.9 percent of the people in this country, from the fiercest liberal to the most apolitical blob, would be standing next to you preventing their creation.

There are no plans to take your insurance away from you. There will be no rationing of care. There will be no health choices commissioner, and he will not be able to transfer money electronically out of your bank account.

There will be nobody coming into your house and telling you what to eat.

There will be no euthanasia.

And the people to whom you are listening with half an ear are telling you half the truth, on a good day!

The euthanasia scare comes from something as benign as a proposal to let you put in for insurance if you have to consult a doctor about what to do if you or a loved one is fatally ill. If you are where I was last March—when I sat down with the doctors to talk about my mother: fatally ill, not awake, not aware—the health care reform will now reimburse you for the doctor's fee for that consultation. And it will pay, whether you decide to let your loved one go or you insist to the doctors that they keep that dear one alive at all costs, to treat her for months or years or decades more.

And this part of this bill actually was originally co-sponsored by a Republican congressman. And from that caring bipartisan starting point, through her own paranoia or for her own political gain, Sarah Palin has invented the bogeyman of "death panels."

Think, please. Think before something horrible happens. As you move to bellow that which you know not to be true, as you try to shout down a congressman who is there to answer your concerns, as, God forbid, you think there has been enough talking and not enough of something else; think of how Lincoln closed his first inaugural address, and remember that wise words stand the test of time.

> If it were admitted that you who are dissatisfied hold the right side in the dispute, there is still no single good reason for precipitate action. Intelligence, patriotism, Christianity, and a firm reliance on Him who has never yet forsaken this favored land are still competent to adjust, in the best way, all our present difficulty.
>
> In your hands, my dissatisfied fellow-countrymen, and not in mine, is the momentous issue. The government will not assail you. You can have no conflict without being you yourselves the aggressors. We are not enemies, but friends. We must not be enemies. Though passion may have strained, it must not break our bonds of affection. The mystic chords of memory, stretching from every battlefield and patriot grave to every living heart and hearthstone, all over this broad land, will yet swell the chorus of the union, when again touched, as surely they will be, by the better angels of our nature.

It's Not a Lie If You Believe It's True

AUGUST 20, 2009

Brought to you by Glenn Beck. His radio people deny he was suspended for calling the president a racist, or more likely for angering enough sponsors that 20 of them canceled their commercials. But sources tell the industry Web site TVNewser that "it was Beck himself who was telling Fox staffers last week that he was 'forced to take the week off.'"

Our bronze to Karl Rove, newly inducted into the Scandinavian American hall of fame, and described by that group as one of the most prominent Norwegian American statesmen in the United States. He has been emboldened enough to demand apologies from two newspapers, because he has yet to be indicted in the political prosecution of former Alabama governor Don Siegelman. "Perhaps then Judiciary Democrats will focus on more important issues and the *Times* and *Post* will admit their mistakes. It would be the responsible thing to do."

I'll apologize for them. I'm sorry you haven't been indicted yet, Karl. There's plenty of time remaining.

Our runner-up: Senator John Cornyn of Texas, still pumping the paranoia that the White House offer to correct any spurious e-mails about health care reform was a "fishy way to collect e-mail addresses of its opponents." The same collection of addresses, by the way, is done at the Web site of Senator John Cornyn of Texas. You want to write a letter of complaint to the senator, you oppose him, you're his enemy? You have to leave your e-mail address and your real-life address too, street address and everything, where you live. One thing left out of this equation: people, some of them people who work for insurance companies, are sending out these mass spam e-mails and urging recipients to send them on to everybody they know. You got your wish, shut up.

But our winner . . .

Congressman Roy Blunt of Missouri. The minority whip has told this one to the editorial boards of newspapers in Springfield, Missouri, and St. Louis. "I'm 59," he says. "In either Canada or Great Britain, if I broke my hip, I couldn't get it replaced."

Two-thirds of the hip replacements done by the National Health Service in Great Britain last year were done on people 65 or older; 63 percent of those done in the Canadian system were done on people 65 or older; 1,200 of them in Canada were done on people older than 85.

Confronted with the astonishing inaccuracy of his bullcrap, Congressman Blunt did not live up to his name. "I didn't just pull that number out of thin air. It came from some people who were supposed to be experts on Canadian health care."

You didn't just pull that number out of thin air? You pulled it out of your backside. This illustrates how much those public servants owned by the insurance and health care industry are expected to try to kill reform. They have not merely suspended the supposed minimum standard, don't lie, they've now suspended even the pretense of getting away with the lie. Like Senator Blunt, who just lied to his constituents, lied to the entire nation, lied to the media, and lied stupidly, and in such a way that his lying would be caught within minutes.

It's too bad we're more worried about lies like those of Senators John Ensign or David Vitter. Their lies might eventually cost them their office. Senator Blunt's lie is egregious enough, insulting enough, that in a perfect world, it would force him to resign.

Congressman Roy Blunt, liar, today's worst person in the world!

Not a Great American

AUGUST 24, 2009

The bronze to Bill-O the Clown. It's not the sophistry of this simpleton's worldview that infuriates people. It's the refusal to use any intellectual energy in arriving at it. We do a brief translation:

"President Obama's health care vision is confusing. It may also bankrupt the nation. That does not sound smart to me. The American people do not want to invest trillions of dollars in a big government program that's confusing. That would be insane."

In other words, Bill-O doesn't like reading anything longer than five paragraphs unless there are pictures in it of puppies or girls. And who said it may also bankrupt the nation? What authority are you quoting? Did you pose that possibility about, say, the pointless war in Iraq?

"The Far Left doesn't want to hear it because those loons want income redistribution and see government run health care as a way to do that." What Bill-O here is saying—if you take taxpayer money and give it by the billions to Blackwater and Halliburton and KBR and Lockheed, through the advent of convenience—that's patriotism. If you take the same amount of money out of corporate profits and give it back to the people, that's income redistribution.

"But clear-thinking Americans understand this whole deal is screwed up. The country needs a fresh start on health care." Billy goes insane any time anybody accuses him of reading or simply regurgitating Republican talking points, yet there it is. "The country needs a fresh start on health care." A virtual word-for-word repeat of the talking points from last week, as presented by Republican senator Jon Kyl.

Our runner-up: Glenn Beck. The Lonesome Rhodes of 2009 now with 33 sponsor cancellations, including a Fox News–wide one from UPS. Back from suspension today with his tin foil hat all polished and freshly recrinkled. "You can be rich. You can be poor. But these czars are pushing people around, this system of government that is going on right now. We are building, at best, a thug-ocracy. We are dealing with massive unions. We are dealing with radicals, revolutionaries. They don't care. They've gone into this cloak of credibility. If you're afraid now, you will cower in fear for the rest of your life. Your children will also cower in fear. And they will serve masters.

"Do not cower in fear. The worst thing you can do is die without honor. And we are truly responsible for the freedom in this country. We are truly responsible. We will be held responsible, not only by God, but also the founders, when we cross the other side. And they will say, what was more important than your children's freedom? The answer is nothing."

There he is, fomenting more violence against the government. Glenn, you do realize when you go off on those paranoid, comical rants, you begin to sound like one of the mullahs, right? Mullah Glenn Beck. Is that better than Lonesome Rhodes, or is it too offensive to mullahs?

But our winner . . .
Republican congressman Wally Herger of California. In front of 2,000 people in Redding, scared into believing that their own crap insurance and health care are better than having a choice between those and plans that are cheaper and better, Herger not only said, "Our democracy has never been threatened as much as it is today." But then some idiot in the crowd stood up and said, "I am a proud right-wing terrorist."

Congressman Herger replied, "Amen. God bless you. There is a great American."

No, sir. That is not a great American. That is a man calling himself a right-wing terrorist. Even if he was being allegorical or hyperbolic, you're a U.S. congressman, damn it. You're bound by oath to uphold the Constitution. And if some buffoon in your audience describes himself with the word "terrorist," you are, at minimum, required to remind him what that means and how many Americans have died at the hands of terrorists. And you have to tell him to shut the hell up until he can come close to living up to what you told everybody in that crowd when your little fascist rally started— that they have to respect each other's opinions.

If you can't, Congressman Herger, you're not entitled to serve as Redding's dogcatcher, let alone be in the House of Representatives.

Congressman Wally "A Right Wing Terrorist Is a Great American" Herger, of the California Second District, today's worst person in the world!

Not a Great Spokesman

AUGUST 25, 2009

The bronze to Lonesome Rhodes Beck of Fox Noise. He used his program yesterday to attack Van Jones, White House environmental adviser on green issues, co-founder of a group called Color of Change. Beck asked, "Why is it that such a committed revolutionary has made it so high in the Obama administration, is one of his chief advisers?"

Beck pretended he was just criticizing an Obama appointee, never mentioning he has a personal vendetta against Jones, because it is the group Jones co-founded but has not been affiliated with for two years which has led the protest against Beck for calling the president a racist, a boycott that has now cost Beck 36 advertisers.

Beck didn't mention that. Beck is crack.

Our runner-up: The ever-hilarious beauty pageant contestant from Fixed News, Gretchen Carlson. Talking about the Obama White House, "There still are a lot of positions available there. A lot of the top players are still anonymous because they haven't been named yet to certain posts. Now, we're talking about the assistant treasury secretary for financial markets, the inspector general, the army secretary."

Obama named his army secretary on June 2, Congressman John McHugh, Republican congressman John McHugh. Even Fox covered it. Gretchen missed it. And she missed that the confirmation of Army Secretary John McHugh has been held up by Republicans. Gretch isn't good with the, you know, facts.

But our winner . . .
Matt Lavoie, the spokesman for yesterday's worst, Congressman Wally Herger of Chico, California. After a constituent now identified as Burt Stead of Redding, California, stood up at a Herger town hall meeting and identified himself as a "proud right-wing terrorist," Congressman Herger responded not with any rebuke but by saying, "Amen. God bless you. There is a great American."

His spokesman, Mr. Lavoie, now says the congressman has no intention of apologizing for praising a self-described terrorist. He says, "The comment was in jest. The man was using satire to make his point," which does not have a damn thing to do with it. As I said last night, even if he was being allegorical or hyperbolic, this is not language to bandy about, not when people on both sides are showing up with submachine guns or guns at town halls. Not when members of right-wing militias are showing up at town halls.

When faced with this crap on the eve of last year's election, even Senator McCain's conscience got the better of him and he reprimanded a woman spouting hate speech against McCain's rival. Congressman Herger and his spokesman need to do the same. Until they do, they're contributing to this climate of paranoia and violence enveloping our political system.

Until they say something, Congressman Herger and this spokesman are not defending the Constitution, they are threatening it.

Matt Lavoie, the spokesman for Congressman Wally Herger, Second District of California, today's worst person in the world!

Not a Great Congressman

AUGUST 27, 2009

The bronze goes to Bill-O the Clown: "Tuesday night on MSNBC, someone said that people who watch Fox News are paranoid and racists. That should tell you everything you need to know about the entire NBC situation. Pinhead does not even begin to cover it."

That would have been me. I said that. That quoted exactly, "Since Fixed News has now migrated completely over to serving propaganda to tin foil hatters, conspiracy theorists, paranoids and racists, it is not a news organization."

Mr. O'Reilly is upset, and he has a right to be upset. Tin foil hatters, conspiracy theorists, paranoids and racists, I'd like to apologize. I left out loons. Fox Noise is only in the business now of serving propaganda to tin foil hatters, conspiracy theorists, paranoids, racists, and loons. Oh, and pinheads. People who watch Fox News thinking there is news in it are tin foil hatters, conspiracy theorists, paranoids, racists, loons, and pinheads.

Our runner-up: So are many of the hosts, like Lonesome Rhodes Beck here, with a twofer. About the advertiser protest after he called the president a racist with a deep-seated hatred of white people: they are now up to 46 advertisers who bailed out. In his words: "They can take my job and they can take my wealth. But that's okay. Even if the powers that be right now succeed in making me poor, drum me out and I'm just a worthless loser, which I'm just about that much above right now—I will only be stronger for it."

Hey, Glenn, you know there's great wisdom in that old tasteless joke. Just remember, when you put yourself up there, you can never drive in the last nail yourself.

Part two: "If you watch MSNBC, I contend that you will see the future, because they are laying the groundwork for a horrible event that will—what they're laying the ground for—anything from the Right there—some awful event. And I fear this government. This administration has so much framework already prepared that they will seize power overnight before anybody even gives it a second thought."

Look, this administration has a comfortable majority in both houses and it still hasn't even been able to show the ability to seize health care. So when you say stuff like that, you don't just sound crazy, you sound really poorly informed and crazy. By the way, that horrible, awful event from the Right, by the way, that has already happened. It's called *The Glenn Beck Show*.

But our winner, once again . . .
Congressman Wally Herger of the Second District of California, still defending his actions and those of that guy at his town hall, Burt Stead. Conveniently, videotape has finally surfaced showing their exchange:

Stead said: "I have been known to say things fishy. I have been known to even attend ReddingTeaParty.com protests. And I want to say that I'm a proud right-wing terrorist.

"I didn't come prepared with a lot of notes tonight. I left them actually at home when I was looking for—while I was looking for my birth certificate."

And Representative Herger responded: "Amen, God bless you. There's a great American."

Well, now we know Mr. Stead is a birther, too, and a Tea Partyer. Congressman Herger not only still thinks he should not have been gently asked not to throw the term "right-wing terrorist" around, he's blaming, who else, the Obama administration. Herger's office has issued yet another statement, nobody's name attached to it this time. "Mr. Burt Stead," it says, "is a taxpayer and veteran, who, like so many others, is rightfully fed up with being called un-American, or extremist, or a political terrorist by liberals in Washington for simply exercising his First Amendment rights. Mr. Stead served his country and therefore, he is a great American. The congressman doesn't at all regret commending him for standing up, exercising his free speech rights, and expressing his strong concerns with the direction liberals in Washington are taking our country."

Except, no liberal called him un-American. That was a lie. It was a misquoting of the Speaker of the House. It was designed to give people like Stead an excuse to get out his "Don't tread on me" paranoia. And no liberal called him an extremist or a political terrorist. That was a report from the Department of Homeland Security, a report that was commissioned while George Bush was still president, noting evidence that the right-wing militias might attempt to indoctrinate veterans just back from Afghanistan or Iraq.

Mr. Stead clearly is not just back from Afghanistan or Iraq. Mr. Stead can be excused for not knowing any of this or choosing not to know any of it. He's been spoon-fed this crap from the Right for seven months, at least. But if Congressman Herger doesn't know this or is choosing not to know it, he is violating his Constitutional responsibilities. He is fomenting violence. If he will not speak out in favor of law and order in this country, he should resign his seat.

Wally Herger, Congressman, California Second, today's worst person in the world!

The Force Is Not Strong with This One
AUGUST 31, 2009

The bronze to Betsy McCaughey, the shameless, factless health industry shill, back on CNBC, allowed to again spew the stuff she made up, or more likely that was handed to her by her pharma overlords, claiming pages 16 and 17 of the reform bill will "force everyone under the age of 65 to buy the same, one size fits all, government plan." Except it doesn't say that. It describes how you can keep your current insurance if you like it for some reason.

When a pro-reform advocate repudiated McCaughey's lie, the interview was suddenly capped by the host. But the real question is why is she still allowed on TV when her shill-dom is so well known that even one of her own health care employers fired her from its board in embarrassment? She is a paid employee?

The runner-up: Columnist and singer Pat Boone, describes cancer cells he saw under a microscope once as "a bunch of little orphan Annie eyes, perfectly round, clear circles." Described the cancer cells he saw as "little black iridescent globs, almost radiant from within, pulsing with menace, looking like miniature Darth Vaders from *Star Wars*."

Then he concluded, "I have to ask the obvious question. Do we know how cancer starts, where the black, filthy cells come from?"

He then compares the miniaturized Darth Vaders, the black iridescent globs, the black filthy cells, to a political virus. And concluded, "I call it liberalism." And when there is an African American president, Pat, the rest of us call those filthy black references racism.

But our winner . . .
Michael Scheuer, ex-CIA staffer, back with another remark about a terrorist attack here, which if uttered by a liberal would be the subject of diatribes on every Fixed News show and every right-wing radio hate-cast all day long. "Oh, sure we're going to be attacked. Rahm Emanuel wants an attack. He loves crisis and in a crisis, the Democrats, he says, can get all their programs through. These people simply do not care. For the first time, I think a sitting president is giving aid and comfort to the enemy, both psychologically and materially. The president obviously does not care."

This is the same lunatic who last month said, without anybody as much as reproaching him, "The only chance we have as a country right now is for Osama bin Laden to deploy and detonate a major weapon in the United States." Mr. Scheuer, you do realize that it is now self-evident you are rooting for terrorism to take place in this country and thus rooting for the terrorists?

Former CIA bin Laden station chief and evidently former American, Michael Scheuer, today's worst person in the world!

The *H* Is for Hypocrisy

SEPTEMBER 8, 2009

The bronze to Orly Taitz. The first actual Obama Kenyan birth certificate she produced was apparently a forgery. We say this because she has now produced another actual Obama Kenyan birth certificate. Somebody stepped on it. See, you can tell it's really Obama's birth certificate because the baby's footprint is black.

This one is so much worse that even the serial birther Jerome Corsi has pronounced it a fake and said that the guy Taitz got it from also once tried to sell one of his own kidneys.

The two biggest mistakes on this one—it says Mombasa British protectorate of Kenya, and yet the dates are offered in American style, with month, then day number, rather than the British style, which is day number and then month. And also Mombasa was not in Kenya in 1961 when Obama was born. Mombasa was in Zanzibar.

I would give Ms. Taitz the benefit of the doubt here if she would just come back and echo that old Doritos ad: "Eat all you want. We'll make more."

Our runner-up: Michele Bachmann. Another great wild guess from the Minnesota congresswoman. She has announced that while the ratio of tax payments to earned income can now hit 50 percent, it was only 5 percent in 1950. "This is slavery, nothing more than slavery, the Constitution provides freedom."

The top tax rate in 1950 was 84 percent. You're off by 79. The current rate is 35 percent. It is lower than it has been for all but 5 of the last 77 years. She just made the numbers up. Which is it, is she crazy, is she stupid, or is she on something?

But our winner . . .
Sean Hannity. Listen to this self-righteous humbuggery about the governor's race in Virginia. "There's been an all-out war

declared by the *Washington Post* against Bob McDonnell, a solid conservative, and the effort to smear, besmirch, demonize and impact that election is under full sway here, and a lot of this has to do—well, they went through this great effort to dig up a graduate school thesis he wrote, and they're claiming that, well, he's saying that homosexuality, working women, and abortion are detrimental to traditional American families.

"That was—let's see, 20 years ago. We'll go back to opinions that he might have held at a time when he's writing the thesis. You see how abusively biased the media can be? It's unbelievable."

Sure is, Sean. Here's Sean Hannity—July 1, 2007: "Chapter six, the thesis," he said as he read from Hillary Rodham's grad school thesis. "It's a 38-year-old document that's been rumored about. 90 pages, steeped in intrigue and mystery. Hillary's thesis, elevated to mystical status from years of secrecy. It allows readers to decipher the true thinking of the former First Lady and now 2008 presidential hopeful."

You see how abusively biased the media can be? It's unbelievable. It's unbelievable. Wait a minute, I can't say that now. I contradicted myself. I just pooped my pants.

Sean "The *H* Is for Hypocrisy" Hannity, today's worst person in the world!

Special Comment

The Line Joe Wilson Crossed

SEPTEMBER 10, 2009

The 43rd president of the United States lied the nation into the war, lied 4,343 of his fellow citizens to death in that war, lied about upholding the Constitution, and lied about weapons of mass destruction.

He lied about how he reacted to Al Qaeda before 9/11, and he lied about how he reacted to Al Qaeda after 9/11. He lied about getting bin Laden, and he lied about not getting bin Laden.

He lied about nation-building in Iraq, lied about the appearance of new buildings in the nation of Iraq, and lied about embassy buildings in nations like Iraq. He lied about trailers with mobile weapons labs in them, and he lied about trailers with Cuban prostitutes in them.

He and his administration lied—by the counting of one nonprofit group—532 times about links between Al Qaeda and Iraq. Only 28 of those were by that president, but he made up for that by lying 231 times about WMD.

And yet not once did an elected Democratic official shout out during one of George W. Bush's speeches and call him a liar. Even when the president was George W. Bush, even when he was assailed from sidelines like mine, even when the lies came down so thick the nation needed a hat, he was still the president, and if he didn't earn any respect, the office he held demanded respect.

Moreover, that president and his congressional tools, like Congressman Addison Graves "Joe" Wilson of South Carolina, insisted on not just unquestioned respect for the office; they wanted unanimous lockstep compliance with the man.

And when the blasphemy of mere respectful criticism somehow came anyway—say, by, or built on that by, the real Joe Wilson—Lord help he who might have made the slightest factual error in that criticism.

Congressman Wilson and his masters and the flying monkeys of right-wing media would pursue the erroneous critic to the ends of their careers, firing hot accusations of moral or intellectual confusion and incompetence at the unbelievers.

And that is the line Congressman Wilson crossed last night when he shouted "You lie" at this president of the United States. Not the respect line. The stupid line. Hey, Mr. Wilson!

"This evening I let my emotions get the best of me when listening to the president's remarks regarding the coverage of illegal immigrants in the health care bill," you hurriedly said last night as a nation caved in on you and your own party's leadership coerced you into saying something.

"While I disagree with the president's statements, my comments were inappropriate and regrettable. I extend sincere apologies to the president for this lack of civility." For the lack of civility, Congressman? Is that what you think this is about?

Of course your comments were inappropriate and regrettable. You are a Republican trying to delegitimize the elected president of the United States—that's all you do, and that's all you've got.

Of course you let your emotions get the best of you. At a figure of $435,296 in campaign donations from the health sector, of course your emotions would take over when your gravy train was threatened. It isn't about "inappropriate and regrettable," sir!

Your comments were inappropriate and regrettable and wrong! You got up in front of the world, embarrassed your district, embarrassed your state, embarrassed your party, embarrassed your nation, shouted at the president like he was a referee at a ballgame and you were a drunk in the stands, and you were wrong.

House Bill 3200 specifically says, sir, in language made precise and binding—in section 246—under the heading "No federal payment for undocumented aliens."

Look, Congressman! All capital letters! For the benefit of the factually challenged! "Nothing in this subtitle shall allow Federal payments for affordability credits on behalf of individuals who are not lawfully present in the United States."

You got it wrong! There is no ambiguity, sir. There is no disagreement! The bill says those here illegally will not be covered; yet whether through stupidity or a willful attempt to mislead the gullible, you decided to spend whatever credibility remained to you on a position in which you are utterly, inarguably, and—in a manner obvious to newborns and the more sophisticated of farm animals—wrong!

You apologize for your lack of civility? When are you going to apologize for your lack of being right? Wrong-Way Wilson. Whatever it is, it's congenital. Wrong-Way Wilson just wrote an op-ed, on August 27 for the Columbia, South Carolina, newspaper the *State*, about the nonexistent death panels that he and Mrs. Palin saw in their dreams—or something:

"Those who have stood up and shown up to have their voices heard have already made a difference in this debate." Perhaps henceforth Mr. Wilson should soft-pedal the "have their voices heard" part.

"Citizens have discovered and brought to light numerous aspects of the health care overhaul (H.R. 3200) that are deeply troubling. These include the end of life counseling program, which has been correctly highlighted by former Alaska Governor Sarah Palin as a program which could lead to seniors being encouraged to seek less care in order to protect the government's bottom line."

Perhaps henceforth Mr. Wilson should soft-pedal the Palin Paranoia, since he caught enough of it last night when he made himself look like an uninformed eight-year-old screaming at an adult.

"Americans . . . want and deserve this honest debate." Perhaps henceforth Mr. Wilson should remember that the word "honest" is as important as the word "debate." The latter without the former is better known as Political Tourette's Syndrome.

The evidence that Wrong-Way Wilson and reality are strangers goes back much further than last night. When Congressman Rob Filner said the U.S. had helped supply Saddam Hussein's chemical and biological weapons, Wilson went nuts. Worse, he accused Filner of a "hatred of America," and insisted, "You shouldn't say that" and "You should retract it" and "You know it is not true."

It was true. It had been confirmed by the Commerce Department in 1994. Wrong-Way Wilson was wrong. A year later, when it was asserted that Senator Strom Thurmond from Wrong-Way's home state had fathered a daughter with a black woman, Mr. Wilson called the assertion a "smear on the image" of Senator Thurmond.

This was after Senator Thurmond's family had acknowledged not just paternity, but the fact that the senator had maintained a secret relationship with his daughter, and provided her money, for decades. After this was admitted, Congressman Wilson considered references to it a "smear" and said Thurmond's daughter should have kept it to herself.

Coincidence, of course, Wrong-Way, that it would be you who would consider the confirmed, acknowledged biracial child of Strom Thurmond as a "smear." And then it would again be you who—in the middle of a festival of blind racial rage dressed up as a health care debate—would shout out "You lie" at a biracial president of the United States as he addressed Congress.

And just a coincidence that you're a member of a radicalized, insurrection-glorifying group, accused of harboring white supremacists, called Sons of Confederate Veterans.

Back to this incident. You have swallowed some of the Kool-Aid you mix up for those damn fools who believe you, Congressman. You sounded as pathetic as one of those poor souls, stampeded by corporate funding from the insurance and health care industries, who shout out nonsense at those demonstrations of willful stupidity that have been mislabeled "town halls," these places where a citizen's life is reduced to acting out that ridiculous maxim "If you're going to be wrong, be wrong at the top of your voice."

But Congressman—you're not supposed to be a town hall panicker, you're not supposed to be a rube defending the efficacy of the snake oil, you are a congressman—and still you were wrong at the top of your voice! Town halls, death panels, oligarhys [sic], a multiracial president who is accused of hating half his own ancestry, neuroses about communist artwork, the idea that fascism and socialism aren't mutually exclusive, grassroots protests bought and paid for by lobbyists and corporations, scared seniors terrified enough to turn to insurance companies for protection against reformers who want to increase their coverage and cut their rates, Birchers, birthers, deathers, the voices in Michele Bachmann's head, the Republican rebuttal to the president of the United States given by a guy who thought he could become "Lord Boustany" by paying a couple of English con men.

And now to top off this pile of stupidity: Congressman Wrong-Way Wilson, who—when a president publicly, and ostentatiously, gave credit for part of his health care reform proposal to the very Republican he swamped in the election last year—followed that bipartisan gesture by shouting "You lie!" as soon as he heard the truth.

It is this week evident that the greatest threat to the nation is not terrorism nor the economy nor H1N1 nor even bad health care. It is rank, willful stupidity. When did we come to extol stupidity ahead of information and rely on voodoo, superstition, and prejudice ahead of education?

How many Republicans believe in death panels and brownies and elves? When did we start to elect the impregnably dense?

I was almost too fearful of using the word "impregnably" because of the prospect that Governor Palin would go after me the way she went after Letterman.

The time has come to rise up and take this country back, to again make it safe for people who actually completed the seventh grade. The crime of Wrong-Way Wilson was not reflected in his emotions, nor his disagreement, nor his inappropriate conduct, nor in his incivility. It was in his prideful wrongness.

There are many vague portions of this bill, but Section 246 says it plain: "No federal payment for undocumented aliens." I defend Congressman Wilson's right to incivility. A little incivility six years ago might have stopped the Iraq War. He can shout anything he wants, at anybody he wants, in any circumstances he wants.

Providing that he is willing to suffer the consequences of his actions, I am willing to suffer him.

This nation can survive a president being disrespected by some nickel-and-dime congressman from Beaufort; the shame falls onto the shouter and not the one shouted at. But this nation cannot survive the continued acceptance, the continued endorsement, the continued encouragement, the continued institutionalization, of stupidity

I think if Mr. Lincoln were alive, he might recast his most famous imagery in the light of the truest of our present crises: A house divided against itself cannot stand. I believe this government cannot endure, permanently half-smart, and half-stupid.

Section 246 is written expressly that there will be no health care funding for those who are here illegally; that there will be no mechanism created to establish such funding. I fear Section 247 will have to be written expressly that there will be a mechanism created to establish stupid panels.

Maybe Beck Knows Section 8

SEPTEMBER 24, 2009

The bronze to Sean Hannity, demagoguing live from California's Central Valley. He accused the administration and radical environmentalists of causing a drought there in order to protect a fish called the delta smelt:

"Today, their water is gone. Shut off by the government. With all the money being spent on a failed stimulus, health care reform and bailing out Wall Street banks, the solution here is relatively simple. Turn the water back on."

The Department of the Interior turned the water back on on the 30th of June. The pumping restrictions ended nearly three months ago. You missed it, Sean. So too did the *Washington Times*, Michelle Malkin, the *Wall Street Journal* editorial page, and the rest of the moron's echo chamber. Check the water you're standing in, Sean. There is a shark in there that you just jumped.

Our runner-up: Chuck Norris, who describes the 9/12 washout as a "revolutionary movement" and writes that to keep it going you should take down your heathen modern American flag "over the next year, post the 13-star Betsy Ross flag, Navy Jack, or Gadsden's Flag, Don't Tread on Me, or any representation that tells the story of Old Glory, and makes a stand for our founders' vision of America. If you insist on posting a modern USA flag, too, then get one that is tea-stained to show your solidarity with our founders."

Stain the U.S. flag? Deliberately desecrate Old Glory? Why does Chuck Norris hate the American flag?

But our winner . . .

Lonesome Rhodes Beck, quoting, praising, embracing Article I, Section 9, Clause 1, of the Constitution, which reads, "The migration or importation of such persons as any of the states now existing shall think proper to admit, shall not be prohibited by the

Congress prior to the year 1808. But a tax or duty may be imposed on such importation, not exceeding 10 dollars for each person."

You know what that part of the Constitution was about? Glenn doesn't. "That's right," he writes. "The founders actually put a price tag on coming to this country, ten dollars per person. Apparently they felt like there was a value to being able to live here. Not anymore. These days, we can't ask anything of immigrants, including that they abide by our laws."

Glenn, Article I, Section 9, Clause 1 of the Constitution is a little confusing. It is, after all, 18th-century legalese. But the key word in there is at the start, "The migration or importation of such persons." Importation of persons? Buying slaves from other countries. The clause Beck thinks has something to do with a price tag on coming to this country was, in fact, a clause that made it illegal to ban the importation of slaves until at least 1808 but gave Congress the right to tax a slave owner ten bucks for each slave he brought in.

This is the fool who thinks he is Thomas Paine or Thomas Jefferson or somebody, or he thinks he and he alone is interpreting the intentions of the founders of the country. And he thinks that clause requiring the continuation of slavery and making it Constitutional for one American to own another is about immigration! This guy may well be the dumbest man on the planet.

Glenn Beck, today's worst person in the world!

Worst Person in the World

Republican Doesn't Translate Well into Spanish

OCTOBER 1, 2009

The bronze to Boss Limbaugh, whose listeners continue to have a fun-house mirror view of the world because this schmuck keeps lying to them. "Obama's safe school czar is a guy promoting homosexuality in the schools and encouraged a 15-year-old kid to have a homosexual relationship with an older man and even facilitated it."

The Obama schools adviser—the term *czar* originated with Nixon and Reagan—is named Kevin Jennings. Fifteen years ago, he wrote that while he was a high school counselor, he met a male student who had a relationship with an older man. The boy was 16, past the legal age of consent. So Jennings did not call the cops. For this, Limbaugh says he was promoting homosexuality in the schools.

As to Limbaugh's fascination with that topic, I refer you again to the Limbaugh comedy routine by the late Bill Hicks.

The runner-up: Abdul Tawala Ibn Ali Alishtari, who has pleaded guilty to charges of terrorism financing and conspiracy to commit wire fraud and now faces up to 25 years in jail. He thought he was transferring $152,000 to Pakistan and Afghanistan to buy night vision goggles and other equipment for a terrorist training camp. He was arrested by Homeland Security in February of 2007, but oddly, the Bush administration did not make a big deal about it, possibly because he also had transferred $15,000 to the National Republican Congressional Committee, and $20,000 more to the National Republican Senatorial Committee. Thus becoming one of the latter group's "inner circle members for life."

And our winner . . .
Michael Steele, chairman of the Republican National Committee, celebrating National Hispanic Heritage Month in that tone-deaf way that has made him the idol of every Democrat. The RNC has released a video titled *A Tradition of Firsts: Hispanic Accomplishments in America.*

However, they left out the nation's first Hispanic Supreme Court justice, Sonia Sotomayor, and labor leader Cesar Chavez, and former Florida Republican senator Mel Martinez, who is on the outs with the party at the moment. And instead of writing a press release in Spanish, Steele's guys simply tried to translate the English one into Spanish, resulting in roughly 25 errors in five sentences, including getting the name of this country wrong in the Spanish translation.

Michael Steele, chairman of the RNC—*esta noche*—can you tell I took seven years of French? *Esta noche el peor persona en este mundo.*

I Know What You Did Last Summer
OCTOBER 6, 2009

The bronze to the fabulous disingenuous insurance industry shill Betsy McCaughey. She's the one who fabricated the infamous death panel lie. Now she has stepped into it neck-high again, writing an op-ed in which she quotes gloom and doom from Dr. David McKalip, a Florida neurosurgeon and a board member of the Florida Medical Association.

She left something off Dr. McKalip's résumé: Dr. McKalip sent out that picture of the president dressed up as a witch doctor to other anti-reformers, and then tried to claim he had no racist intent. We should note also that Dr. McKalip has consulted with Georgia congressman Dr. Paul "Take Your Chronic Depression to the ER" Brown.

Our runner-up: Rupert Murdoch. In February, his vanity newspaper, the *New York Post*, printed a political cartoon showing two cops over the body of a dead chimpanzee they had shot, with one officer saying, "They'll have to find someone else to write the next stimulus bill."

Many *Post* staffers protested, but only Sandra Guzman, the editor of a monthly insert in the *Post* called "Tempo," did so publicly and on the record. Even Murdoch himself at the time noted that "as the chairman of the *New York Post*, I'm ultimately responsible for what is printed in the pages. The buck stops with me. Last week, we made a mistake," matey. "We ran a cartoon that offended many people. Today I want to personally apologize to any reader who felt offended," Jim, me boy, "and even insulted. We will seek to be more attuned to the sensitivities of our community."

Now, nearly eight months later, there's a new statement about this in-house protester Ms. Guzman. No spokesman is quoted, but since Mr. Murdoch says the buck stops with him, we will attribute it to him: "Sandra is no longer with the *Post* because the monthly in-paper insert, 'Tempo,' of which she was the editor, has been," shiver me timbers, "discontinued."

In other words, after it all quieted down, Murdoch eliminated Ms. Guzman's department and fired her.

But our winner . . .
Congresswoman Michele Bachmann. Speaking about how Speaker Pelosi might handle Blue Dog Democrats over health care reform, Bachmann says, "She will either beat them to death, bludgeon them to death, or she'll try to buy them off."

Yes, don't let that out-to-lunch look behind the eyes fool you. There's some sort of slasher-movie obsession going on inside that congresswoman. This is at least the second time she has applied violent imagery to the public discourse. Just last month, she had told her fellow Republicans that to stop health care reform, they needed to make "a covenant to slit their wrists."

Congresswoman Michele "I Know What You Did Last Summer" Bachmann, today's worst person in the world!

Special Comment

Why Are We Making It Harder?
OCTOBER 7, 2009

Since August 23 of this year, I have interacted daily with our American health care system and often done so to the exclusion of virtually all other business. It's not undercover reporting. It's not an expert study of the field.

But since that day when my father slid seemingly benignly out of his bed onto the floor of his home, I've experienced with growing amazement and with multiplying anger the true state of our hospitals, our doctors' offices, our insurance businesses, our pharmacies. My father's story as a patient, and mine as a secondary participant and a primary witness, has been eye-opening and jaw-dropping, and we are among the utterly lucky ones—a fact that by itself is terrifying and infuriating.

And thus, for all those we have met along the way, those with whom we have shared the last two months inside the belly of the beast, and for everyone in this country who will be here and right soon, a show-length "Special Comment" on the subject of health care reform in this country.

I do not want to yell. I feel like screaming, but everybody is screaming. Everybody is screaming that this is about rights or freedom or socialism or the president or the future or the past or political failure or political success. We have all been screaming.

I have been screaming, and we have all been screaming, because we do not want to face—we cannot face—what is at the heart of all of this, what is the unspoken essence of every moment of this debate. Why are we truly driven to such intense, ineffable, inchoate, emotions? Because ultimately, in screaming about health care reform—pro or con—we are screaming about death.

This ultimately is about death. About preventing it, about fighting it, about resisting it, about grabbing hold of everything and anything to forestall it and postpone it, even though we know that the force will overcome us all, always has, always will.

Health care is at its core about improving the odds of life in its struggle against death, of extending that game which we will all lose, each and every one of us, onto eternity, extending it another year or month or second. This is the primary directive of life, the essence of our will as human beings. Or perhaps it is a measure of our souls, the will to live.

And when we go to a doctor's office or a hospital or storefront clinic in a ghetto, we are expressing this fundamental cry of humanity: I want to live. I want my child to live. I want my wife to live. I want my father to live. I want my neighbor to live. I want that stranger I do not know and never will know to live.

This is elemental stuff, our atoms in action, our survival mode in charge. Tamper with this, and you are tampering with *us*. And so we yell and scream and try to put it all into political context or expand it to some great issue of societal freedom or dress it up in something that would be otherwise farcical, like a death panel, but this issue needs no expansion and no dressing up. The Democrats need to draw no line in the sand, the Republicans need to calculate no seats to be gained, and the Blue Dogs need to anticipate no campaign contributions lost.

This issue is big enough as it is. This is already life and death.

Of all the politicians of the previous century, none fought harder to prevent an administration that had promised to involve itself in health care from ever gaining power than England's Winston Churchill. He equated his opponents in the party that sought to introduce national health to the Gestapo of the Germans that he and we had just beaten, just as those opposing reform now have been invoking Nazis as frequently and as falsely as if they were invoking zombies.

Churchill cost himself the election because he did not realize he was overplaying an issue that people were already damn serious about.

Irony this, because a decade earlier, Churchill had made the greatest argument ever for government intervention in health care, only he did not realize it. He was debating in parliament the notion that the British government could not increase expenditures on military defense unless the voters specifically authorized it. Just as today's opponents of reform are claiming they speak for the voters of today, even though those voters spoke for themselves eleven months ago.

Churchill's argument was this: "I have heard it said that the government had no mandate. Such a doctrine is wholly inadmissible. The responsibility for the public safety is absolute and requires no mandate."

And there is the essence of what this is. What on the eternal list of priorities precedes health? What more obvious role could government have than the defense of the life of each citizen?

We cannot stop every germ that seeks to harm us any more than we can stop every person who seeks to harm us; but we can try, damn it. And government's essential role in that effort, to facilitate it, reduce its costs, broaden its availability, improve my health and yours, seems ultimately self-explanatory.

We want to live. What is government for, if not to help us do so? Indeed, Mr. Churchill, the responsibility for the public safety is absolute and requires no mandate, and yet, today at this hour, somebody, somewhere in this country, is arguing against or protesting against or yelling against health care reform because the subject is really life and death, and they're scared and they've been scared and they've been misled by the overly simple words of one side and misinformed by the overly complex words of the other side.

And that one person—at least that one person—who is tonight so scared that somehow sickness and pain and death will come sooner because of reform, they do not understand, that one person, if his or her argument is successful and reform is again squashed, that one person arguing against health care reform will die sooner because they argued against health care reform—just as you and I have largely failed to understand the terror, the fear of death, that underlies this debate in the minds of so many.

The leadership of the reform effort has also failed to understand it and failed to lead, not just in practical terms but in rhetorical ones.

If you did not know what something called the "public option" was, you might instinctively oppose it. Option—my health care is now optional? Doesn't that mean it can go away somehow? Doesn't that mean that when I need it, it won't be there? Doesn't it mean somebody is trying to take it away from me?

And this insurance that might go away is public? I'm giving control to the government somehow? No private, just public?

And so, in seconds, with mental reflexes as acute and natural as any mechanism of fight or flight, something that will expand health care and reduce its costs, something that will help fight death and pain becomes misunderstood as exactly the opposite.

You can blame the one doing the misunderstanding all you want, but the essence of communication is reducing the chance of misunderstanding, and the term the "public option" has been as useless and as full of holes and as self-defeating as has been the term "global warming."

It is political-speak. It is legalese. It is designed not for the recipient but for the speaker. It is the ego of the informed strutting down the street and saying, "Look at me, I talk smart."

Just as global warming is really bad climate change, the public option is, in broad essence, Medicare for everybody. Frame it that way, sell it that way, and suddenly, it doesn't sound like a threat turning the seemingly solid insurance which people have now, for better or worse, into something optional and turning anything private into everything public.

Once you said "Medicare for everybody," there would be just as much to explain. If you were under 65, you'd pay for it. You wouldn't *have* to buy it. You wouldn't have to change from whatever you have now. There are just as many caveats. Still, the intent of this all would be clearer.

Much of the criticism of health care reform is coming from those who have, or are about to get, Medicare, and in confusion, in fear, and in the kind of indescribable realization that we are far closer to the end than we are to the beginning, they are suddenly mortally afraid that health care reform will take it away from them.

"Medicare for everybody" may not be literally true, but instead of terrifying, it would be reassuring, and the explanations and the caveats would be listened to and not shouted down as anger and fear.

Fear—remember—of death. Fear that wells up inside.

This rhetorical ship, of course, has sailed, and frankly, those leading the effort to reform health care have been so outflanked, out-argued, out-terrorized by its opponents that their reflexes seem shot. They are, to use to Mr. Lincoln's words about General Rosecrans, "Frozen in place like a duck hit on the head."

And yet, even from the most insurrectionary of the infamous town halls of August, there came report after report of proponents of health care reform responding to Tea Partyists and the genuinely confused, in voices calm with genuine empathy and honest inquiry, by asking, "What are you afraid of? What do *you* think we can do to improve health care?"

Setting aside the professional protesters, the shameless mercenaries of this equation, the LaRouche bags, and the hired guns, the results were uniform and productive. Dialogue, conversation, admission of fear, admission that we are indeed talking about pain and sickness and life and death—admission that we are seeking the same things and that this should not be left to the politicians who almost to a man reek of the corruption of campaign contributions from the very monopolies they are supposedly trying to control.

And something else would come up—something that you'd never hear included in the debate over reform, in the debate about insurance and bankruptcy, and even in the debate over the remorseless rapaciousness of companies that are forever increasing premiums and deductibles while reducing what they give back to the person who is sick. What you never hear about is the person who is sick.

Have you ever stayed overnight in a hospital? All data suggest that in a given year, only about one in ten of us does. It's not a universal experience.

Could you sleep in a hospital—with constant noise, with sharing a room with strangers, perhaps, with contemplating mortality and, more immediately, the fog of germs in the place with staph infections and MRSA, and nursing staffs cut to the minimum, and overworked doctors, and medical record-keeping so primitive it might as well be done on blackboards?

And the bills? What about the person who is sick and the bills? How are they supposed to get better while they are sitting there inside a giant cash register? How do you heal? How do you kill a cancer when the meter is running so loudly you can hear it?

When a system of health care has been so refined, so perfected, as to find a way to charge for almost everything and to reimburse for almost nothing—how does the person who is sick not worry always, always, about where he is going to get the money? And how is somebody worrying always about where he's going to get money supposed to also get better?

Yet our neighbor in that hospital bed hoping tonight half for health and half for the money to pay for it is still in better shape than at least 122 Americans who might be watching this right now and who will not be with us tomorrow because they will die—because they do not have insurance.

I will pick it up there and then move on to the question of whether, if health care is not reformed, we should force the issue by bailing out of this stylized blackmail that is insurance.

Sometime around one in the morning on Saturday, the 22nd of August of this year, my father, struggling with knee problems, generalized weakness, lack of appetite, and lethargy, tried to use the portable urinal he kept by his bed to limit those middle-of-the-night trips to the toilet. It sounds a little gross, I know. But certainly not when the alternative is a 10- or 20-minute ordeal of struggling to the bathroom and wondering what in the hell you're going to do if you don't make it there in time.

But that night, there was an additional problem. He was having trouble going. He tried to adjust his position sitting on the edge of the bed, and suddenly the mattress shifted underneath him and deposited him gently on the floor. He might have been in nothing more threatening than a seated position there.

With his knees as bad as they are, there was almost no chance he was going to get out of it without help. For reasons that would later become apparent, my father would pretend to himself that wasn't true. He decided to believe that he would soon be feeling better and would be able to get up on his own. He thinks he dozed much of the night.

As it got light out, he realized his cell phone was within grasp, and he called me. Not to say he was in trouble—he never mentioned it. But only to talk about the move we were planning for him to his own place closer to me. He never mentioned the precariousness of his position. He'd now been stuck on the floor for about seven hours.

Sometime in the afternoon, between the dehydration and exhaustion, the hallucinations started. He heard my sister and her family in the hallway outside his bedroom. He could feel the vibrations of the footsteps of his grandkids running up and down.

In a startling tribute to the imagination's ability to make hallucinations like this one completely self-contained and impervious to logic, he heard his daughter say, "Don't bother Grandpa. He's resting."

He thinks he smelled cooking. My sister and her kids were in fact in Upstate New York at the time. My dad found himself increasingly angry and finally, sometime after midnight on the morning of Sunday, August 23, he phoned her and demanded to know why she had been in the house without so much as giving him the courtesy of peeking her head in to see if he was all right.

Only after her repeated insistence that she had been, and was still, 330 miles away and had been all day did reality regain control. My father apologized. My sister called the neighbor. The neighbor called the cops.

There was never an official diagnosis of that one incident that night. But I've gone into such excruciating detail because of what I was told that night by the doctors at the ER when I joined my father and what I have been told by other health professionals since. The hallucinations almost certainly were provoked by dehydration, if not renal failure per se, and certainly a kind of temporary shutdown of the kidneys.

By the time he got there, it had been more than 24 hours since he had triggered this cascade of problems by trying to adjust the position of his body so he could urinate. And still he had not done so. My father's kidneys were in trouble. Considering that kidney disease was what killed his father, this was very bad news.

We heard just yesterday about kidneys and insurance. The Waddington brothers, Travis of New York and Michael of Santa Fe—the *New York Times* reported their dad, David, needed a kidney transplant because of congenital renal disease. Each of the sons was ready to donate, of course, but they were warned not even to get tested to see if they matched, for if they did, transplant or no, they would conceivably be denied insurance for the rest of their lives because they might test positive for the same congenital renal disease that threatened their father and thus they would have a preexisting condition.

And still, the Waddingtons and their dad and my dad were all luckier than at least 45,000 Americans, because, as discovered in a new study conducted by Harvard University and the Cambridge Health Alliance, that's how many of us are dying each year—because we don't have insurance.

The number is horrible. But when it's contrasted with what faced my father that night, it is unforgivable, because as Cambridge's summary of the findings put it: deaths associated with lack of health insurance now exceed those caused by many common killers such as kidney disease.

My father had less to fear that night from bad kidneys than he would have if he hadn't had insurance. And yet we let this continue. You and I, this society, our country, Democrats, and Republicans, this is the study that a congressman from Florida quoted, about which the Republicans demanded an apology when they should have been standing there shrieking, demanding that we fix this.

Uninsured working-age Americans have a 40 percent higher risk of death than their privately insured counterparts. People, in short, are dying for lack of money.

Dying as surely as they did when Charles Dickens wrote about the exact same problem: of a boy who couldn't get sufficient medical care for his affliction; of the underprivileged, suffering not just privation but death, as the comfortable moved silently and unseeingly through the streets of London. The book was called A Christmas Carol, and the boy Dickens imagined was called Tiny Tim. And it was published on the 19th of December, 1843.

It is 166 years later, and the problem is not only still with us, it is getting worse. The mortality rate among Americans under the age of 65 who are uninsured is 40 percent higher than for those with insurance. In 1993, a similar study found the difference was only 20 percent. We are moving backwards.

We are letting people die because they do not have insurance? What's worse is that barring meaningful health care reform now, this will only grow. The difference between the surveys from 1993 and now suggest that this fatal insurance gap is growing by about 1 percent per year. Your chances of dying because you don't have insurance are now 40 percent higher than those who have it. By extrapolation, three years from now, your chances will be 43 percent higher.

Your chances of dying because you used to smoke, compared to those who never smoked, are only 42 percent higher. You heard that right. At the current rate in 2012, you will be more fortunate, more secure, more long-lived if you used to smoke than if you don't have insurance. It is mind-boggling and mindless.

This is the country you want? This is the country you will accept? Do those other people in this country have meaning to you? Or are they just extras in your movies? Backgrounds in your painting? Choruses in your solo?

Without access to insurance for all of us, and the only way we achieve that is with the government filling in the gaps—just like it does with flood insurance, for God's sake—that fatal gap will just keep growing. A 45 percent higher likelihood of death for the uninsured compared to the insured by 2014. By 2022, the figure will be 53 percent higher—53 percent.

In the 1840s, as Dickens wrote *A Christmas Carol*, in a time upon which we now look back with horror, the city of Manchester in England commissioned a crude study of mortality among its residents; a doctor, P. N. Holland, studied the sanitary conditions of the houses in the streets of Manchester and divided them into three categories. And when he compared the death rate in the first-class houses in the first-class streets to the death rate in the second-class houses in the third-class streets, he found that the mortality in those worse locations was 53 percent higher.

If we do not reverse this trend in 14 years' time, we will not be living in the America of 2022. The shadows of the things that may be tell us that we will instead be living in an insurance-driven version of the Dickensian England of 1843—again.

God bless us, everyone.

I told my father the other night that the insurance I really want to get for him and me is called corporate-owned life insurance, C-O-L-I, COLI, like E. coli. How fitting.

With or without your consent, your employer is permitted by law to take out life insurance on you. It can, in fact, take out life insurance on everybody who works for it. Who gets the money when you all die? Your employer does.

Dad pointed out that, theoretically, this would give them motivation to kill you. That, of course, would be for the same reason, as Michael Moore points out in his new movie *Capitalism: A Love*

Story, that you can't buy fire insurance on the house of the guy who lives next door to you. Golly gee, that's right. Suddenly, you'd have a motive to burn down his house, and the world is already too much like that symbolically to make it a little bit like that in reality.

No, it's really unlikely that even the most evil corporation would think of killing you to get a payout from the COLI insurance plan. It exists for much more mundane and passive reasons. You're going to die anyway, and the tax laws of this country are such that if your company has 100,000 employees, it can take out small whole life policies on everybody and just let the actuarial tables do the work for it—$10,000 here, $20,000 there, maybe $50,000 back here, and all of it is tax-exempt.

Your employer can borrow the money to pay the premiums on secret insurance it has on you, and the interest on that loan is tax-deductible. Your employer can, in essence, overpay the premium it has on you and your fellow drones, and the extra money in the kitty is called "cash value." It can be stuck into a pension benefit plan or other product of the mad, mad world of accounting, and "cash value" is also tax-deferred. It can be returned to your employer later as a tax-free loan. And if your employer goes bankrupt, the "cash value" in those insurance policies is protected by tax laws from creditors.

In short, your employer can get a tax-deductible loan to buy insurance on you that until this past June it didn't have to tell you about, and the money is first tax-deferred and then tax-free, and then when you die, the payoff it gets is tax-exempt, and when the company dies, the boss still gets to keep the money from the creditors even if somehow, you, the guy on whom your boss has surreptitiously taken out an insurance policy, happen to be one of the creditors—tough.

And even though it's based on insurance on *your* health and *your* life, all that tax-free, tax-exempt, tax-deferred money not only does not go to you, it also does not go to the government. And so, if we are really ever going to do anything about federally supported health care as an alternative to these private insurers, there is that much less tax money to do that with. Some of the money that isn't going to you and isn't going to the government is going to strengthen the already monolithic insurance companies.

Just in case this isn't a sweet enough deal, the government is almost silent about telling that employer of yours what kind of health insurance it must give you. And year after year, the companies get smarter and more audacious about either cutting what your health insurance covers or cutting the number of employees the health insurance covers, or both.

If that is still not sweet enough, there is also something called the National Association of Insurance and Financial Advisers, and it has a political action committee, IFAPAC. Last year, IFAPAC had $1,492,000 worth of campaign money with which to buy politicians. And you'd be amazed how many of them you can buy with even $1,492,000.

These are the same kind of people who are not only influencing the health care debate, spending more than $1 million a day to defeat reform, they are also the same people who—by raising your premiums and cutting your reimbursements, by manipulating prices at hospitals and doctors' offices for everything from tongue depressors to enemas, and by influencing health care in this country more effectively and more selfishly than a dictator could ever do—decide what kind of health care you get, how much you pay for it, and whether they would rather not see you get it.

It is your skin, literally, and it is in the hands of people, insurance companies, who can still make money by betting against your good health. There's only one comfort here, and it's cold, indeed. Profit while you can, insurers. Sickness and death wait not just for your customer. They also wait for you, and they are double-parked.

The doctor who treats you and the pharmacist who makes you pay through your nose are not your enemies in this. It proves they are as much victims as you and I are. The time has come to realign this battle here so that it is not just us versus the entire medical and health care establishment. It's us and the doctors and the nurses and the pharmacists and maybe even some of the hospitals against the real enemy, the insurance companies.

The insurance companies who are right now at war against America.

• • •

Dr. Albert Sabin was, by his own description, pretty full of himself when he managed to temporarily stop the testing of the Salk polio vaccine after a bad batch sickened and killed some children during the first tests in the 1950s. Sabin recounted this in a TV interview in the '80s. He was weeping.

He had believed he was doing right. He had convinced himself that the fact that Salk's vaccine, the so-called inactivated polio vaccine, had been chosen for use instead of Sabin's own live polio vaccine was irrelevant to his efforts.

He was weeping as he recounted this, too. Ultimately, there proved nothing wrong with Salk's vaccine. The one batch had been improperly handled and manufactured. Sabin and others delayed all further testing for weeks.

Sabin was weeping as he remembered that. For in 1983, Dr. Sabin had contracted a rare disease of his own. Surgeons operated, relieved the intense pain and muscle weakness, and then ten days later, it came back, ten times worse, enough for him to be yelling and crying virtually all the time. The pain, he said, "made me want to die."

Dr. Albert Sabin suddenly remembered that the stopping of the Salk vaccine experiments had led to the deaths of children. More immediately, though, it had led to pain, both physical and emotional for the children *and* the parents. And he said it had not occurred to him then that the first thing doctors must do, the first thing the health care system must do, is stop pain.

He vowed to spend the rest of his life relieving pain. His own searing agony and paralysis gradually, inexplicably faded.

They moved my father this afternoon. I don't mean they moved him to another hospital. They moved him in his bed into a different position. It was agony for him. Agony enough that he could barely see us. Agony enough they had to give him all the painkiller he could handle, and he couldn't talk anymore.

Another moment when somebody like me wonders about what it would be like if he was going through that, and I was watching, worrying about whether we could afford the painkillers, or the doctors, or that hospital, or any treatment at all.

What kind of society do we live in where millions of us face questions like that, and politicians glibly talk about incremental improvements while they slowly reshape the new laws that are supposed to reduce the number of us faced with pain untreated due to money into laws that take more money out of our pockets and give it to the corporations who are profiting off health care, without contributing one second to the relief of pain or the curing of disease.

The pimps of the equation taking their 20 percent off the top—the health insurance cartel.

How would our politicians react if there were millions of Americans in pain getting insufficient care to relieve that pain because of interference from insurance corporations and those millions had just been injured in a natural disaster or an attack on this country? How fast would the politicians rush their portable podiums to the driveways outside the emergency rooms? How quickly would the money come?

You know the answer. And you know what the answer has been about rushing to help those millions of Americans in pain tonight, attacked not by another country or a terrorist or even a flood, but attacked merely by life. Half of the politicians are dedicated to protecting the corporations from having to help our relatives and our neighbors in pain. The other half are calculating how much they can anger our insurance overlords before our insurance overlords stop contributing to their campaigns.

May all their CEOs, may all the wavering political frauds, suffer ten minutes of Dr. Sabin's pain or my father's.

That's another part of the story you just haven't seen: the doctors. For all of the jokes over all of the years, these guys really are on our side in this, especially the ones in the hospitals, especially the ones without whose skills you would heal up just as fast in a bowling alley as in the best of the medical centers.

The man who took out my appendix two years ago—a messy, dangerous job that took more than two hours, from which I recovered fast enough that I only missed four days of work—left three little scars, one of which I can't find anymore. I wrote all the checks. I know how much he got out of the whole price, about 10 percent.

A very good friend of mine is a doctor in California. He wrote me about all of this the other day. "You can see," he said, "why doctors who want to make a living or cover increasing costs, labor, overhead, et cetera, have only one choice: see more patients, spend less time, answer fewer calls, because there is no other way to increase revenue."

"Plus," he wrote, "if you order tests, patients think they're getting better care, and doctors think that testing saves them time in thinking or talking with people. You have chest pain? Instead of asking you questions, why don't we go ahead and do this stress test that I get paid much more for than some little office visit to do, and make sure it's not your heart."

And so, like us, the doctors are slaves to insurance. That's not even talking about malpractice. We have to help them on that. Maybe we do need to cap damages. We do it, though, maybe so that everybody benefits. You set the cap at whatever it works out to be now, and then you lower it each year by exactly how much the entire cost of a patient's health care is lowered in this country. Incentivize the doctors to help make health care available to everybody.

We patients and the doctors have to be on the same side again, to stop pain, to heal disease, and not be simply customers and salesmen. We patients need doctors to help us with thinking long-term, too. People want to discuss their end-of-life preferences well in advance, my friend the doc says. And doctors should be paid to have these discussions.

And then my friend the doctor wrote something that hadn't occurred to me. "We spend a lot of money on doing things that people would not have wanted us to do to them."

That hit home. My mother died in the spring. Bless her. She lived without symptoms until nearly two weeks before she went, and we had all talked about what to do and when to do it and what not to do. And so when they said there's breast cancer and there's five lesions in her brain and there's nothing we can do that will wake her, but we can do a lot to lessen her pain, or we can do things that might extend her life but also won't cure and also won't wake her, but might be hurting her—we can't tell—it took five seconds to decide.

And then I thought of all the people who never had that discussion with their mother or father, who don't know that those are the choices they might face, and how it might help to have a doctor who says, blandly, "Here it all is." You say, "Doc, thanks. I have decided I still want you to keep me alive forever, even if I'm suffering and comatose." He says, "Got it."

Only now he can send you a bill and you can have insurance pay you back for it. So your mother and you will know, when the time comes, exactly what each choice would bring. And some buffoon decided to call that a death panel.

On the list of preventable deaths—diabetes, stroke, ulcers, appendix, pneumonia—we're 19th in the world. Canada is 6th. England, 16th. We're 19th. Portugal is 18th. You're better off in Portugal.

Death panels? We have them now. They're called Wellpoint and Cigna and United Health Care and all of the rest.

Ask not for whom the insurance companies' cash register bell tolls. It tolls for thee.

I do not know who the two women were, yet they are indelibly burned into my memory now. They stood outside on a crisp New York morning last week, middle-aged, short, looking more than a little weary. They were wearing lab coats, and they were leaning against what those coats told me was their place of employment, the Mortimer B. Zuckerman Research Center at Memorial Sloan Kettering Cancer Center.

The women in the cancer researcher lab coats were smoking cigarettes. I've seen a lot of startling things in my more than 40 days and 40 nights alongside my ailing father inside this nation's fractured health care system, but nothing seemed to me to better symbolize the futility, the ram-your-head-against-the-wall futility, of this gigantic medical entity that we have created, that seems to not only have broken free from human control but which has, to some great measure, enslaved us.

Twenty-three stories tall, built partly with a $100 million gift from the publisher of the *New York Daily News* and *US Magazine*, and two of the cancer researchers are standing in front smoking.

That isn't the only picture that haunts my dreams. A man walks out of another hospital, casual, purposeful, in control. The red stitches on the left side of his shaved head outline a space as big as a large potato and at least an inch higher than the rest of his skull. I don't know if he was getting better or he was getting worse. I don't know if he had just gotten good news or bad. I don't know if tonight he's healthy or he's dead.

Months ago, I got in line at a drugstore here. A woman ahead of me, obviously a familiar figure to the young pharmacist behind the counter, tried, with mixed success, to take in the gentle explanation. You have maxed out your prescriptions on that insurance, the professional said slowly. I can't give it to you.

The customer shook her head in resignation. It was like the medieval courts of Chancery, where, if you were poor, you could take your lawsuit against the rich or the government and hope that when they heard the handful of cases to be heard that year, they somehow picked yours.

If they didn't, you could try again next year or, in some cases, every year for the next 20 years.

The woman who needed the prescription spoke even more slowly than the pharmacist just had. She had almost no hope in her voice. "Try the Cigna, please."

Another drugstore late at night, and the pharmacist there was a friend of mine. "You have to do something about this," he said loudly as he handed me my refill. He reached for somebody else's prescription. "You see this? Antifungal cream. I just filled this. You know what this costs wholesale? Four dollars. You know what I sell it for? Two hundred sixty-three dollars. I sell it for less and I get fired, and maybe we lose our license."

And then this. Last Saturday, I leave my father 24 hours after serious surgery that probably saved his life, serious enough that he was still under sedation, and it would be another 24 hours before he knew where he was or who I was. Yet I knew he was okay, because I had gotten him the best care in the world. Literally—his surgeon is considered among the top five guys in his field alive today. Even I can tell you he absolutely nailed the operation.

And I know that after my father was to wake up, when postoperative fluids would get into his lung and he had trouble breathing and he had to inhale after every word, they would give him a drug called Lasix that would start to drain the fluids. And within five minutes, he would be breathing easier. And within 15, it would be like nothing was ever wrong, and that this was just one of 20 drugs they can use on him, not just to make him better long-term, but, just as importantly, and twice as imperatively, to stop his pain short-term.

I marveled that we had come so far that you can barely take care of your life, like he would admit he hasn't for 80 years, and you can even be as dumb as those two women outside of the cancer research center smoking away, yet there's still a kaleidoscope of drugs and therapies and nurses and diagnosticians and psychiatrists and X-ray techs and surgeons, and all of them are capable of undoing the pain and curing the sickness and forestalling death.

As I walked down the hallway from my dad's room, I allowed myself a brief moment of selfishness. I'm sorry. I'm sorry that I'm happy that I can spend whatever it takes to help my dad get better, to keep him around.

But maybe I can atone for that selfishness by making this case tonight to you, to whoever sees this, that we have to make these wonders of life and health and peace of mind and control of pain available to everybody.

This is boiling in my brain that day. I take the shortcut out to the street through the emergency room. And that's when I hear my name called. It's a man roughly my age, and he looks worried to death and really familiar.

I haven't seen him in 32 years. He was the nephew of the two brothers from Brooklyn who used to run the baseball card shows when we were both kids. His uncles were businessmen. But he, like me, was just another kid collecting mostly for the fun of it. It's amazing to see him again, joyous almost, just for the sake of the continuity that the accident of our running into each other provides to us both.

And he asks what I'm doing there. I tell him. He smiles, because my father used to go to those card shows with me. Mike remembers him.

Then I ask Mike why he's there. "My daughter is in ICU," he says.

"Three weeks now." The worried look returns to his face. "Lyme disease. It's one thing—they knocked that down—and then it's another." There's a brief pause. "Tomorrow I will have to sell my farm. Did you know I had a farm?" I don't have to ask him why he's selling it.

He then goes the next step. "You want to buy my card collection? I have got some great stuff."

We must reform a system that lets my father get better care than yours does or better care than Mike's daughter does because of the accident of life that I make more money than he does or my checkbook could hold out longer than his does or yours does, as the bills come endlessly, like some evil version of the enchanted water buckets from *Fantasia*.

The resources exist for your father and mine to get the same treatment, to have the same chance, and to both not have to lie there worried about whether or not they can afford to live.

Afford to live. Are we at that point? Are we so heartless that we let the rich live and the poor die and everybody in between become racked with fear, fear not of disease but of deductibles?

Right now—right now—someone's father is dying because they don't have that dollar to spend. And the means by which the playing field is leveled, and the costs that are just as inflated to me as they are to you are reduced, and the money that I then don't have to spend anymore on saving my father can go instead to saving your father, that's called health care reform.

Death is the issue. How can we not be united against death? I want my government helping my father to fight death. I want my government to spend taxpayer money to help my father fight to live. I want my government to spend taxpayer money to help your father fight to live.

I want it to spend my money first on fighting death. Not on war. Not on banks. Not on high-speed rail. Spend our money. Spend my money first on the chance to live.

And we must be unanimous in this, not to achieve some political triumph for one side against the other, but to save the man or the woman or the child who will be dead by morning in this country, in this century, on our watch, because we're not spending that money tonight.

I will not settle for a compromise bill. I will extend my hand to those who are scared of the inevitability of death, but who have been told they are scared of reform, those who been exploited by the others, paid or forced to defend the status quo.

We must recognize the enemy here. It's an enemy capable of perverting reform meant for you and me into its own ATM that mandates only that more of us become slaves to the insurance companies, the moneyed interests that have bled their customers white and used their customers' money to buy the system, to buy the politicians, to buy the press.

It cannot now even be checked by the government. Ordinarily the solution would be obvious. We would have to do it for the government. We would have to bring insurance companies to their knees, to organize, to pick a date when we say, "Enough," and then at a given hour, on a given day, stop paying the premiums: an insurance strike.

But the insurance companies' stranglehold on us is so complete right now that lives would be risked. Lives would be lost by the very act of protest. What parents could risk the cancellation of their child's insurance? What adult could risk giving his insurer the chance to claim that everything wrong with him on the day of an insurance strike was now suddenly a preexisting condition?

Even as the payouts move inexorably downward to being less than what you have paid in over the years, we are such serfs to the insurance companies that just to invoke the true spirit of the founding of this nation is to give them *more* power and not less.

So I propose tonight one act with two purposes. I propose we, all of us, embrace the selfless individuals at the National Association of Free Clinics. You know them. They conducted the mass health care free clinic in Houston that served 1,500 people.

I want a health care clinic every week in principal cities of the states of the six senators key to defeating a filibuster against health care reform in the Senate. I want senators Blanche Lincoln and Mark Pryor to see what health care poverty is really like in Little Rock.

I want Senator Max Baucus to see it in Butte.

I want Senator Ben Nelson to see it in Lincoln.

I want Senator Mary Landrieu to see it in Baton Rouge.

I want Senator Harry Reid to see it in Las Vegas.

I'll donate. How much will you donate? We enable thousands of our neighbors to have just a portion of the bounty of good health, and we make a statement to the politician, forgive me William Jennings Bryan: "You shall not press down upon the brow of America this crown of insurance. You shall not crucify mankind upon a cross of blue."

We think these events will be firmed up presently. You will be able to link from our Web site. Trust me. I will remind you.

Because in one party, in one demographic, in one protest movement, we're all brothers and sisters. We are united in membership in the party that insists that every chance at life be afforded to every American seeking that chance. We are united in membership in the party that insists on the right of everyone to the startling transcendent blessings of the technological advance of medical science.

We're united in membership in the party that is for life, that is against death, that is for lower premiums, that is against higher deductibles, that is for the peace of mind that can be provided only by the elimination of the fear that costs will decide whether we live or we die.

Because that's the point, isn't it? It is hard enough to recover, to fight past pain, and to stave off death, if just for a season or a week or a day. It is so hard that eventually for you, for me, for this president, for these Blue Dogs, for these protesters—it is so hard to recover that for all of us, there will come a time when we will not recover.

So why are we making it harder?

A follow-up: Thanks to viewers donating nearly $2 million, there was a health care clinic at the State House Convention Center in Little Rock, Arkansas, a two-day-long free health fair in Kansas City, Missouri, and a fair in Hartford, Connecticut.

And because of your generosity, there was a free health fair in a major city of a state that ranks 49th in overall health care, out of the 50 in the United States, plus the District of Columbia and Puerto Rico—this according to the Commonwealth Fund's independent research. Louisiana ranks 45th for prevention and treatment. It ranks 37th for access to health care. But because of the generous donations to the National Association of Free Clinics, a free health fair was held in New Orleans.

We can go further still. To donate, go to Countdown.msnbc
.com or Freeclinics.us.

It's Not the Chamber of Accounting

OCTOBER 19, 2009

The bronze to Bill-O, claiming that he has the best research staff
in the business, and they declared Rush Limbaugh racism-free.
"Playing the race card is easy and hateful. The only thing we can
find about Rush Limbaugh is that he thinks quarterback Donovan
McNabb is overrated by some people who want black quarter-
backs to succeed."

Yes, well, of course, that is the fatal quote for which the NFL
considers Mr. Limbaugh inappropriate for ownership, since it was
expressed far more strongly than that, and it's racism, and it's racism pertaining to football.

But that was the only racist quote? The Media Matters Web site
found 28; from the "We are being told that we *have* to hope Obama
succeeds" quote or the "We have to bend over, grab the ankles
because his father was black" quote, or the calling the president
and other people "Half-rican Americans" quote, or saying the NFL
all too often looks like a game between the Bloods and the Crips.

Bill, your research staff couldn't find the relative whereabouts
of the ass and the elbow.

The silver to Congressman Jack Kingston of Georgia. One of the
most vociferous opponents of the stimulus plan, he issued a news
release boasting about $245,187 in federal funding for new police
officers in the cities of Alma and Jesup, Georgia. Congressman
Kingston said in the press release, "We've seen from experience
that local initiatives go a lot further toward solving problems than
policies set in Washington. This funding will provide tax relief by
saving local tax dollars."

So local, local—the money was raised locally? It was from the stimulus.

But our winner . . .
Tom J. Donahue, president of the U.S. Chamber of Commerce. Despite the implication of its name, it's not a part of government, just a group of businesses archly opposed to, well, everything. It has for years claimed that its membership, which largely opposes things like health care reform, is "three million businesses of all sizes, sectors and regions." It has included that figure in testimony to Congress, implying that, well, with three million businesses and businesspeople, that's pretty much all the businesses and business-people in the country, and represents almost everybody.

No. After a series of investigations by various media outlets, specifically *Mother Jones*, using the Chamber's own data and history, the Chamber has had to admit that membership is not quite three million:

It's 300,000. Nice.

Tom J. "Give or Take 2.7 Million" Donahue, president of the U.S. Chamber of Commerce, today's worst person in the world.

Worst Person in the World

The Fightin'est Man the Top 40 Ever Knew

NOVEMBER 2, 2009

The bronze to Pat Boone, the ex-teeny-bopper singer. He's now authored one of those dog-whistle, you know, assassination, insurrection columns for the deplorable Newsmax site, writing that exterminators need to go to the White House and kill its "varmints and unwelcome creatures. . . . I believe figuratively, but in a very real way, we need to tent the White House. To the dismay of millions of us, this occupant seems to think we need an emperor.

Our White House is being eaten away from within. We urgently need to throw a tent, a public remonstration and outcry over that hallowed abode, to cause them to quake and hunker down inside, and then treat the invaders, the alien rodents, to massive rodent gas, the most lethal antidote to would-be tyrants and usurpers. We must clean house, starting with our own White House."

Funny he uses the word *usurpers*. Pat Boone has now personally done more to try to incite violence against the elected representatives of the United States government than the entire country did during the two terms of George W. Bush. He should be ashamed of himself, particularly in his distrust of democracy and his distrust of the American way of life.

The runner-up: The infamous Congresswoman Virginia Foxx of North Carolina. She's the one who claimed health care reform would lead to the murder of seniors. She's the one who claimed that the conclusion that the murder of Matthew Shepard was homophobia was a "hoax." This just in from the senile lady from the North Carolina Sixth District: "I believe the greatest fear that we all should have to our freedom comes from this room, this very room, and what may happen later this week in terms of a tax increase bill masquerading as a health care bill. I believe we have more to fear from the potential of that bill passing than we do from any terrorist right now in any country."

Well, Ms. Foxx, clearly your employers in the insurance industry do have that fear. And honestly, when I said Fox News, no relation, had done more long-term damage to this country than Al Qaeda, meaning the nation was strong enough to survive Al Qaeda fundamentally unchanged, but Murdoch was eating away at our national soul, the skulls of several conservative apologists exploded.

You've now got an actual elected congresswoman with her lips so firmly attached to the insurance butt that she could make this insane analogy. So where are the conservative screamers now?

But our winners . . .
Amanda Carpenter of the *Washington Times*, Michael Goldfarb of the *Weekly Standard*, Mary Katharine Ham of O'Reilly's show,

and Ed Morrissey of the Hot Air Blog. Here are their tweets on Friday, as rounded up by Think Progress, after the administration voluntarily released a list of 500 visitors to the White House from January through July:

Wrote the condescending Miss Ham: "Friday afternoon visitor logs have two visits by Bill Ayers, one by Jeremiah Wright." From Ed Morrissey, supergenius: "Jeremiah Wright has visited the White House more often than McChrystal and Petraeus combined." From Miss Carpenter, a modest woman with much to be modest about: "WH visits: Kim Gandy, 12; Immelt, 5; Bill Ayers, 2; John Podesta, 17; George Soros, 2; Andy Stern, 22; Trumka, 7; Oprah, 2; Jeremiah Wright, 1."

From the breathless Mr. Goldfarb, "I tried to warn you, America."

Why didn't we hear more about this? Jeremiah Wright at the White House? Bill Ayers? Bill Ayers? Wouldn't we be able to hear Sarah Palin's rapture from Alaska without microphones, just coming through the walls and windows of our homes? As the White House ethics counselor, Norm Eisen, wrote in an introduction that none of the conservative rocket scientists apparently bothered to read, "Given this large amount of data, the records we are publishing today include a few false positives, names that make you think of a well-known person, but are actually someone else. In September, requests were submitted for the names of some famous or controversial figures. For example, Michael Jordan, William Ayers, Michael Moore, Jeremiah Wright, Robert Kelly—R Kelly—and Malik Shabazz. The well-known individuals with those names never actually came to the White House. Nevertheless, we were asked for those names and so we have included records for those individuals who were here and share the same names."

And there is your conservative intelligentsia in action. Shoot first, figure out if it was too good to be true later.

Amanda Carpenter of the *Washington Times*, Michael Goldfarb of the *Weekly Standard*, Mary Katharine Ham of O'Reilly's show, and Ed Morrissey of the Hot Air Blog, or, as we call them here, *clowns*, today's worst persons in the world.

Beck, Shark, Jump

NOVEMBER 3, 2009

The bronze shared tonight by Governor Tim Pawlenty and Congressman Wrong-Way Wilson of South Carolina—different guys, same hypocrisy. Pawlenty defining a Republican: "You can't get endorsed by ACORN. You can't support the stimulus bill. You can't be for bank bailouts." George W. Bush's bank bailouts, sir, supported by Governor Tim Pawlenty, all $700 billion of it. I guess, Governor, you're not a Republican.

Congressman Wilson on the slow accumulation of H1N1 vaccine in this country: "The current administration is solely responsible. They can't blame this on any prior administration. This is the responsibility of the current administration. They put the lives of Americans at risk."

In June, Wilson voted against the supplementary appropriations bill, which contained special funding for more H1N1 vaccine. By the way, the congressman's wife now has H1N1. I think this is in the Bible somewhere.

The runner-up: Congresswoman Cathy McMorris Rodgers of Washington State, and the GOP House leadership, clarifying Congresswoman Foxx's lunatic statement yesterday that health care reform was greater than any threat to this country posed by any terrorist anywhere. Congresswoman Rodgers disagrees. "I would say it's the difference between an internal versus an external attack. Yes, this is rocking our foundation."

Judging by your willingness to exploit terrorism for politics, Congresswoman, and your status as one of those crazy birthers, I would say your foundation was rocked quite a while ago.

Speaking of which, our winner . . .
Lonesome Rhodes Beck, on health care reform: "Ten years ago, I could have shouted every single day about Osama bin Laden and his wacky, crazy threats to kill Americans in New York.

And nobody would have been willing to stand in line for two hours while some security officer made Grandma take her shoes off. No one would have done it. But don't you see, while the government is still not willing to do these things, today America is different. America has changed. Washington, we're not going to let you get away with it anymore. The 9/12ers are willing to stand in line and take our shoes off before the plane actually hits the tower."

Beck, shark, jump. You and the 9/12ers have the nerve to exploit 9/11 for your lousy TV ratings? You cannot make light of 9/11, nor bandy it about as if your petty political grievances are comparable to it, and still be an actual patriotic American.

In short, Glenn, 9/12ers, if you're invoking 9/11 to oppose health care reform, go to hell.

Glenn Beck, today's worst person in the world!

Good Bet

NOVEMBER 9, 2009

The bronze to Orly Taitz Limbaugh. Those interstitial periods of vague rationality, they are getting shorter and shorter. "The Muslim shooter [at Fort Hood] was being teased. He was really being teased. He's a psychiatrist. He was really being teased. I don't know if you talk to people in the military. It's like being in a professional sports locker room. Their teasing is merciless. Oh, it's part and parcel of it. Everybody gets teased."

They keyed his car at his apartment and had an ALLAH IS LOVE bumper sticker pulled off his car, that we know of. And by the way, what in the hell does Orly Taitz Limbaugh know about life in the military? He got a deferral.

"By the way, I mean playing the game the way the media, the Democrats do, we could almost say this is Obama's fault, because this guy said that he believed Obama was going to get us out of

Iraq and Afghanistan. Obama hasn't done it. And that's one of the reasons why the guy cracked."

Except nobody's playing this that we could almost say that this was Bush's fault. This is Dr. Hasan's fault. The rest of the world is trying to be patient enough to find out what the hell Hasan thought his motives were, and then try him in court. But not this idiot Limbaugh, or these knee-jerk racists like Bryan Fischer of the American Family Association, who called for a purge of Muslims from the U.S. military. They are busily trying for the Jack Ruby route.

Our runner-up: Lloyd Blankfein, the CEO of Goldman Sachs, which, after you and I and two presidents bailed them out, reports a $3.19 billion profit and expects to pay out just under $22 billion in salaries and bonuses this year. Mr. Blankfein has now told the *Times* of London that Goldman Sachs is providing an important social purpose and he is just a banker, "doing God's work."

I don't know who that creature is you're working for, Mr. Blankfein, but I'll bet my soul on the premise that it ain't God.

But our winner . . .
Rupert Murdoch, interviewed by one of the Australian networks he owns, questioned about one of the American networks he owns.

Political editor David Speers noted: "Glenn Beck has called Barack Obama a racist. He helped organize protests against him."

Murdoch's response: "On the racist thing, that caused a grilling, but he did make a very racist comment about, you know, blacks and whites and so on, which he said in his campaign he would be completely above. And that was something which perhaps shouldn't have been said about the president. But if you actually assess what he was talking about, he [Beck] was right."

Perfect! Beck was wrong to say it, but really, he was right, because Obama was racist in what he said, even though Murdoch offers no evidence of what was racist about it, and Murdoch can't even remember what it was Obama said. And that pretty much defines Fox Noise, doesn't it?

Rupert "Glenn Beck Called Obama a Racist, Glenn Beck Was Right" Murdoch, today's worst person in the world.

A Bundle of Interconnected Mistakes

NOVEMBER 10, 2009

The bronze to Rupert Murdoch. Just isn't his week. First he defended Glenn Beck calling the president racist. Now he's been caught flat-footed in a lie about another reference to Obama, a lie on one of his own networks, Sky News Australia.

When political editor David Speers said: "It was on Fox. And [Beck had] likened [Obama] to Stalin. Is that defensible?" Murdoch retorted: "No, no, not Stalin, I don't think. Uh, I don't know who that is. Not one of our people."

So this guy doing the promo for the April 2, 2009, *Glenn Beck Show* on Fox News is a Glenn Beck impersonator?

As images of Obama, Hitler, Stalin, and Lenin flashed on the screen, Beck read: "Is this where we are headed? Those who don't know history are destined to repeat it."

To that point about repeating history, the last guy there, that was Stalin. The first guy was Obama. That would be a comparison of Obama to Stalin, Rupe, by one of your people. You might want to watch your own network, if you can risk your soul jumping out of your body and smacking you in the face.

The runner-up: Congresswoman Sue Myrick of North Carolina. David Gaubatz, co-author of the book *Muslim Mafia*, has responded to the Fort Hood nightmare with another one of these screw-the-Constitution, screw-waiting-for-any-investigation, revenge fantasies, complete with book burnings. Says Gaubatz, "Now is the time for a professional and legal backlash against the Muslim community and their leaders. If Muslims do not want a backlash, then I would recommend a housecleaning. Stack every Saudi, Al Qaeda, Pakistani, Hamas, and Muslim Brotherhood piece of material from their mosque and have a bonfire."

Hard to tell if Gaubatz hates or is just looking to make money off this. But Congresswoman Myrick, in theory, is an elected representative of the people of the United States. She wrote the foreword to this piece of crap and is thus endorsing racial hatred, guilt by association, attacks on freedom of religion, book burning, professional and legal backlashes, and housecleanings, all of which once let loose on this society could, she has obviously forgotten, easily be redirected against thin-brained congresswomen from North Carolina.

But our winner, back after too long an absence . . .
Bill-O the Clown.

He decided to talk health care reform with Brit Hume, and hilarity ensued.

Bill-O: "They call it the public sector."

Hume: "Public option, you mean?"

Bill-O: "Public option, whatever. The folks don't want it."

Hume says, "The public option—actually, some polls show that the public option standing by itself is not at all unpopular, but it is kind of popular."

Holy crap. O'Reilly was lying so much, Brit Hume had to correct him twice. Holy crap. And public sector? That might not be the dumbest thing ever said on Fox. That's still Glenn Beck citing the university of "I don't remember." But citing the public sector insurance plan? Holy crap.

Bill "What's All This about a Public Option" O'Reilly, today's worst person in the—what's the word here—world!

Think of the Children

NOVEMBER 19, 2009

The bronze: Rupert Murdoch. The Media Matters folks tried to pin him down today on his defense of Beck's claim that President Obama was a racist. Murdoch said he didn't think the president was a racist, but he did think Beck was responding to a racist comment made by the president. Now he's apparently denying that.

First, what he said to his own reporter, political editor David Speers: "On the racist thing, that caused a grilling, but he did make a very racist comment."

Then what he says he didn't after being asked, "Mr. Murdoch, could you be more specific about what racist comments the president allegedly made?" To which he responded: "I deny that absolutely."

"What?" the interviewer said. "You deny that you did?"

Looks like the pirate trolley has come off the pirate track, matey.

The runner-up: Congressman Louie Gohmert of Texas, one of the gang of six idiots complaining to Fox Noise about the terrorism trials in New York. "You got millions of New Yorkers who will be put at risk. Unless they're trying to create a new jobs bill by allowing terrorism back in New York. This is insane. And even that would be insane."

Well, Gohmert knows he's insane. He claims he was joking, but by the way, Congressman, thanks to you and that troglodyte president you supported the last eight years, we're at risk all the time here in New York. When did you suddenly start caring?

But, our winner . . .
Lonesome Rhodes Beck. Norah O'Donnell interviewed a teenage girl at a Sarah Palin book signing. The girl read what was written on her own T-shirt, "The U.S. handed out $700 billion in Wall Street bailouts and all I got was this lousy T-shirt." Norah correctly pointed out that Palin supported the bailout, to the surprise of the young girl. Beck took umbrage—not with Norah's observation, nor with Palin's hypocrisy. The comical actor whined, "They gotta go after 13-year-olds . . . a 13-year-old, you gotta go after a 13-year-old?" His sycophant co-host asks, "And did they ever do this, did they ever do this to Barack Obama supporters during the campaign?"

"You gotta go after a 13-year-old—this is child abuse. I want to report this father to some sort of, you know, department of health and children's service or whatever it is, for child abuse."

What's the name of the young man who appeared in the pro-SCHIP ad, Graham Frost, the one Michelle Malkin attacked?

How old was he, 47? No, he's 12. That's right, 12. How old was the girl with the heart condition that the *National Review* attacked for being in the other SCHIP ad, Bethany Wilkerson? Twelve? No, she was two. How old was the gal that Congressman John Shadegg brought to the floor the other day to complain about health care reform? Held her up like a human shield. Maddie? How old was she? Two? No, she was 7 months old. Child abuse in politics is a right-wing requirement.

Lonesome Rhodes "When We Do It, It's Cool, When You Do It, You're Hitler" Beck, today's worst person in the world!

Worst Person in the World

Fool's Gold
NOVEMBER 24, 2009

The bronze to the fired Hewlett-Packard CEO, Carly Fiorina, who is now running for the Senate from California as a Republican. Ms. Fiorina on the bank bailout on Fox Noise, October 14, 2008: "The bank bailout was, unfortunately, necessary, because credit is tight for hardworking Americans and small businesses."

Eight days later, she credited the bailout with unlocking credit. Now that the bailout has worked, she addressed a breakfast held by the conservative *American Spectator*, and according to that publication, "Fiorina said she was opposed to bailouts and President Obama's economic stimulus package."

Ma'am, you're embarrassing yourself, and you explain again why Hewlett-Packard dumped you.

The runner-up: Bill-O, really earning that epithet *Clown* on this one. Bill Moyers has announced that at the age of 75, after 38 years in television news, he will be retiring from his weekly program on PBS. "No, I think we, Jesse Waters, drove him out of PBS. I think Jesse Waters is responsible for Bill Moyers leaving. Now, Bill Moyers is hammering Bush and Cheney. They wanted them impeached, this and that, and, you know, taking shots at the *Factor*. So we sent Jesse out to talk with him."

In the ambush interview from O'Reilly's stalker producer, Moyers mopped the floor with the kid. He invited Waters to come on the show because O'Reilly didn't have the courage to do so, he said. A year later, O'Reilly sent his other flunky, Porter Berry, to try to sideswipe Moyers, and no one has seen Berry since.

And these interviews from two and three years ago, that's what Bill-O thinks drove Moyers out of PBS. Bill also thinks he has his own police force and that he schedules the tides. Notice, O'Reilly never does these ambush interviews himself because, well—here kitty, kitty, kitty.

But our winner . . .
A twofer from Lonesome Rhodes Beck. As a fairly recent survivor of an emergency appendectomy, I think I can say this—I don't think what they took out of him was his appendix. Predicting a collapse of the American economy, he advised, "I like to call it the three-G system for this; it's God, gold, and guns. Now, personally, you might take God and put him as an umbrella over the whole thing. Then you've got your gun and your gold down here, too."

Once again, Beck's dirty little secret is that American society means as much to him as faith means to a televangelist. It's a scam. It's a cash cow. He's in it for the money. He keeps trying to sell people gold, largely because a disproportionate number of his advertisers sell people gold.

Here's a fact Beck never mentions: the gold sellers will buy gold back from you at about 60 or 70 percent of the going wholesale price they charge you. In other words, if you buy gold and the price doesn't go up 30 or 40 percent, you will never make your money back, let alone a profit.

Part two, Beck called Mary Landrieu a prostitute again, did it on the radio, using the word itself. Then on television: "So we know you're hooking, but you're just not cheap." At the end of the same attack of verbal diarrhea, Beck concluded, "I guess shame is dead. Shame died."

What would you know about shame? And where are the conservative feminists? A woman politician is called a prostitute and you're okay with that? It's okay if I call Sarah Palin that? The hell it is.

Lonesome Rhodes Beck, traveling gold salesman, today's worst person in the world!

Declare Victory and Get Out

NOVEMBER 30, 2009

Mr. President, it now falls to you to be both former Republican senator George Aiken and the man to whom he spoke, Lyndon Johnson. You must declare victory and get out.

You should survey the dismal array of options in front of you—even the orders given out last night—sort them into the unacceptable, the unsuccessful, and the merely unpalatable, and then put your arm down on the table and wipe the entire assortment of them off your desk—off this nation's desk—and into the proverbial scrap heap of history.

Unless you are utterly convinced—willing to bet American lives on it—that the military understands the clock is running, that the check is not blank, and that the Pentagon will go to sleep when you tell it to, even though the Pentagon is a bunch of perpetually 12-year-old boys desperate to stay up as late as possible, by any means necessary—unless you're sure of all that, get out now.

We are at present fighting, in no particular order, the Taliban, a series of sleazy political/military adventurers, not the least of whom is this mountebank election-fixer Karzai, and what National Security Adviser James Jones estimated in October was around eight dozen Al Qaeda in the neighborhood.

But poll after poll, and anecdote after anecdote, of the reality of public opinion inside Afghanistan is that its residents believe we are fighting Afghanistan. That we, sir, have become an occupying force. Yes, if we leave, Afghanistan certainly will have an occupying force, one way or the other, whether it's from Pakistan or consisting of foreign fighters who will try to ally themselves with the Taliban.

Can you prevent that? Can you convince the Afghans that you can prevent that? Can you convince Americans that it is the only way to undo Bush and Cheney policy catastrophes dating back to Cheney's days as secretary of defense in the '90s?

If not, Mr. President, that way lies Vietnam. If you liked Iraq, you'll love Afghanistan with 35,000 more troops, complete with the new wrinkle, straight from the Minderbinder lingo of Joseph Heller's *Catch-22*.

President Obama will be presenting an exit strategy for Afghanistan. The exit strategy that begins by entering still further. Lose to win, sink to swim, escalate to disengage. And even this disconnect of fundamental logic is predicated on the assumption that once the extra troops go in, when the president says, "Okay, time for adult swim, generals, time to get out of the pool and bring the troops with you," that the Pentagon is just going to say, "Yeppers."

The Pentagon, often to our eternal relief, but just as often, sadly, to our eternal regret, is in the war business. You were right, Mr. President, to slow the process down, once a series of exit strategies had been offered to you by men whose power and in some case livelihoods are predicated on making sure all exit strategies, everywhere, forever, don't really result in any serviceman or -woman actually exiting.

These men are still in the belly of what President Eisenhower so rightly, so prophetically, christened the military-industrial complex. Now—and later as the civilian gray eminences with "retired" next to their names, formally lobbying the House and Senate, informally lobbying the nation through television and the printed word, to "engage" here, or "serve" there, or "invest" everywhere—they are, in many cases, just glorified hardware salesmen.

It was political and operational brilliance, sir, to retain Mr. Bush's last secretary of defense, Mr. Gates. It was transitional and bipartisan insight, sir, to maintain General Stanley McChrystal as a key leader in the field.

And it was a subtle but powerful reminder to the authoritarian-minded war hawks like John McCain, and the blithering idiots like former governor Palin, of the civilian authority of the

Constitution. It was a picture drawn in crayon for ease of digestion by the Right, to tell our employees at the Pentagon to take their loaded options and go away and come back with some real ones.

You reminded them, Mr. President, that Mr. Gates works for the people of the United States of America, not the other way around. You reminded them, Mr. President, that General McChrystal is our employee, not our dictator. You've reminded them, Mr. President. Now, tonight, remind yourself.

Stanley McChrystal. General McChrystal has doubtless served his country bravely and honorably and at great risk. But to date, his lasting legacy will be as the great facilitator of the obscenity that was transmuting the greatest symbol of this nation's true patriotism, of its actual willingness to sacrifice, into a distorted circus fun-house mirror version of such selflessness.

Friendly fire killed Pat Tillman. Mr. McChrystal killed the truth about Pat Tillman. And that willingness to stand truth on its head on behalf of "selling" a war, or the generic idea of America being at war, to turn a dead hero into a meaningless recruiting poster, should ring essentially relevant right now.

From the very center of a part of our nation that could lie to the public, could lie to his mother, about what really happened to Pat Tillman, from the very man who was at the operational center of that plan, comes the entire series of plans to help us supposedly find the way out of Afghanistan? We are supposed to believe General McChrystal isn't lying about Afghanistan?

Didn't he blow his credibility by lying, so obviously and so painfully, about Pat Tillman? Why are we still believing the McChrystals? Their reasons might sound better than the ones they helped George Bush and Dick Cheney fabricate for Iraq. But surely they are just as transparently oblivious to the forest.

Half of them insist we must stay in Afghanistan out of fear of *not* repeating Iraq, while the other half, believing Bush failed in Iraq by having too few troops, insist we must stay in Afghanistan out of fear of *repeating* Iraq. And they are suddenly sounding frighteningly similar to what the Soviet generals were telling the Soviet politicos in the 1980s about Afghanistan.

Sure, it's not going well. Sure, we need to get out. We all see that. But first let's make sure it's stabilized and then we get out.

The Afghans will be impressed by our commitment and will then take over the cost of policing themselves, even though that cost would be several times their gross national product. Just send in those extra troops, just for a while. Just 350,000.

I'm sorry, did I say 350,000? I meant 35,000. Must be a coffee stain on the paper.

Mr. President, last fall, *you* were elected. Not General McChrystal, not Secretary Gates, not another Bushian drone of a politician. You. On the Change Ticket, on the pitch that all politicians are not created equal.

And upon arrival you were greeted by a Three Mile Island of an economy, so bad that in the most paranoid recesses of the mind one could wonder if the Republicans didn't plan it that way, to leave you in the position of having to prove the ultimate negative, that you staved off worldwide financial collapse, that if you had not done what you so swiftly did, that this "economic cloudy day" would have otherwise been the "biblical flood of finance."

So, much of the change for which you were elected, sir, has thus far been understandably, if begrudgingly, tabled, delayed, made more open-ended. But patience ebbs, Mr. President. And while the first one thousand key decisions of your presidency were already made about the economy, the first public, easy-to-discern, mouse-or-elephant kind of decision becomes public tomorrow night at West Point at eight o'clock.

You know this, Mr. President: we cannot afford this war. Nothing makes less sense to our economy than the cost of supplies for 35,000 new troops. Nothing will do more to slow economic recovery. You might as well shoot the revivified auto industry or embrace the John Boehner Health Care Reform and Spray-Tan Reimbursement System.

You know this, Mr. President: we cannot afford this war. Nothing makes less sense to our status in the world than for us to re-up as occupiers of Afghanistan, and for you to look like you were unable to extricate yourself from a military Chinese Finger Puzzle left for you by Bush and Cheney and the rest of Halliburton's henchmen.

And most of all, and those of us who have watched these first nine months trust both your judgment and the fact that you know this, Mr. President: unless you are exactly right, we cannot afford this war. For if all else is even, and everything from the opinion of the generals to the opinion of the public is even, we cannot afford to send these troops back into that quagmire for second tours, or thirds, or fourths, or fifths.

We cannot afford this ethically, sir. The country has, for eight shameful years, forgotten its moral compass and its world purpose. And here is your chance to reassert that there is, in fact, American exceptionalism. We are better. We know when to stop making our troops suffer in order to make our generals happy.

You, sir, called for change, for the better way, for the safety of our citizens, including those citizens being wasted in war-for-the-sake-of-war, for a reasserting of our moral force. And we listened. And now you must listen. You must listen to yourself.

That's Not What Christmas Is All About

DECEMBER 7, 2009

The bronze to Alisyn Camerota, news model over there at Fox Noise. This is what happens when Roger Ailes lets the news models ad-lib rather than making sure they just read the talking points. "If," she asks a conservative columnist, "there's no federal money used to subsidize abortion for low-income women, doesn't that mean there will be more low-income babies? And do any of these amendments talk about the health care for them, then? Meaning," she explained to dumbfounded guest conservative Kate Obenshain, "that low-income women do rely on subsidies often for abortion?"

To her credit, Ms. Obenshain said, "No, they don't." Actually, "No, low-income women pay for their own abortions," she said, "and that won't change." Everybody move away from news model Camerota and her conviction that the problem of this country today is all those low-income babies. Damned slacker infants.

The silver to Lonesome Rhodes Beck, clearly more than slightly off the tracks after his recent ratings plummet and that big total of 17 tickets sold to his movie in New York, comparing efforts to control climate change to—well, to everything, as usual. "What kind of Salem Witch Trials are we in? McCarthy, you call me McCarthy. No, no. Don't you remember, McCarthy was part of the government, the all-powerful government. For the first time in American history that I know of—and I know American history pretty well. For the first time in American history, we are on the wrong side. We're on the Axis power globally and we are on the wrong side internally. I never thought I'd see this day come."

Okay. I know you think you know American history pretty well, but you don't. This is the guy who thinks a clause in the Constitution that protected slavery was actually a tax on immigrants. This is a guy who said he thought Thomas Paine was opposed to the redistribution of wealth. This is a guy who does not realize nearly all of Joe McCarthy's victims were in the government. And this is the guy for whom everything and every day is Armageddon. It confuses his little mind, he screams. I think we may need a new nickname for him. Car alarm, Car Alarm Beck.

But our winner . . .

Mayor Russell Wiseman of Arlington, Tennessee, a suburb of Memphis. Apparently it's small enough to be suffering from a severe politician shortage. In a conspiracy theory from which Glenn Beck would recoil, Mr. Wiseman has posted on his Facebook page the following:

"This is total crap. We sit the kids down to watch *The Charlie Brown Christmas Special* and our Muslim president is there. What a load. Try to convince me that wasn't done on purpose."

The mayor of a place where they wear shoes and everything. He thinks the president of the United States sent 30,000 more troops to Afghanistan so he could preempt the telecast of *A Charlie Brown Christmas* last Tuesday, so the mayor and his children couldn't watch it. The mayor also went on, saying the president's supporters should move to a Muslim country. Then he said the U.S. had become a Muslim country, which, if it were true, would certainly help a lot of people who had to move.

But let's get back to the assertion by Mayor Wiseman, whose brother is the chair of the Tennessee Shelby County Republican Party, that the president conspired to keep Russell Wiseman and all the little Wisemans from ever seeing *A Charlie Brown Christmas*, which has now been shown on network television every year since 1965, which you can get on a DVD from Amazon for $9.83, or less if you buy used, which you can get as a download from iTunes for ten bucks. Seriously. You're a grown-up who can brush his own teeth, probably, and you think this was deliberate, Mayor? An Obama plot to keep your kids from seeing *A Charlie Brown Christmas*. Did anybody tell you ABC's running it tomorrow night, and next Tuesday night? Do they not pay you $9.83, sir?

Have you seen a psychiatrist lately, Mayor? Have you checked to see if your head is still attached at the shoulders, or if it kind of swings loose when there's a strong breeze? It's a plot! A plot to keep your kids from hearing Linus read the Nativity story from Luke.

Mayor Russell "Maybe the Last Name Is Meant Ironically" Wiseman from Arlington, Tennessee, who also may believe in brownies and elves, today's worst person in the world!

Worst Person in the World

It's Only a Joke When No One Laughs

DECEMBER 8, 2009

The bronze to Bret Stephens of the *Wall Street Journal*, trying to extend the Right's belief that it's found the holy grail in these e-mails stolen from climate change experts. It's holy *something*. He employs the classic ploy of I'm not saying what I'm obviously saying, but those who acknowledge climate change have "what I would call the totalitarian impulse. This is not to say that global warming true believers are closet Stalinists, but their intellectual methods are instructively similar. For the anti-Semite, the problems of the world can invariably be ascribed to the Jews. For the Communist," he writes, "to the capitalist."

And as the list above suggests, global warming has become the fill-in-the-blank explanation for whatever happens to be the problem. I'm not saying Mr. Stephens is an intellectual midget who has prostituted himself out to Rupert Murdoch, who will do anything to defend big polluters, and whose myopia could lead to the destruction of the atmosphere. I'm just saying—

The runner-up: The fine folks at Cluster Fox and Friends again. A poll from the right wing–manipulated Rasmussen Reports wasn't good enough for them. "Did scientists falsify research to support their own theories on global warming?" Fifty-nine percent somewhat likely, 35 percent very likely, 26 percent not very likely. That would be 120 percent who believe it's possible, 94 percent of whom believe it's somewhat or very likely.

So this poll question follow-up: Does Fox falsify the news to support its own theories on everything? One hundred percent of the respondents were unable to stop laughing long enough to answer.

But our winner, in an all-time first . . .
The same guy as last night for the same thing, Mayor Russell Wiseman of Arlington, Tennessee, the man who posted on Facebook that President Obama is a Muslim and that's why he spoke to the nation last Tuesday night at 8:00 Eastern, so he could preempt the showing of *A Charlie Brown Christmas* for the 45th year in a row.

He's it again, because I wasn't finished. When the Memphis newspaper called him for comment, Mayor Wiseman said they're making a mountain out of a molehill. The molehill, sir, is between your ears. They showed *A Charlie Brown Christmas* tonight and they're showing it again next Tuesday. And if you were a real American, sir, you'd have seen it so many times already you'd be able to cite it from memory.

His city has now disavowed this mayor. Posted on its official Web site, "The mayor's comments were not made on a town computer or using town computer services. The town recognizes Barack Obama as the president of United States, and in accordance with the Constitution, recognizes both the freedom of religion and freedom of speech. We welcome all law-abiding people to our town. We do not discriminate. We provide essential services to all town of Arlington people, without regard to their religion, race, color, age, gender, sex, or national origin."

Ample parking day and night. People shouting, "Howdy neighbor." Now, Mayor Wiseman has sent a statement to local media: "Regarding all the reports about my recent Facebook remarks, I want to take this opportunity to say how much I regret that I offended anyone with my poor attempt at tongue-in-cheek humor amongst friends. While my comments were certainly blown way out of proportion, I do recognize that I allowed things to go too far. I trust we have probably all experienced things getting out of hand from time to time. And I do regret it. I also take some measure in comfort in knowing that the people who know me best understand that I am a progressive and tolerant person, who believes wholeheartedly in the rights and equality of all people."

Ample parking day and night, people. So it was a joke? It was a progressive joke. The president's a Muslim; he preempted *A Charlie Brown Christmas* because it has Bible readings in it; his supporters should all move to a Muslim country. Ha, ha, ha, a joke. A joke, Mayor, would be this: Do you know how stupid the people who think Obama is a Muslim really are? They're so stupid they think he went on TV at 8:00 so he could preempt *A Charlie Brown Christmas* because it's got Bible readings in it. I mean, there are a lot of stupid sons of bitches in this country. But those people would have to be so stupid that they'd be serving as the local chairman of the National Stupid Sons of Bitches Club.

That, Mayor Wiseman, is a joke.

Mayor Russell "Yes, the Name Is Meant Ironically" Wiseman, of Arlington, Tennessee, once again, today's worst person in the world!

In Gold We Trust

DECEMBER 9, 2009

The bronze to Lauren Petterson, executive producer of Cluster Fox and Friends. After one of the otherwise comical, but sadly politically propagandistic, "mistakes," one of her bosses over there established a zero-tolerance standard. But when this graphic went up on her show, suggesting 94 percent of people believed it was likely or very likely that climate change scientists had distorted facts, and one of the hosts said the number could easily reach 100 percent, and also that 120 percent said they believed it was possible, Ms. Petterson said there was no error in that graphic. "We were just talking about three interesting pieces of information from Rasmussen"—the pollsters—"we didn't put on the screen that it added up to 100 percent." Thus no one at Cluster Fox will even be reprimanded. So the zero tolerance policy must mean that when it comes to how much journalistic integrity they must maintain at Fox, they'll tolerate zero.

Our runner-up: Lonesome Rhodes Beck, speaking of which, Goldgate is gathering momentum. Now the *LA Times* is questioning why he's telling his audience that the economy is about to collapse and they should buy gold, while many of his advertisers just happen to sell gold, and one of them uses a convicted felon as a spokesman.

Beck mocked the reporting, claiming that the advertising and what he says in the noncommercial parts of his shows are unconnected. Well, not according to one of the advertisers. Reading from Politico.com, "Peter Epstein, president of Merit Financial Services, which advertises on Beck's shows, says gold retailers expect favorable coverage from commentators on whose shows they pay to advertise. 'You pay anybody on any network, and they say what you pay them to say,' said Epstein. 'They're bought and sold.'"

So Beck is saying his argument for gold is organic. But one of the men who sponsors his program is saying he's paying Beck to say that, that Beck is "bought and sold." Maybe more sold than bought; Beck's ratings have plummeted 30 percent from the first week of November to the first week of December.

But tonight's winner . . .
Correspondent David Wright of ABC's *World News Tonight*, with the same kind of selective editing and dishonesty usually reserved for the cesspools of the *Wall Street Journal* and the right-wing blogs. Tonight, Mr. Wright of ABC tried to make Jon Stewart of *The Daily Show* look like a climate change denier. This is the sound bite they played in Mr. Wright's report this evening:

"Poor Al Gore," Stewart said, "global warming completely debunked, via the very Internet you invented. Oh!"

This is the fuller comment, not edited to stand Jon Stewart's meaning on its head: "Poor Al Gore, global warming completely debunked via the very Internet you invented. Oh! Oh, the irony, the irony. Actually, the real story is not quite that sensational. Now, does it disprove global warming? No, of course not!"

No, of course not, unless you have (A) no journalistic qualifications, (B) no journalistic ethics, or (C) you are falsifying the news to fit a personal political agenda. At Fox, when they do that, they make an excuse. At the *Wall Street Journal*, they don't even bother to do that. At ABC, when they do, they're supposed to fire somebody. Might have been a producer, but the piece has his name on it.

David Wright of ABC News, until we hear otherwise, today's worst person in the world!

Special Comment

Not Health, Not Care, Not Reform

DECEMBER 16, 2009

To quote Churchill after Munich: "I will begin by saying the most unpopular and most unwelcome thing: that we have sustained a total and unmitigated defeat, without a war."

On my program Howard Dean said that with the appeasement of Mr. Lieberman of Connecticut by the abandonment of the Medicare buy-in, he could no longer support HR-3590. Dr. Dean's argument is informed, cogent, heartbreaking, and unanswerable.

Seeking the least common denominator, Senator Harry Reid has found it, especially the "least" part. This is not health, this is not care, this is certainly not reform. I bless the Sherrod Browns and Ron Wydens and Jay Rockefellers and Sheldon Whitehouses and Anthony Weiners and all the others who have fought for real reform. And I bleed for the pain inflicted upon them and their hopes. They have done their jobs and served their nation.

But through circumstances beyond their control, they are now seeking to reanimate a corpse killed by the Republicans, and by a political game played in the Senate and in the White House, by men and women who have now proved themselves poorly equipped for that fight. The "men" of the current moment have lost to the "mice" of history.

They must now not make the defeat worse by passing a hollow shell of a bill just for the sake of a big-stage signing ceremony. This bill, slowly bled to death by the political equivalent of the leeches that were once thought state-of-the-art medicine, is now little more than a series of microscopically minor tweaks to a system which is the real-life, here-and-now version, of the malarkey of the Town Hallers. The American Insurance Cartel is the Death Panel, and this Senate bill does nothing to destroy it. Nor even to satiate it.

It merely decrees that our underprivileged, our sick, our elderly, our middle class, can be fed into it, as human sacrifices to the great maw of corporate voraciousness, at a profit per victim of 10 cents on the dollar, instead of the current 20.

Even before the support columns of reform were knocked down, one by one, with the kind of passive defense that would embarrass a touch-football player—single-payer, the public option, the Medicare buy-in—before they vanished, the Congressional Budget Office estimated that the part of the bill that would require you to buy insurance unless you could prove you could not afford it would cost a family of four with a household income of $54,000 a year 17 percent of that income, $9,000 a year, just for the insurance!

That was with a public option. That was with some kind of check on the insurance companies. That was before—as Howard Dean pointed out—the revelation that the cartel will still be able to charge older people more than others; will—at the least—now be able to charge much more, maybe 50 percent more, for people with preexisting conditions—preexisting conditions; you know, like being alive.

You have just agreed to purchase a product. If you do not, you will be breaking the law and subject to a fine. You have no control over how much you will pay for that product. The government will have virtually no control over how much the company will charge for that product. The product is designed like the Monty Python sketch about the insurance company's "Never-Pay" policy— "Which, you know, if you never claim, is very worthwhile. But you had to claim, and, well, there it is."

And whom do we have to blame for this? There are enough villains to go around, men and women who, in a just world, would be the next to get sick and have to sell their homes or their memories or their futures just to keep themselves alive, just to keep their children alive, against the implacable enemy of American society, the insurance cartel.

Mr. Grassley of Iowa has lied, and fomented panic and fear. Mr. DeMint of South Carolina has forgotten he represents people, and not just a political party. Mr. Baucus of Montana has operated as a virtual agent for the industry he is charged with regulating. Mr. Nelson of Nebraska has not only derailed reform, he has tried to exploit it to overturn a Supreme Court decision that is, in this context, frankly none of his goddamned business.

They say they have done what they have done for the most important, the most fiscally prudent, the most gloriously phrased, the most inescapable of reasons. But mostly they have done it for the money. Lots and lots of money from the insurance companies and the pharmacological companies and the other health care companies who have slowly, deliberately, and effectively taken this country over.

Which brings us to Mr. Lieberman of Connecticut, the one man at the center of this farcical perversion of what a government is supposed to be. Out of pique, out of revenge, out of betrayal of his earlier wiser, saner self, he has sold untold hundreds of thousands of us into pain and fear and privation and slavery, for money. He has been bought and sold by the insurance lobby. He has become a senatorial prostitute.

And sadly, the president of the United States has not provided the leadership his office demands. He has badly misjudged the country's mood at all ends of the spectrum.

There is no middle to coalesce here, sir. There are only the uninformed, the bought-off, and the vast suffering majority for whom the urgency of now is a call from a collection agency or a threat of rescission of policy or a warning of expiration of services.

Sir, your hands-off approach, while nobly intended and perhaps yet someday applicable to the reality of an improved version of our nation, enabled the national humiliation that was the Town Halls and the insufferable Neanderthalian stupidity of Congressman Joe Wilson and the streetwalking of Mr. Lieberman.

Instead of continuing this snipe hunt for the endangered and possibly extinct creature "bipartisanship," you need to push the Republicans around or cut them out or both. You need to threaten Democrats like Baucus and the others with the ends of their careers in the party. Instead, those Democrats have threatened you, and the Republicans have pushed you and cut you out.

Mr. President, the line between "compromise" and "compromised" is an incredibly fine one. Any reform bill enrages the Right and provides it with the war cry around which it will rally its mindless legions in the midterms and in 2012. But this Republican knee-jerk inflexibility provides an incredible opportunity to you, sir, and an incredible license.

On April 6, 2003, I was approached by two drunken young men at a baseball game. One of them started to ask for an autograph. The other stopped him by shouting, "Screw him, he's a liberal." This program had been on the air for three weeks. It had, to that point, consisted entirely of brief introductions to correspondents in Iraq or to military analysts. There had been no criticism, no political analysis, no commentary. I had not covered news full-time for more than four years. I could not fathom on what factual basis I was being called a "liberal," let alone being sworn at for being such.

Only later did it dawn on me that it didn't matter why, and it didn't matter that they were doing it. It only mattered that if I was going to be mindlessly criticized for anything, the reaction would be identical whether I did nothing that engendered it or whether I stood for something that engendered it.

Mr. President, they are calling you a socialist, a communist, a Marxist. You could be further to the right on this than Reagan—and this health care bill, as Howard Dean put it here last night, this bailout for the insurance industry, that sure invites the comparison—and they will still call you names.

Sir, if they are going to call you a socialist no matter what you do, you have been given full, unfettered freedom to do what you know is just. The bill may be the ultimate political manifesto, or it may be the most delicate of compromises. The firestorm will be the same. So why not give the haters, as the cliché goes, something to cry about.

But concomitant with that is the reaction from Democrats and Independents. You have riven them, sir. Any bill will engender criticism, but this bill costs you the Left and anybody who now has to pony up 17 percent of his family's income to buy this equivalent of Medical Mobster Protection Money.

Some speaking for you, sir, have called the public option a fetish.

They may be right. But to stay with this uncomfortable language, this bill is less fetish and more bondage. Nothing short of your reelection and the reelection of dozens of Democrats in the House and the Senate hinges in large part on this bill. Make it palatable or make it go away or make yourself ready, not merely for a horrifying campaign in 2012, but also for the distinct possibility of a primary challenge.

Befitting the season, sir, these are not the shadows of the things that will be, but the shadows of the things that may be. But at this point, Mr. President, only you can make certain of that. There is only one redemption possible. The mandate in this bill under which we are required to buy insurance must be stripped out.

The bill now is little more than a legally mandated delivery of the middle class—and those whose dreams of joining it slip ever further away—into a kind of Chicago stockyards of insurance. Make enough money to take care of yourself and your family and you must buy insurance, on the insurers' terms, or face a fine.

This provision must go. It is, above all else, immoral and a betrayal of the people who elected you, sir. You must now announce that you will veto any bill lacking an option or buy-in but containing a mandate.

And Senator Reid, put the public option back in, or the Medicare buy-in, or both, or single-payer, for that matter. Let Lieberman and Ben Nelson and Baucus and the Republicans vote their lack of conscience and preclude 60 "ayes." Let them commit political suicide instead of you.

Let Mr. Lieberman kill the bill, then turn to his Republican friends only to find out they hate him more than the Democrats do. Let him stagger off the public stage to go work for the insurance industry. As if he is not doing that now.

Then, Mr. Reid, take every worthwhile provision of health care reform you legally can, and pass it via reconciliation, whenever and however you can. And by the way, a Medicare buy-in can be legally passed via reconciliation. The Senate bill with the mandate must be defeated, if not in the Senate, then in the House.

Health care reform that benefits the industry at the cost of the people is intolerable. And there are no moral constructs in which it can be supported. And if the bill and this heinous mandate still become law, there is yet further reaction required. I call on all those whose conscience urges them to fight, to use the only weapon that will be left to us if this bill becomes law. We must not buy federally mandated insurance if this cheesy counterfeit of reform is all we can buy.

No single-payer? No sale. No public option? No sale. No Medicare buy-in? No sale. I am one of the self-insured, albeit by choice. And I hereby pledge that I will not buy this perversion of health care reform. Pass this at your peril, Senators, and sign it at yours, Mr. President. I will not buy this insurance. Brand me a lawbreaker, if you choose. Fine me, if you will. Jail me, if you must.

But if the Medicare buy-in goes, but the mandate stays, the people who fought so hard and so sincerely to bring sanity to this system must kill this mutated, ugly version of their dream, because those elected by us to act for us have forgotten what must be the golden rule of health care reform. It is the same one to which physicians are bound by oath: First do no harm.

Tauntin' the Christmas City

DECEMBER 17, 2009

The bronze to Orly Taitz Limbaugh. One of the great historians, he described the second Reagan term and the only George H. W. Bush term as eight years of prosperity. "Now after eight years of prosperity under Bush 43, we're again seeing the seething hate for profits."

Let's see. The recession from July 1990 to March 1991. The recession from March 2001 to November 2001. And the current George Bush recession, which started in December 2007. Oh, oh, I forgot, when Limbaugh talks about prosperity and profits, he means his own personally; screw the rest of you.

The runner-up: Sean Hannity. This is special; he was outraged— outraged—because "the president has a new pen pal, North Korean Dictator Kim Jong Il." Now according to the *Washington Post*, "the president wrote Mr. Kim a secret letter that was delivered last week to the communist dictator by the administration's special envoy to North Korea."

This month is the second anniversary of the day Kim Jong Il got another personal letter hand-delivered in secret. It was from President George W. Bush. I guess that was okay. Maybe he had better penmanship or something.

But our winner . . .
Michelle Malkin. She has exposed more persecution of Christians trying to celebrate Christmas, in this case a little boy who had been asked to draw something that reminded him of the holidays. In her words, "Public school lunacy of the day; a second-grader in Taunton, Massachusetts, was kicked out of school, suspended and ordered to undergo a mental evaluation for drawing a picture of Jesus Christ on the cross."

It's the freaking Roman Colosseum out there for Christmas-fearing celebrants, people. While Ms. Malkin's readers are threatening the teacher, there is one small problem with the Malkin story—actually five small problems. According to the superintendent of schools in Taunton, Mass., the nine-year-old was not kicked out. He wasn't suspended. And his class had not been asked to draw something that reminded them of the holidays. And actually he didn't draw a picture of Jesus Christ on the cross.

He drew a picture of himself on the cross. Just in case his message was not clear enough, he wrote his name right above the picture. You know, maybe you want a doctor to ask him if everything is okay at home. Also, since 1914, Taunton, Massachusetts, has been known as the Christmas city, because of the huge Christmas display set up each year on Taunton Green, at town expense.

Michelle "Facts, What Are Facts?" Malkin, today's worst person in the world!

Not Since Burr

JANUARY 4, 2010

We are at war, and Dick Cheney came down last week from Mount Megalomania to announce that "when President Obama pretends we aren't, it makes us less safe."

If Mr. Cheney believes we are at war, then he, as the most recent former occupant of the vice presidency, is under the strictest obligation to put aside his case of terminal partisanship and rally to the support of his president at a time of war. Instead, his remarks not only give encouragement to the enemies of this country, they give them an exact measure as to how successful they have been in damaging our freedoms.

In a previous time, Mr. Cheney's pathetic exploitation of human fears, his undermining of our courage and resolve and clearheaded calm thinking, would have resulted in his being chased off the national stage by a public sick to death of the personal industry he has made of undermining American freedom and of undermining the authority of this elected government.

And in a previous, more resolute time, among journalists in this country, nobody would be pretending that this obvious fact was not true. It would have been in every newspaper, and on every broadcast—after his disgraceful performance since Christmas, when a terrorist attempted an attack in this country, Dick Cheney is the beneficiary. And if he cannot summon exactly the same kind of absolute apolitical patriotism he demanded of everyone else while he was in office, he is, by his own terms, nothing more or less—morally, if not legally—than a traitor to the United States of America.

Who Are the Terrorists?

JANUARY 5, 2010

Each day it seems the lunatic fringe finds a new way to rationalize its penchant for viewing the rest of us as less than human. We don't count as much as they do. Ordinary Americans don't matter.

Newest example, hate-radio host Neil Boortz yesterday: "Obama-care will do more damage," he said, "than a successful terrorist bombing of an airliner and kill more people as well."

So, rather than count how many things are wrong with that statement or how many times Neil Boortz must have been abused for him to wind up so dehumanized for him to say such a thing, let us answer it on his terms.

What would you do, sir, if *terrorists* were killing 45,000 people every year in this country? The current health care system, the insurance companies, and those who support them, are doing just that.

Let's frame this in language even conservatives can understand. Those fighting health care reform—not those debating its shape nor its nuance but people who demand the status quo—they are killing 45,000 Americans a year. If they were killed all at once, or even 100 at a time, Neil Boortz would be demanding martial law and government by the generals. Instead, because they die individually because of disease and not disaster, Neil Boortz and all those who ape him approve this. Forty-five thousand a year in America.

Remind me again, who are the terrorists?

U.S. Government for Sale

JANUARY 21, 2010

On the cold morning of Friday, March 6, 1857, a very old man who was born just eight months and thirteen days after the Declaration of Independence was adopted, a man who was married to the sister of the man who wrote "The Star Spangled Banner," a man who was enlightened enough to have freed his own slaves and given pensions to the ones who had become too old to work, read aloud, in a reed-thin voice, a very long document.

In it, he ruled on a legal case involving a slave, brought by his owner to live in a free state, yet to remain a slave.

The slave sought his freedom and sued. And looking back over legal precedent, and the Constitution, and the America in which it was created, this judge ruled that no black man could ever be considered an actual citizen of the United States.

"They had for more than a century before been regarded as beings of an inferior order, and altogether unfit to associate with the white race, either in social or political relations, and so far unfit, that they had no rights which the white man was bound to respect."

The case, of course, was *Dred Scott*. The old man was the fifth chief justice of the United States of America, Roger Brooke Taney. And the outcome, he believed, would be to remove the burning question of the abolition of slavery from the political arena once and for all.

The outcome, in fact, was the Civil War. No American ever made a single bigger misjudgment. No American ever carried the responsibility for the deaths and suffering of more Americans. No American was ever more quickly vilified. Within four years Chief Justice Taney's rulings were being ignored in both the South and the North.

Within five, President Lincoln, at minimum, contemplated arresting him. Within seven, he died, in poverty, while still chief justice. Within eight, Congress had voted to not place a bust of him alongside those of the other former chief justices.

But good news tonight, Roger B. Taney is off the hook.

Today, the Supreme Court of Chief Justice John Roberts, in a decision that might actually have more dire implications than *Dred Scott v. Sandford*, declared that because of the alchemy of its 19th-century predecessors in deciding that corporations had all the rights of people, any restrictions on how these corporate-beings spend their money on political advertising are unconstitutional.

In short, the First Amendment—free speech for persons—which went into effect in 1791, applies to corporations, which were not recognized as the equivalent of persons until 1886. In short, there are now no checks on the ability of corporations or unions or other giant aggregations of power to decide our elections.

None. They can spend all the money they want. And if they can spend all the money they want—sooner, rather than later—they will implant the legislators of their choice in every office from president to head of the Visiting Nurse Service.

And if senators and representatives and governors and mayors and council members and everyone in between are entirely beholden to the corporations for election and reelection to office, they will soon erase whatever checks might still exist to just slow down the ability of corporations to decide the laws.

It is almost literally true that any political science fiction nightmare you can now dream up, no matter whether you are conservative or liberal, is now legal. Because the people who can make it legal can now be entirely bought and sold, no actual citizens required in the campaign fund-raising process.

The entirely bought-and-sold politicians can change any laws. And any legal defense you can structure now can be undone by the politicians who will be bought and sold into office this November, or two years from now. And any legal defense which honest politicians can somehow wedge up against them this November, or two years from now, can be undone by the next even larger set of politicians who will be bought and sold into office in 2014, or 2016, or 2018.

Mentioning Lincoln's supposed ruminations about arresting Roger B. Taney, he didn't say the original of this, but what the hell:

Right now, you can prostitute all of the politicians some of the time, and prostitute some of the politicians all the time, but you cannot prostitute all the politicians all the time. Thanks to Chief Justice Roberts, this will change. Unless this mortal blow is somehow undone, within ten years, every politician in this country will be a prostitute.

And now let's contemplate what that perfectly symmetrical, money-driven world might look like. Be prepared, first, for laws criminalizing or at least neutering unions. In today's Court decision, they are the weaker of the nonhuman sisters unfettered by the Court. So, as in ancient Rome or medieval England, they will necessarily be strangled by the stronger sibling, the corporations, so they pose no further threat to the corporations' total control of our political system.

Be prepared, then, for the reduction of taxes for the wealthy, and for the corporations, and the elimination of the social safety nets for everybody else, because money spent on the poor means less money left for the corporations.

Be prepared, then, for wars sold as the "new products" which Andy Card once described them as, year after year, as if they were new Fox reality shows, because military-industrial-complex corporations are still corporations. Be prepared, then, for the ban on same-sex marriage, on abortion, on evolution, on separation of church and state. The most politically agitated group of citizens left are the evangelicals, throw them some red meat to feed their holier-than-thou rationalizations, and they won't care what else you do to this corporate nation.

Be prepared, then, for racial and religious profiling, because you've got to blame somebody for all the reductions in domestic spending and civil liberties, just to make sure the agitators against the United Corporate States of America are kept unheard.

Be prepared for those poor dumb manipulated bastards, the Tea Partyers, to have a glorious few years as the front men, as the corporations that bankroll them slowly roll out their total control of our political system. And then be prepared to watch them be banished, maybe outlawed, when a few of the brighter ones suddenly realize that the corporations have made them the Judas Goats of American Freedom.

And be prepared, then, for the bank reforms that President Obama has just this day vowed to enact to be rolled back by his successor purchased by the banks, with the money President Bush will have wound up giving to Obama's successor through the judgment of the chief justice Bush appointed. I presume that successor will be President Palin, because if you need a friendly face of fascism, you might as well get one that can wink, and if you need a tool of whichever large industries buy her first, you might as well get somebody who lives up to that word "tool." Be prepared for the little changes, too. If there are any small towns left to take over, Walmart can now soften them up with carpet advertising for their Walmart town council candidates, brought to you by Walmart.

Be prepared for the Richard Mellon Scaifes to drop such inefficiencies as vanity newspapers and simply buy and install their own city governments in the Pittsburghs. Be prepared for the personally wealthy men like John Kerry to become the paupers of the Senate, or the ones like Mike Bloomberg not even surviving the primary against Halliburton's choice for mayor of New York City.

Be prepared for the end of what you're watching now. I don't just mean me, or this program, or this network. I mean all the independent news organizations, and the propagandists like Fox for that matter, because Fox inflames people against the state, and after today's ruling, the corporations will only need a few more years of inflaming people, before the message suddenly shifts to "Everything's great."

Glenn Beck and Rush Limbaugh don't even realize it: today, John Roberts just cut their throats, too. So, with critics silenced or bought off, and even the town assessor who lives next door to you elected to office with campaign funds 99.9 percent drawn from corporate coffers—what are you going to do about it? The Internet!

The Internet? Ask them about the Internet in China. Kiss Net neutrality goodbye. Kiss whatever right to privacy you think you currently have, goodbye. And anyway, what are you going to complain about, if you don't even know it happened? In the new world unveiled this morning by John Roberts, who stops Rupert Murdoch from buying the Associated Press?

This decision, which in mythology would rank somewhere between "The Bottomless Pit" and "The Opening of Pandora's Box," got next to no coverage in the right-wing media today, almost nothing in the middle, and a lot less than necessary on the Left.

The right wing won't even tell their constituents that they are being sold into bondage alongside the rest of us. And why should they? For them, the start of this will be wonderful.

The Republicans, conservatives, Joe Liebermans, and Tea Partyers are in the front aisle at the political prostitution store. They are specially discounted old favorites for their Corporate Masters. Like the first years of irreversible climate change, for the conservatives the previously cold winter will grow delightfully warm. Only later will it be hot. Then unbearable. Then flames.

The conservatives will burn with the rest of us. And they'll never know it happened. So what are you going to do about it? Turn to free speech advocates? These *were* the free speech advocates! The lawyer for that homunculus who filed this suit, Dave Bossie, is Floyd Abrams.

Floyd Abrams, who has spent his life defending American freedoms, especially freedom of speech. Apparently his life was spent this way in order to guarantee that when it really counted, he could help the corporations destroy free speech.

His argument, translated from self-satisfied legal jargon, is that as a function of the First Amendment, you must allow for the raping and pillaging of the First Amendment by people who can buy the First Amendment.

He will go down in the history books as a quisling of freedom of speech in this country. That is, if the corporations who now buy the school boards which decide which history books get printed approve. If there are still history books.

So what are you going to do about it?

Russ Feingold told me today there might yet be ways to work around this, to restrict corporate governance and how corporations make and spend their money. I pointed out that any such legislation, even if it somehow sneaked past the last U.S. Senate not funded by a generous gift from the Chubb Group, would eventually wind up in front of a Supreme Court, and whether or not John Roberts is still at its head would be irrelevant.

The next nine men and women on the Supreme Court will get there not because of their judgment nor even their politics. They will get there because they were appointed by purchased presidents and confirmed by purchased senators.

This is what John Roberts did today. This is a Supreme Court–sanctioned murder of what little actual democracy is left in this democracy. It is government of the people by the corporations for the corporations. It is the Dark Ages. It is our *Dred Scott*. I would suggest a revolution, but a revolution against the *corporations*? The corporations that make all the guns and the bullets?

Maybe it won't be this bad. Maybe the corporations legally defined as human beings, but without the pesky occasional human attributes of conscience and compassion, maybe when handed the only keys to the electoral machine, they will opt *not* to redesign America in their own corporate image.

But let me leave you with this final question: After today, who's going to stop them?

Quick Comment

Let's Talk about John Edwards's Love Child

JANUARY 22, 2010

I worked full-time in sports for about 20 years, and I've worked full-time in news for about 10 years. And after yesterday, I must finally say aloud what I have long thought but have been reluctant to voice. The average person in the American news industry appears to be about one-fifth as plugged into the world he or she covers as the average person in the American sports industry is to his or hers.

If yesterday the Supreme Court had ruled that the salary and payroll caps in football, basketball, and baseball were unconstitutional and that teams could thus spend any amount of money they chose on the players they wanted, every sports outfit from ESPN to the local cable access show in Sandusky, Ohio, would have been on the air with a special report about the obvious big-as-Mount-Kilimanjaro consequences of this: that the big-city teams would quickly corner the market in talent, and a place like Green Bay, Wisconsin, would shortly lose the ability to keep its franchise, let alone win anything.

But when the Court instead ruled that the equivalent of salary and payroll caps for corporate political advertising were unconstitutional, guaranteeing that corporate donations would soon turn every other kind of donation into a kind of bankrupt Green Bay Packers, America's crack political reporters went, "Supreme Court, boring. Let's talk about John Edwards's love child. That will affect people's lives."

Not the Court *and* John Edwards. I can live with that. I'm in TV.

I've made choices like that.

Nightline and *Good Morning America*—reports the *Huffington Post*—between them two minutes of coverage of the Supreme Court decision, more than half an hour on Edwards. Newspapers and online sites were nearly as blinkered.

Some people rightly fear right-wing media bias. Some claim there is a left-wing equivalent. The real threat to journalism, and thus to democracy, is the media's blinding lack of thought, of effort, of imagination. As I said in sports—get a roll of stamps and mail it in.

Summoning His Inner Bill-O

JANUARY 26, 2010

The bronze to Orly Taitz Limbaugh. After claiming that "for people who are prejudiced, when you say banker, people think Jewish," he then revealed himself as one of them. "Guess who Obama is assaulting," he said. "He's assaulting bankers. He's assaulting money people. A lot of those people on Wall Street are Jewish." So the Anti-Defamation League rightly called out Limbaugh—pretty gently, actually—calling his remarks borderline anti-Semitic.

Not only did Limbaugh lie in trying to claim he didn't say anything offensive, he then had his flunky guest host, Mark Steyn, attack the national director of the Anti-Defamation League, by saying "this disgusting craven little twerp thinks that the font of anti-Semitism is Rush Limbaugh. This guy is a buffoon. The ADL should be ashamed of themselves, should be embarrassed at having this guy."

ADL protests borderline anti-Semitic remarks. Limbaugh bootlicker twists that into "the font of anti-Semitism is Rush Limbaugh." Nice job, Rush, having your flunky do your dirty work for you.

The runner-up: Nancy "I Still Know What You Did Last Summer" Grace. She's to give a deposition Thursday in a case in which she's being sued for wrongful death by the family of Melinda Duckett, the woman who committed suicide in 2006 after appearing on Grace's everybody-is-guilty program on CNN's Headline News. Grace strongly questioned Ms. Duckett about the disappearance of her son, and Ms. Duckett went home and killed herself. Or, as Nancy Grace would tell the story, if it had not been about herself: Nancy Grace hounded Melinda Duckett to death and should go to jail for 960 lifetimes. No one is innocent.

This is beside the point. Ms. Grace has made a nice living parading the lurid and tawdry crimes of the worst and saddest people of the country in front of a camera, figuratively dragging dead children in front of the studio lights, and positioning herself as the avenging angel in pancake makeup, with consummate and awful skill merging the worst of criminals with the worst of television. So naturally, for the deposition Thursday, in a case in which she may be the guilty party, she doesn't want the deposition videotaped. A woman who exploits victims and perpetrators alike on TV will not defend herself on camera.

But our winner ...

Bill-O, summoning his inner Bill-O. At a public appearance on Long Island, O'Reilly fantasized about being the main adviser to President Obama and, to make it easier for Republicans to achieve "détente" with Democrats, calling in the CIA director Leon Panetta and giving him a secret job to do.

He said, "You've got to kidnap Pelosi and Reid. Don't hurt them. Don't hurt them, okay? But take them to an undisclosed location. No waterboarding. Well, maybe with Nancy. So that's what I would do, I'd kidnap Reid and Pelosi."

I know, every time I tell you about O'Reilly, somebody says, oh, it's just posturing, you're trying to get ratings, you're obsessed with O'Reilly, you're a less crazy version of him. Then you hear a tape like that, from an unguarded moment, in an environment in which he thinks he's among friends, and he starts with the violence fantasies.

Just like the Tiller the Killer drumbeat, Bill O'Reilly is, at heart, a danger to the safety of elected leaders in this country. Ha ha ha, how funny it is to joke about kidnapping the Speaker of the House and waterboarding her. He says it because he wants somebody to do it. When I call him on it, I don't care if fewer people watch this show as a result. This man is dangerous, year in, year out. He was dangerous to George Tiller, a physician who performed late-term legal abortions. He is dangerous to Nancy Pelosi. And if you want to live in a country where people like Bill O'Reilly can encourage hatred and violence, just pretend this is a phony showbiz feud. It isn't.

Bill O'Reilly, who said all that in public, today's worst person in the world!

Scott Roeder, Fraud

FEBRUARY 1, 2010

Regarding Friday's conviction of the terrorist who assassinated Dr. George Tiller, yes, Scott Roeder was convicted, and the jury needed only 37 minutes to decide. But largely overlooked was the fact that Mr. Roeder was also convicted on two counts of aggravated assault. After murdering Tiller in a place of worship, Scott Roeder pointed his gun at two church ushers.

And in that action lies the truth of what Scott Roeder did. He was not someone willing to give up everything he had to stop what he saw as an unforgivable sin. He was not acting from some deeply felt conviction. He was a man who simply, like a million men before him, latched on to a cause, used God as an excuse, and murdered someone, and then tried to get away.

If you are really laying down your life for a principle, you do not take your action, whatever it is, then point your weapon at two innocent bystanders and try to save yourself. Scott Roeder, terrorist, murderer, assassin, is also Scott Roeder, fraud.

Hot Air

FEBRUARY 2, 2010

And now a quick visit to the land of the former half governor of Alaska, the world's foremost taker of umbrage, Sister Sarah. She has called for the White House to fire Chief of Staff Rahm Emanuel after his unacceptable use of a term which Miss Palin aptly describes as offensive to special-needs kids and their families.

In doing so, she has done three things: she has proved once again that she will use her kids for political hay, at any time, under any circumstances; she has reminded us all that her ex-future-son-in-law, whom she also once used for political hay, quoted her as having called her own youngest child her "retarded baby"; and thirdly, her credibility is so slight, she's probably just guaranteed Mr. Emanuel his job for life.

But perhaps her real intent in going after Emanuel's boneheadedness has failed. She was trying to divert attention from her latest skivvy scandal, in which she used $63,000 of contributions to her political action committee to buy copies of her own book wholesale from her publisher and give them to donors. The blog Hot Air, one of the greatest sources for sophistry on the Web, says this is no big deal because it would only involve about 4,700 books.

The number of books is not the question. It's the royalties on the books. At her publisher, HarperCollins, a division of News Corp, an author can set herself up as a special sales client, buy her own book in bulk, and then get a 10 percent royalty on the deal.

In other words, there's a way for Sarah Palin to tithe all the donations to her political action committee and keep it for herself. It's only $6,300. And, of course, this is not the kind of person who would do something unethical for only $6,300.

Ducking without Cover
FEBRUARY 5, 2010

The bronze to Governor Mark Sanford of South Carolina. Back before he made his name hiking, he announced last summer that his accepting money from the Obama stimulus would be "fiscal child abuse" and would lead to "a thing called slavery."

News item: Governor Mark Sanford of South Carolina has flown to Washington to meet with Obama's secretary of education and to demand that South Carolina be given $300 million in stimulus money. At least that's where Sanford's people *say* he was.

Finishing ahead of the governor, Robert J. Kiesel of Basking Ridge, New Jersey, who was arrested after committing what amounts to the worst person's driving trifecta: charged with driving while intoxicated, driving while intoxicated and crashing into a parked truck, a liquor truck, and driving while intoxicated and crashing into a parked liquor truck in front of Sterling's Fine Wines.

But our winner . . .
Senator John Cornyn of Texas, the Republicans' top campaign strategist. *Politico* reported that the president has now invited Republican senators to the same televised question-time session that he had with their counterparts in the House. A GOP insider told the Web site, "They don't want anything to do with it. They want the whole thing to just go away."

Cornyn answered, "We're always happy to hear from the president, but I don't really feel any compelling need to do it. For what purpose? Was it for a photo op or is it serious? The president can invite Mitch McConnell or John Boehner or anybody he wants for a serious talk about issues."

Yeah, Senator, but, of course, Boehner is a congressman. Besides which, there is the bigger issue. Here, kitty, kitty, kitty, kitty.

Senator John Cornyn, today's worst person in the world!

Quick Comment

Shelby Throws Homeland Security under the Airbus

FEBRUARY 8, 2010

Once again, your Senate to the highest bidder. "Inaction on these nominees," the senator said, "is a disservice to the American people exacted by members of the opposing party who choose to block the process for political gain."

The complaining senator was Richard Shelby of Alabama. The year was 2005. The nominees were President Bush's. The opposition senators choosing to block the process for political gain were Democrats. But now another senator is holding up President Obama's nominees, choosing to block the process for political gain. This other senator has put a blanket hold on 70 to 80 of them, from appointees at Homeland Security to appointees to the Department of Justice Intel Division, because he wants, of all things, an earmark.

A $35 billion contract for tankers is going to the American firm Boeing. This senator is delaying counterterrorism appointees because he wants the contract taken from Boeing and given instead to the makers of Airbus, a firm based in France. Airbus just happens to have assembly plants in the senator's state. It just happens to have given that senator at least $34,000 in personal and PAC donations since 2000. It just happens to use the lobbying firm that employs the senator's former legislative director.

The senator deliberately keeping American intelligence understaffed so he can get $35 billion to go to a foreign company from whose teat he sucks is Senator Shelby of Alabama.

The system of senatorial holds has outlived its usefulness. So have this-senator-for-rent hypocrites like Richard Shelby.

Worst Person in the World

Regular Business
FEBRUARY 8, 2010

The bronze to Ed Sheehy, the president of the group of 173 auto group members called Southeast Toyota. You can understand that Mr. Sheehy is a little upset lately. But his response to the Toyota apocalypse? To pull his group's commercials off local ABC-TV affiliates because of what Southeast Toyota called excessive stories on the Toyota issues by Brian Ross of ABC News. Now, it's their advertising money and they can spend it any way they want.

But when you want to punish journalists for trying to keep the public from getting killed in your lame-ass cars, try to keep that a secret, because otherwise every news organization in the country is going to pick it up and pick on it, and remind the country whenever possible that if you want a car that doesn't stop, visit Ed Sheehy, especially at his dealership, JM Toyota/Lexus of Margate, Florida, where the Toyotas are literally driving themselves out of the showroom.

Runners-up: Bill-O and Karl Rove. You recall they led off the Bill O'Reilly autobiographical-history-of-the-world show by attacking the Research 2000 poll for Daily Kos in which disturbingly large numbers of Republicans admitted they believe Obama is a socialist, was not born here, and should be impeached.

You remember Bill-O memorably said, "Did you know that Republicans are stupid and evil?"

He added, "The poll is a fraud, as is the Web site." Yesterday Fox News found a poll result favorable to the candidate it has decided to elect as the next president, and Chris Wallace ran with it. Republicans' favorites for the nomination in 2012, as you saw it on Fox—Palin and Romney. Whose poll? Research 2000, the same poll O'Reilly branded a fraud, as is the Web site. Not that *one* result in it.

But our winners . . .
The United States Senate Committee on Indian Affairs. Where are you guys? Three major Native American reservations in South Dakota, particularly the Cheyenne River Reservation, have been buried under snow and ice with major power failures for two weeks. Power lines down, thousands of Lakota and other tribespeople who were already facing 75 to 85 percent unemployment *before* a blizzard, and an ice storm that added six inches of ice weight to utility poles, hit—it's been two weeks since those lines were knocked down and most of the electricity went with it. They managed to get the water turned back on at Cheyenne River. Unfortunately, most of the water goes into a pipe system that failed during the storm. The pipes are broken.

With the wind chill, it was minus 19 there today. What will you find out about this at the Web site of the Senate Committee on Indian

Affairs? Some means of donating to the affected tribes? A means of underwriting the energy companies now distributing propane tanks by hand? An emergency hearing on the crisis there? Nothing. There is a committee meeting Thursday to discuss regular business.

The Senate Committee on Indian Affairs, AWOL, today's worst persons in the world!

Where Are They?

FEBRUARY 15, 2010

I think having now been one for 51 years, I am permitted to say I believe prejudice and discrimination still sit defeated, dormant, or virulent, somewhere in the soul of each white man in this country. Sixty-three years after Jackie Robinson, and 56 years after *Brown v. Board of Education*, and 46 years after the Civil Rights Act, and a year and a half after the presidential election, this is not a popular thing to say.

This is also not a thing that should be true, even as a vestige of our sad past on this topic. But it is. Discrimination is still all around us in so many ways, openly redirected toward immigrants who are doing nothing more than following the path that brought my recent ancestors here and probably yours, too.

Or it's focused on gays, predicated on a mumbo jumbo of biblical misinterpretations.

Or it's leaching out still against black people in things like the Tea Party movement. I think the progress we have made in the last 60 years in this country has been measurable and good, but I think discrimination has been tamed, perhaps, but not eradicated.

For our society still emphasizes our differences as much as our similarities. We may be 63 years from Jackie Robinson, but we are not 63 days from a man going on national radio and telling us the president of the United States was elected only because of the color of his skin.

Discrimination, I have always thought, is a perversion of one of the most necessary instincts of survival. As a child, put your hand on a red-hot stove and you'll quickly learn to discriminate against red-hot stoves. But at that age, if you're also told you need to beware of, say, black people, you will spend your life having to fight against wiring created in your brain for no reason other than to reflect someone else's prejudice.

And it need not even be that related to trauma.

The other night in the hospital, my father was talking about seeing Satchel Paige pitch. At Yankee Stadium this was. The time was about 1941, and the team was the New York Black Yankees, and my father shook his head in amazement as he told me this. "It never occurred to me—it never occurred to anybody I know that he *couldn't* play for the other Yankees," my dad said. "We just assumed he didn't want to, that none of them wanted to."

These thoughts still linger in our lives, still actively passed on to some of us by people who are not like my father, who never questioned their own upbringing or parents or school or world. That older, brutal prejudice-with-impunity world, which reappears somewhere every day, like *Brigadoon*—sometimes with virulence, like in Don Imus's infamous remarks; sometimes with utter, arrogant tone deafness, as in John Mayer's *Playboy* interview; sometimes with a kind of poorly informed benign phrase, like Harry Reid's comment about dialect; sometimes with the boneheadedness of surprise that no one is screaming, "MF-er, I want more iced tea at a Harlem restaurant."

But it's still there. I'm not black, so I can't say for sure, but my guess is the reverse feeling still exists, too. The same doubt and nagging distrust, only with the arrow pointing the opposite way. And I guess it's still there too among Hispanics and Asians and every other self-identifying group, because since the Civil War this country has not only become ever increasingly great, not merely for dismantling the formalized racism of our first 200 years on this continent, but because we have been dismantling a million years of not fully trusting the guys in the next cave because they are somehow different.

This all still lingers about us, all of us, whether we see it or not. And since it's no longer fashionable, indeed no longer acceptable, it oozes out around the edges, and those who speak it don't even realize that, as good as their intentions might be, as improved as their attitudes might be from where they used to be or where their parents or grandparents used to be, or where America used to be, it's still racism.

Thus it has become fashionable, sometimes psychologically necessary, that when some of us express it, we have to put it in code or dress it up or provide a rationalization to ourselves for it. We say that this has nothing to do with race or prejudice—the man's a socialist, he's bent on destroying the country, and he was only elected by people who can't speak English. Or was it that he was only elected by guilty whites?

The rationalizations of the racist are too many and too contradictory for the rest of us to keep them straight. The whole of the anger-at-government movement is predicated on this. Times are tough. The future is confusing. The threat from those who would dismantle our way of life is real, as if we weren't, to some extent, doing it for them now.

And the president is black, but you can't come out and say that's why you're scared. Say that, and in all but the lifeless fringes of our society, you are an outcast. So this is where the euphemisms come in. Your taxes haven't gone up. The budget deficit is from the last administration's adventurous war. Grandma is much more likely to be death-paneled by your insurance company than by the government. And a socialist president would be the one who tried to buy as many voters as possible with stupid tax cuts.

But facts don't matter when you're looking for an excuse to say you hate this president. But not because he's black. Anything you can say out loud without your family and friends bursting into laughter at you will do.

And this is where those Tea Parties come in. I know I've taken a lot of heat for emphasizing a particular phrase which originated at a FreeRepublic.com rally a year ago this month—it originated with a Tea Partyer. And I know phrases like "Tea Klux Klan" are incendiary, and I know I use them in part because I'm angry.

But at so late a date we still have to bat back that racial uneasiness which has come to envelop us all. And I know if I could only listen to Lincoln on *this* of all days [Presidents' Day] about the better angels of our nature, I would know that what we're seeing at the Tea Parties is, at its base, people who are afraid, terribly, painfully, cripplingly, blindingly afraid.

But let me ask all of you who attend these things, how many black faces do you see at these events? How many Hispanics, Asians, gays? Where are these people? Surely there must be blacks who think they're being bled by taxation? Surely there must be Hispanics who think the government should have let the auto industry fail. Surely there must be people of all colors and creeds who believe in cultural literacy tests and speaking English.

Where are *they*? Where *are* they? Do you suppose they agree with you, but they've just chosen to attend their own separate meetings, that they're not at *your* Tea Party because they have a Tea Party of their own to go to? Are you thinking, as my father did about Satchel Paige and the Black Yankees, that they want this?

My father had an excuse for that. He was 12 years old. It was 1941. Are you at the Tea Party 12 years old? For you, is it 1941? You're scared, and you're in a world that has changed in a million ways. The most obvious one is something unforeseeable a decade ago, the election of a black president.

Yet you are also in a world inherited, installed by generations that knew only fear and brutality and prejudice and difference and suspicion. The generations have gone, but the suspicion lingers on.

Not all of our heritage is honorable. Not all the decisions of the founding fathers were noble. Not very many of the founding fathers were evolved enough to believe that black people were actually people. The founding fathers thought they were, and fought hard to make sure they would always remain, slaves.

Fear is a terrible thing. So is prejudice. So is racism. And progress toward the removal of any evil produces an inevitable backlash. The Civil War was followed not by desegregation but by Jim Crow and the Klan. The civil rights legislation of the '60s was followed not by peace but by George Wallace and anti-busing overt racism.

Why should the election of a black president be without a backlash? But recognize what this backlash is, and maybe you can free yourself from this movement, built on inherited fears and echoes of 1963 or 1873.

Look at who is leading you and why, and look past the blustery self-justifications and see the fear, this unspoken, inchoate, unnecessary fear of those who are different.

If you believe there is merit to your political argument, fine. But ask yourself when you next go to a Tea Party rally or watch one on television or listen to a politician or a commentator praise these things or merely treat them as if it was just a coincidence that they are virtually segregated, ask yourself, where are the black faces? Who am I marching with? What are we afraid of?

And if it really is only a president's policy and not his skin color, ask yourself one final question. Why are you surrounded by the largest crowd you will ever again see in your life that consists of nothing but people who look exactly like you?

Quick Comment

Something Is Wrong

FEBRUARY 18, 2010

Something is really wrong with me here. I'm beginning to love the Tea Party. Senator Orrin Hatch of Utah told a crowd at American Fork Junior High last night that they had better get in line. "If we fractionalize the Republican party," he told this group, "we're going to see more liberals elected."

Somebody in the crowd of 300 shouted, "I think you guys are as out of touch as you can get."

Hatch doesn't get it. The Tea crowd doesn't want reform. It doesn't want to be heard. It wants something for nothing. In fact, it wants everything for nothing, including violence.

A woman speaker at the Take Back America rally in eastern Washington State underscored that point. Speaking of her state's Democratic senator, she asked rhetorically, "How many of you have watched the movie *Lonesome Dove*? What happened to Jake when he ran with the wrong crowd? What happened to Jake when he ran with the wrong crowd? He got hung. And that's what I want to do with Patty Murray."

So which one of the founding fathers advocated that, ma'am? John Quincy Molotov?

And then, of course, there are the political leaders of that movement. Speaking at the Conservative Political Action Conference, Florida Tea Party Senate candidate Marco Rubio said the recent Washington snowstorm crippled the Obama administration because "the president couldn't find anywhere to set up a teleprompter to announce new taxes, ha-ha."

Mr. Rubio appeared to have read this cheap shot off one or both of the two teleprompters in front of him while giving his speech. Hearing Rubio speak, South Carolina senator Jim DeMint said, "I was standing backstage with tears."

I know how you feel, Jim. Symbolically, the rest of us were there with you, and our eyes also filled with tears—of laughter.

Quick Comment

Even Their Ignorance Is Big
FEBRUARY 22, 2010

A mind may be a terrible thing to waste, but if you waste 15 million of them, apparently you get Texas. If a University of Texas poll is correct, that is how many Texans, 60 percent of the population, either believe humans and dinosaurs lived at the same time or are not sure.

Oh, this gets much worse. Evolution does okay in Texas; 68 percent believe in it, with or without the "guiding hand from god." Human evolution? Not so much; 50 percent with or without.

I'd like to be able to pin this on political affiliation, but it's almost a tie; 51 percent of Democrats said they either never go to church or only go once or twice a year; 45 percent of Republicans said they either never go to church or only go once or twice a year.

When pollsters asked Texans if they disagreed or agreed with the statement "God created human beings pretty much in their present form about 10,000 years ago," 38 percent of Texans agreed. Okay, the joke that goes with that statistic is so obvious, I'll just skip it.

Conclusion, ultimately, Texas may not have to secede from the union.

It may just collectively drop off like a vestigial tail.

Special Comment

Help

FEBRUARY 24, 2010

Last Friday night, my father asked me to kill him. We were just shy of six months since he was hospitalized, and it was the end of a long day at the end of a longer week. Not to get too clinical or too grotesque on you, but he'd had his colon removed at the end of September, and that went so well that it was no more complicated than an appendectomy.

But what followed was a series of infections, like storms in the monsoon season, one arriving, blossoming, inundating him, my dad shaking it off and cheerfully bouncing back, and then within days, another one coming to flatten him once again. Pneumonia, three or four times, I've lost count. Kidney failure, liver failure—the liver failure got better, remarkably enough. Dialysis, feeding tubes, drainage taps, drainage tubes, breathing tubes.

He couldn't talk through that. Then he got strong enough and they could put a cap on a breathing tube, and one day he scared the crap out of a friend of his who didn't know, who came in and gave him the customary "How you doing, Ted?"—only to jump out of his shoes when my father suddenly and gleefully answered him in a strong, full voice, "Surprisingly well."

Sometimes Dad swelled up and looked like he was puffy as a prizefighter who had a really bad night, and sometimes he'd get dialysis that was so effective or an antibiotic so specific that he would look like he did 25 years ago.

Three weeks ago, they found something extraordinary. A nurse noticed what looked like a minor infection just below the surface of his skin, a kind of super pimple, if you will. It was actually the front edge of a series of abscesses which would be drained and would produce, all told, about six liters of infected stuff.

Six liters—you know how much that is? You know what that looks like? You don't want to know.

But you do want to know it's been found because it means the man hasn't been weak all this time, he's been incredibly, inhumanly strong.

The abscesses were like swimming pools for these infections. The strongest one would emerge, then my dad, with the help of the antibiotics, would kill it off. Then the antibiotics would be discontinued, and the next infection would pop out and challenge him. As he pointed out—you know, just like the organized-crime families.

Then last week they found another abscess of sorts in the chest. So they needed to put drains in there, too. This was Friday morning. His surgical team came in to see him. He did his nonverbal caricature of their chief. They all laughed like hell. They numbed him up, snip, snip, plug, plug, and this infection starts draining and they leave him alone for a while.

Then in the afternoon, they changed a few of the plugs, and the IVs attached to them, and the respiratory therapist had been in checking the ventilator and his tubes because there was a leak somewhere. And to improve his dialysis, they changed his dialysis port. And then in the evening, they needed a CAT scan of his chest to make sure those drains were in the right place, and they had to change a dressing on some bad skin. And every hour, of course, the nurse had to come in and draw blood to check how well he was getting oxygen.

And then at night, it was time for dialysis using the new dialysis port. And that's when I showed up after this show. My father was a little annoyed, the way he often gets in there—annoyed about all the activity.

That day, it was like being Sisyphus with that boulder. Only at the top of the hill, when he loses the boulder, it doesn't just roll back downhill, it rolls over him first.

He's brave about pain, provided you warn him in advance and provided the sheer volume of the activity during the day doesn't terrify him. As with terrorism, it is not just *when* terror happens, it's terror that it *might* happen.

So he's annoyed but in a good mood Friday night, and as I usually do, I sit down to read to him, Thurber. I've been reading a lot of James Thurber short stories lately, and he's insisted I should do it on the show—and we'll see about that.

But a few pages in, the X-ray technician shows up. They have to take one more picture of him to see if those new drains in his chest are working, and I have to leave his room for, at most, three minutes.

And I come back in, and my father is thrashing his head back and forth. You can't hear him, he can't speak at the moment, but you become a lip reader in those circumstances. And this one word he keeps repeating is not tough to discern: "Help." He's mouthing the word "help" over and over and over again.

And I get his attention, and he is in full panic. Maybe the X-ray tech hurt his back or touched my dad's new chest drains or, likely, he had done nothing much at all, but it was just too much for my father. "Stop this," he mouths. "Stop, stop, stop."

And I say to him, "I know for a fact they're not doing anything more to you tonight." And he looks at me and he starts thrashing his head again, "Help, help, help." I get his attention once more. I asked him, "Do you want me to stop all of this?" And he looks at me and mouths, "Yes." And I asked him, "Do you understand what happens then?" And he looks at me and again mouths, "Yes."

And I ask him, "Do you realize you are not terminally ill right now? If we do stop all this, it might not be quick." And he mouths, "Stop this." And I say, trying to joke him out of it or through it, and trust me, gallows humor is your best defense in this situation, "What, you want me to smother you with a pillow?" And he mouths, "Yes, kill me."

I told my dad that, obviously, I would not do that. But I would go and talk to the doctors. When I came back, I told him they would really be put out by this, because he wasn't sick enough and all the indications were he could still fight off what remained of those infections. And he went back to thrashing his head and mouthing "help" because clearly I was not giving him the sense of relief, relief from the paradoxical truth that people desperately trying to save your life sometimes manage only, or also, to torture you.

Of course, I actually was trying to get him that sense of relief.

When I went to see the surgical intensive care unit resident, I told him my dad had hit his wall, he couldn't take any new treatments, that it was now terrifying torture, that he needed it to stop. But I said, look, I'm his health proxy, we've had conversations about end-of-life care. We've had them in here, when he was home, and well, I am not operating in the dark here. I said, I think he really wants the one word he keeps mouthing, he wants help. Is there any medical reason not to, I don't know, give him some sedation, some sort of mental vacation from being the patient?

The resident thought that was a damned good idea and said it would also help his breathing, which the respiratory therapist had noticed wasn't quite right that night. So when I came in and gave my father the song and dance about how put out the doctors were, really, I was just stalling. I started to read to him again, and he was still thrashing his head from side to side in utter frustration and then he started to calm down and enjoy the story. And as he began to close his eyes and rest, the nurse slipped in and injected a sedative into one of his IVs.

And as I left the hospital that night, the full impact of these past six months washed over me. What I had done—conferring about the resident in ICU, the conversation about my father's panicky, not-in-complete-control-of-his-faculties demand that all treatment now stop, about the options and the consequences and the compromise, the sedation, the help for a brave man who just needed a break.

That conversation, that one, was what these ghouls who are walking into Blair House tomorrow morning have decided to call death panels. Your right to have that conversation with a doctor, not the government, but a doctor, and your right to have insurance pay for his expertise on what your options are when Dad says, "Kill me"—or what your options are when Dad is in a coma and can't tell you a damn thing. Or what your options are when everybody is healthy and happy and coherent and you're just planning ahead.

Your right to have the guidance and the reassurance of a professional who can lay that all out for you—that's a "death panel." That, right now, is the legacy of the protests of these subhumans who get paid by the insurance companies, who say these things for their own political gain, or like that one fiend, for money. For money!

Betsy McCaughey told people that this conversation about life and death and relief and release, and also about—no, keep treating them no matter what happens, until the nation runs out of medicine. She told people that's a death panel! And she did that for money!

It's a life panel—a *life* panel. It can save the pain of the patient and the family. It is the difference between guessing what happens next and being informed about what probably will. And that's the difference between your being able to sleep at night and second-guessing and third-guessing and thirtieth-guessing yourself.

And it can also be the place where your family says, "We want you to keep him alive no matter what. We believe in miracles." And the doctor says yes. Nobody gets to say no except the patient or the family. It's a *life* panel—and damn those who call it otherwise to hell.

And that brings up the other point of all this. They've rolled my father under every piece of machinery in there except an atom splitter.

They pumped him full of every drug and remedy, plus he's got Medicare and some supplemental insurance, and my out-of-pocket medical bills over the last six months have been greater than my dad's have.

And why in the hell should that not be true for everybody in every hospital in every sickroom in every clinic in this country? What is this country for, if not to take care of its people? Because whatever I've been through these past six months and whatever my dad's been through, not once were our fears or our decisions amplified by the further horror of wondering how the hell would we pay for this.

What about families having these conversations tonight about kids or about uninsured adults, or what about the guy out there whose father is 50 and he's mouthing the word "help" and the guy knows what his father doesn't know, that the insurance company has just declared that the illness the father has is a preexisting condition and he has no more insurance, and when that son goes out to talk to that doctor about what to do next, even if there is a chance of recovery, that son can't afford to pay for it?

That is the goddamned death panel, Sarah Palin.

Since Friday night, my father has been comfortable. He's been breathing well, and there have been no signs of stress or discomfort. He has also not awakened. His white blood cell count, the indicator of infection, is now at about four or five times normal. Doubtlessly, in removing that much infection from him, some of it got loose into his bloodstream, or it came in from another source.

He's not being sedated anymore, but he only has the strength either to fight off the infections or to wake up, but not both. We're hoping he does the first and then the latter. We are prepared for the probability that he will do neither.

His team and I had another life discussion, a life-panel discussion, not six hours ago. And thank God I had those conversations with my father.

Thank God I got his instructions about when to use my judgment and when to stick exclusively with his and when, if he's capable of recovery, to let them use everything they have, and when to make sure they're not just keeping him alive with no hope, when to listen to the instruction "help" first and then the one about "stop" later.

So, considering that if he does not recover, you will not see me here for a while, I have some requests. First, to you, please have this conversation with your loved ones. Don't wait. Do it *now*.

It's tough. It acknowledges death. And it also narrows the gray area you or they will face from infinity to about a foot wide. It is my greatest comfort right now, and I want it to be yours.

And to the politicians who go into Blair House tomorrow for that summit, I have some requests as well. Leave your egos at the door. I want, I demand, that you give everybody in this country a chance at the care my father has gotten. And I demand that you enact this kindest and most generous aspect of the reform proposed, the right to bill the damned insurance company for the conversation about what to do when the time comes, the life panel.

And I want all of you to think of somebody lying in a hospital bed tonight who needed that care and needed that conversation and imagine that is your father or mother or son or daughter or wife or husband or partner—and if you cannot do that, if you cannot put aside the meaninglessness of your political careers for this, my request to you then is that you not come back out of that meeting, for you would not be worthy of being with the real people of this country who suffer, and who suffer again because you have acted on behalf of the corporations and not the people. If you cannot do this, go into that room and stay there, and we will get new ones to replace your worthless roles in the life of our country.

My father cannot speak for himself. He appointed me to do so for him. I haven't the slightest doubt he wants me to say this tonight, right now. He mouthed these words to me, and I will now give them such voice as I have, to you, going into that summit tomorrow: help, help, help, help!

10,000 Men Fell

MARCH 22, 2010

Passing health care reform is a first step—there's a lot wrong with it—but the penalty for not paying the fine for not buying the mandatory insurance has now been reduced to nothing.

So, blessings nonetheless on those who took this first step. Pat yourselves on the back. And, tomorrow morning, get back to work fixing what is still wrong with our American health care system. These remarks are about our political climate in the wake of this bill's passage.

Eight days ago, a 16-year-old kid picked up a courtesy phone at a store in Washington Township, New Jersey, and announced over the public address system, "Attention, Walmart customers: All black people leave the store now." The boy has been arrested and charged with harassment and bias intimidation.

Two days ago, a Tea Party protester shouted the "N" word at Congressman John Lewis of Georgia, one of the heroes of 20th-century America, and Congressman André Carson of Indiana. And another shouted antigay slurs at Congressman Barney Frank of Massachusetts.

Capitol Hill police confirm no arrests were made and there were no serious efforts to identify the vermin involved. Television, print, and radio news organizations will not be asked to turn over their tapes and images of the event nor subpoenaed if necessary.

This is not to dismiss what the 16-year-old did in New Jersey. But it would seem that what was shouted at the congressmen merits at least as much investigation and, hopefully, as much prosecution. After all, it did occur inside the metaphorical center of American government, a place at least as crowded, and as sanctified, as a Walmart.

But in a backward, sick-to-my-stomach way, I would like to thank whoever shouted at Mr. Lewis and Mr. Carson for proving my previous point.

If racism is not the whole of the Tea Party, it is in its heart, along with blind hatred, a total disinterest in the welfare of others, and a full-flowered, self-rationalizing refusal to accept the outcomes of elections, or the reality of democracy, or of the narrowness of their minds and the equal narrowness of their public support.

On Saturday, that support came from evolutionary regressives like Michele Bachmann and Jon Voight. On a daily basis that support comes from the racists and homophobes of radio and television: the Michael Savages and the Rush Limbaughs. Shockingly, that support even came, on a specific basis, from another Congressman, Republican Devin Nunes of the California 21st.

"When you use totalitarian tactics, people, you know, begin to act crazy," he said on C-SPAN. "And I think, you know, there's people that have every right to say what they want. If they want to smear someone, they can do it."

Congressman Nunes, you should resign. You have no business opening a door for a man like John Lewis, let alone serving alongside him. And if you shouldn't resign for your endorsement, your encouragement, of the most vile, the most reprehensible, and the most outdated spewings of the lizard-brain part of this country, you should resign because of your total disconnect from reality.

There have been no "totalitarian tactics," Congressman. People, these few, sad people, have begun to act crazy, because it has been the dedicated purpose, the sole method and sole function of the Republican Party, to entice them to act crazy.

Those shouts against the Congressmen, Mr. Nunes, were inspired not by what people like John Lewis have done in their lives. They have been inspired by what people like you have done in the last year.

And so the Far Right escalates the rhetoric and the level of threat just a little more. And worse still, it escalates the level of delusion.

The election of a Democratic president is socialism. The election of a black president is an international conspiracy. The enactment of any health care reform is an apocalypse. And the willful denial of reality by the leader of the minority party in Congress is the only truth.

A willful denial, incidentally, that includes the leader of the minority party in Congress ignoring the fact that his is the minority party, and that he represents the minority, and that despite having broken all the rules of decorum in place in this nation since the end of the Civil War, that despite having played every trick mean and low—despite having the limitless financial backing of one of the biggest cartels in the world, he and his cronies and the manufactured outrage of the Tea Party failed to derail health care reform.

Failed, Mr. Boehner. You lost. You blew it. "Shame on each and every one of you who substitutes your will and your desires above those of your fellow countrymen," you said last night just before the vote. The will and desire of your countrymen, Mr. Boehner?

If you're one of the leaders of a party that in four years coughed up the Senate Majority, coughed up the House Majority, coughed up the White House, coughed up health care reform, and along the way ignored every poll, and every election result, I would think the "will and desires of your fellow countrymen" should be pretty damn clear by now: your countrymen think your policies are of the past, and your tactics are of the gutter.

But Boehner's teary "shame on you" over the tyranny of the vast majority taking a scrap back from the elite clueless minority, that's just an isolated incident. Just as Congressman Randy Neugebauer shouting "Baby-Killer" or "It's a Baby-Killer" during Congressman Bart Stupak's laudable speech last night was just an isolated incident.

Just as the shouting of the "N" word at Congressmen Lewis and Carson was just an isolated incident. Just as the spitting on Congressman Emanuel Cleaver was just an isolated incident. Just as the abuse of Congressman Barney Frank was just an isolated incident. Just as the ethnic slurs shouted at Congressman Ciro Rodriguez of Texas was just an isolated incident. Just as the oinking by Congressman Joe Wilson during the president's address was just an isolated incident.

Just as whatever's next will be just an isolated incident. You know what they call it when you have a once-a-week series of isolated incidents? They call it two things. They call it a "pattern," and in the United States of 2010 they call it "the Republican Party."

American political parties have disappeared before. They are never forced out by their rivals. They die only by their own hands, because they did not know that the hatred or the myopia or the monomania they thought was still okay wasn't okay anymore.

And so I offer this olive branch to the defeated Republicans and Tea Partyers. It is a cold olive branch. It is scarred. There aren't many olives on it, but it still counts. You are rapidly moving from "The Party of No" past "The Party of No Conscience" toward "The Party of No Relevancy." You are behind the wheel of a political Toyota. And before the midterms, you will have been reduced to only being this generation's home for the nuts.

You will be the Flat-Earthers, the Isolationists, the Segregationists, the John Birchers.

Stop. Certainly you must recognize that the future is with the humane, the inclusive, the diverse. It is with America. Not the America of 1910, but the America of 2010. Discard this dangerous, separatist, elitist, backward-looking rhetoric, and you will be welcomed back into the political discourse of this nation. But continue with it, and you will destroy yourselves and whatever righteous causes you actually believe in. And on the way, you will damage this country in ways and manners untold.

But even that damage will not be permanent. Faubus, and the McNamara brothers, and Bull Connor, and Lindbergh, and Joe McCarthy damaged this nation. We survived, and they were swept away by history. You cannot destroy this country, no matter how hard you seem to be trying to. Nor can you destroy this country's inexorable march toward the light.

The Belgian Nobel Prize winner Maurice Maeterlinck once wrote that "at every cross-roads on the path that leads to the future, tradition has placed 10,000 men to guard the past." Last night those 10,000 men fell.

Quick Comment

Reaping the Whirlwind

MARCH 29, 2010

It's the standard liberal claptrap—somebody on the Far, Far Right goes way too far with their new language of violence, especially gun violence, and then the immediate outcry that we have to back away from the edge of this cliff, because whether or not it was meant as metaphor, there are sickos out there who will happily take it literally.

It is almost a catechism by now, except that in Arizona both parts in the play have now been performed by the same person. Her name is Carmen Mercer, and she is—or was—the president of the MCDC, the Minuteman Civil Defense Corps. Its anti-immigration members stand watch on the U.S. border. Cynics say they stand around.

Anyway, 13 days ago, they got an e-mail from Ms. Mercer urging a change in their own rules that would permit them to not just report illegals and international drug carriers but to track them. Angry over a claim that the border was now secure and, of course, angry over health care reform, Ms. Mercer urged her membership to go to the border to protest.

"You are strongly encouraged," she wrote, "to exercise your rights and duty as an American citizen to carry a long arm and if challenged use it to defend the United States and America." She added the volunteers should come "locked, loaded and ready."

Guess what happened next? Carmen Mercer suddenly found out that a surprisingly large number of her e-mail correspondents took her literally.

"People are ready to come locked and loaded and that's not what we're all about," she now says. "It only takes one bad apple to destroy everything we've done for the last eight years."

Apparently Ms. Mercer misunderstood her membership. When she said "locked, loaded, and ready," she did not think that would translate as "bring your guns" to a bunch of nut bags looking to shoot people who do not look like them, as a Minuteman member allegedly did last year, killing an immigrant and his nine-year-old daughter. Ms. Mercer thought they'd get the subtle imagery she obviously intended.

To her credit, when the scales suddenly fell from her eyes, she did something unexpected. On Friday, Carmen Mercer and her board of directors voted to dissolve the Minuteman Corporation, because, for whatever reason, people taking "locked, loaded, and ready" literally was way too much for her.

Perhaps there is a lesson in this for a much more high-profile agitator who does not understand the stupidity of her own supporters, and who recently advised them, "Don't retreat, instead reload."

Not Too Swift

MARCH 30, 2010

The bronze to Bud Day, Medal of Honor recipient and retired colonel. He has now endorsed Charlie Crist for the Republican Senate nomination in Florida, instead of Tea Partyer Marco Rubio, saying, "You know, we just got through electing a politician who can run his mouth at Mach One, a black one. Now we have an Hispanic who can run his mouth at Mach One."

He expanded upon Mr. Obama, calling him "the black one with the reading thing. He can go as fast as the speed of light and has no idea what he's saying. I put Rubio in that same category, except I don't know if he is using one of those readers."

Colonel Day, of course, appeared in the Swift Boat ads against John Kerry in 2004. You'll remember him. He was the white one with the racism thing.

The runner-up: Ricky Flowers, address not given, who led police in Ohio on a high-speed chase where he was wanted for failing to signal. It ended at Garfield Heights, Ohio, with Mr. Flowers ditching the car and scaling a fence. Unfortunately for Mr. Flowers, the fence was outside the Ohio Northeast Pre-Release Center for Women. When he landed back on the ground, he was inside a prison yard surrounded by corrections officers.

But our winner . . .
Oklahoma state senator Steve Russell. Two weeks ago, that body passed his horrific bigoted bill designed to reduce protections for gays by enabling Oklahoma law enforcement agencies to ignore the broader definition of hate crimes passed by the U.S. Congress a few years ago in the Matthew Shepard Act on the grounds that it denied Oklahoma churches the right to preach against homosexuality.

The Oklahoma bill permits prosecutors to ignore Title 18, U.S. Code Section 245, except the protections for gays are not in Title

18, U.S. Code Section 245. They are in Title 18, U.S. Code Section 249. So what did Oklahoma nullify when its senate attacked Title 18, U.S. Code Section 245?

Title 18, U.S. Code Section 245, protects people against hate crimes based on "race, color, religion or national origin."

So the religious nuts in Oklahoma who tried to strip the rights from gays wound up stripping the rights from the religious nuts in Oklahoma.

Oklahoma state senator Steve "I Wonder What Hoist on His Own Petard Means" Russell, today's worst person in the world!

Mob Rule

APRIL 7, 2010

Several members of the Hutaree, a Christian militia group, have been arrested in Michigan. Yesterday, the authorities announced they'd taken into custody a man after he'd made countless threats against a U.S. senator. Today the FBI arrested another man for making dozens of threatening phone calls to the Speaker of the House, Nancy Pelosi.

But last night a candidate for the Republican nomination for a congressional seat in Florida said this about the Democratic incumbent to the Tea Party crowd: "Let me tell you what you've got to do. You've got to make the fellow scared to come out of his house. That's the only way you're going to get these people to pay attention. You've got to put pressure on them."

That's Allen West talking about Congressman Ron Klein.

We've met Mr. West before. He is the man who claimed that the Al Jazeera network, in offering to send a limousine service car to his home to pick him up for an interview, was actually trying to kidnap him. He is the man who left the U.S. military in shame after he supervised the torture of, and fired a gun near the head of, an Iraqi policeman in custody.

Obviously, at any time, from any point on the political spectrum, West's incitement to violence is unacceptable. And he has just underscored why he and people who have endorsed him, like Sarah Palin, have forfeited their rights to serve in government for the simple reason that they are not dedicated to democracy. They are believers in mob rule.

But the larger question is why are the bullies and the delusionals and the violent fanatics crawling out of the woodwork now? It is frequently posited that this is the residue of the first decade of this century, of the violence, of the paranoia, of the torture, of the phony war, of the simplistic mantra of "You're with us or you're against us."

So, in some respects, this plague has descended upon us because we, as a nation, took no steps to say that the answer, internationally or here at home, cannot just be the fundaments of torture, violence, and fear of violence.

We prosecuted no one in real authority. And so an Allen West was not held up as an example of what this country stands against when he threatened to kill a policeman in Iraq. Instead, he is somehow encouraged to run for office and to threaten a congressman in Florida.

Worst Person in the World

And Sometimes a Blind Squirrel Doesn't Find a Nut

APRIL 14, 2010

The bronze to Orly Taitz. The original birther has been repudiated by the Pleasanton, California, Tea Party. It had invited her to its clan meeting tomorrow, but according to founder Bridgette Nelson, the group had been getting calls from candidates like crazy. "It's not worth it; she's too controversial; this is not what the Tea Party is about at this point."

Wow! Too controversial for the Tea Party. Worse yet, I'm dropping her as Limbaugh's nickname.

The silver medalist: Sean Hannity. "One of the things I fear the most is that Barack Obama catering to the world's dictators is the—literally the Neville Chamberlain of our time." Let me tell you a couple things about Neville Chamberlain. Neville Chamberlain believed that conservatives had a monopoly on truth. He believed in suppressing dissent and disagreement from moderates and liberals. He tried to purge those people from his own government and party who disagreed with him. He was an isolationist who believed his country could do whatever it wanted to and face no consequences in the world. And he was supported by every damned Republican in this country.

Since you don't know what's happening in the world today around you, Sean, you could at least try to get yesterday right. Try Wikipedia, Sonny.

And our winner . . .
Bill-O the Clown. After Senator Tom Coburn spanked him and Fox News for leading an Oklahoma woman to believe she could go to jail if she didn't buy health insurance, O'Reilly condescended to tell the senator, "You don't really know anybody on Fox News because there hasn't been anyone that said people would go to jail if they don't buy mandatory insurance. We researched to find out if anybody has ever said you were going to go to jail if you don't buy health insurance. Nobody has ever said it. But it seems to me you used Fox News as a whipping boy when we didn't qualify there. You were wrong to do that, Senator, with all due respect."

O'Reilly's crack research team, as usual.

Here's Glenn Beck, Fox News, on November 12: "If you don't buy into their government health care, there will be jail time."

Dick Morris, Fox News, November 9: "One of the provisions in the Pelosi bill is you can actually go to jail for not having health insurance, $250,000 or five years in prison."

Andrew Napolitano, Fox News, November 10: "The government may fine you, prosecute you, and even put you in jail."

Greta Van Susteren, Fox News, to Congressman John Shadegg, October 7: "Can you imagine the sheriff going out and running you in, throwing you in jail? I mean, it is theoretically possible under what you tell me."

And Beck again, on November 13, on a certain Fox News show. Beck: "I don't have universal health care." Host: "Well, you will soon." Beck: "Or I'll go to jail."

The host in that conversation was O'Reilly. It was on his show.

"We researched to find out if anybody ever said you were going to go to jail if you don't buy health insurance. Nobody has ever said it."

In other words, Bill couldn't find a quote from his own show with both hands.

Bill-O the Clown, back from retirement and proving he can still bring the stupid, today's worst person in the world!